P9-DWC-831

The Writer's Guide to Everyday Life
From Prohibition Through World War II

The Writer's Guide to
Everyday Life
from Prohibition
through
World War II

Marc McCutcheon

WRITER'S DIGEST BOOKS
CINCINNNATI, OHIO

This hardcover edition of *The Writer's Guide to Everyday Life From Prohibition Through World War II* features a "self-jacket" that eliminates the need for a separate dust jacket. It provides sturdy protection for your book while it saves paper, trees and energy.

Other fine Writer's Digest Books are available from your local bookstore or direct from the publisher.

99 98 97 96 95   5 4 3 2 1

Library of Congress Cataloging-in-Publication Data

McCutcheon, Marc.
    The writer's guide to everyday life from prohibition through World War II / by Marc McCutcheon.
        p.   cm.
    Includes bibliographical references.
    ISBN 0-89879-697-0
    1. United States—Social life and customs—1918-1945—Dictionaries.
    2. English language—United States—Slang—Glossaries, vocabularies, etc.   3.
    Americanisms—Dictionaries.   I. Title
E169.M45   1995
973.91—dc20   95-32559
                                                                          CIP

Edited by Marc Jennings
Cover illustration by Laura Kuhlman
Interior designed by Sandy Conopeotis Kent

Chapter opening collages created using images from the Dover Pictorial Archives Series.

The excerpt from "Zoot Lore" from The Talk of the Town, June 19, 1943 issue of *The New Yorker* appearing on page 173 is reprinted by permission; © 1943, 1971, The New Yorker Magazine, Inc.

DEDICATION

To my parents,
Mary and Errol McCutcheon,
who lived it.

ABOUT THE AUTHOR

Marc McCutcheon is also the author of *The Compass in Your Nose &
Other Astonishing Facts about Humans* (Putnams); *Descriptionary* (Facts
on File); *The Writer's Guide to Everyday Life in the 1800s* and *Roget's Super-
thesaurus* (Writer's Digest Books). He lives in South Portland, Maine
with his wife, Deanna, and two children, Kara and Matthew.

TABLE OF CONTENTS

INTRODUCTION

Writers working on romances, mysteries, thrillers, police procedurals, historical dramas—where do they go to find obscure information on everyday life in what is easily the most story-rich period of the century—Prohibition through World War II?

For example, when did teenagers refuse to wear jeans unless their cuffs were rolled up?

How did people make their own booze during Prohibition?

When was the word *swell* on everybody's lips? And in which decade was something so cool that it had to be called the "cat's pajamas," the "cat's whiskers," "the bee's knees" and a dozen other variations?

What night of the week did the radio program "Fibber McGee and Molly" come on? What time? How about "Inner Sanctum?" "The Shadow?" "The Lone Ranger?"

What soap operas did most women listen to over the radio in the 1930s?

Why did so many people break their arms trying to start a Ford Model T? How did one shift gears in the Tin Lizzy? And why were so many people seen driving over hills in one backward?

When was Flash Gordon serialized in the movie theaters? How about Tarzan? Which movie did Americans flock to see in 1929? 1945?

When did American men stop wearing tee shirts, and what event provoked them to do so?

What year was "Don't Sit Under the Apple Tree" a number one hit? "Jeepers Creepers?" "Chattanooga Choo Choo?"

When did girls go crazy over bobby sox and tight sweaters?

Unfortunately, small, period-illuminating details like these are frequently difficult and time-consuming to find. While there are enough books on political events and general history to fill a fleet of 1930s Lincolns, and enough works on World War II to sink a battleship, few references on *everyday life* during the Prohibition through the World War II era exist.

And that's exactly what the writer of a coming-of-age, rags-to-riches or timeless love story needs in order to avoid spending perhaps hundreds of hours at the library winnowing minutiae; a reference book one can have at his fingertips to find out in an instant the favorite pinup girls of the World War II GI; the cars favored by gangsters; how speakeasys served liquor illegally during Prohibition and got away with it; what kitchen product housewives scraped out of their pots and pans to aid the war effort; when the zoot suit was all the rage; when the Orson Welles "War of the Worlds" radio drama that terrified the nation was broadcast; what hairstyle was "in" in 1940; what year a character would most likely dance the Charleston, sit on a flagpole or swallow a live goldfish; the difference between a tommy gun, a grease gun and a burp gun; popular slang among World War II soldiers in the army, marines and navy; and favorite scams of criminals.

Such particulars will add color, depth and that important "ring of truth" to any fiction (or nonfiction) setting. Of course, such particulars can just as easily trip you up. Indeed, be forewarned here; anachronisms lie in wait to ambush and strip the credibility from an amateur historian at every turn.

For example, could a fictional character fly in a helicopter before 1940? How about 1945? Were there traffic lights before 1925? Talking motion pictures before 1930?

And what about slang and everyday street language? Did people living in the 1920s use words like "hep" and "hip"? Were they "in the groove" as early as the 1930s? Were they "cool" by the 1940s? Did they take "dope" or smoke "reefers" in the 1930s? Before the 1920s, a "fag" was a cigaret and, if you were "gay," you weren't a homosexual, you were simply happy. Be careful!

The conscientious writer double-checks facts before an editor gets a chance to raise a question. To facilitate research, this book is specially designed with anachronistic pitfalls in mind. To avoid such pitfalls, you'll find quick-reference chronologies at the back and also in the larger, general text, in which dates are cited whenever possible.

To illustrate some of the words and slang terms in context, quotations from magazines, newspapers and books from the period appear periodically throughout the text. For example, along with the definition of a Model T is one man's description of how to actually start one up. You'll find similar quotes describing clothing, fads, cars, World War II weapons and more.

Use this reference to verify facts and dates, for ideas and, most of all, for inspiration. Read it through. Feel the period come alive. Borrow from it to make your own work live.

Flappers. Babe Ruth. Prohibition. Lindbergh. The Depression. The advent of radio. The golden age of movies. Aviation. Amelia Earhart. The midwest dust bowl disaster. Jesse Owens. Gangsters. John Dillinger. Pearl Harbor. FDR. Audie Murphy. The War in Europe. The War in the Pacific. The advent of the atomic age.

A thousand stories await. Turn the page and watch the ideas pop.

And now if you'll excuse me, I really must go or, as one generation of Americans used to say, scram.

Or was that beat it?

Marc McCutcheon
S. Portland, ME.

SLANG, COLLOQUIALISMS AND EVERYDAY SPEECH

ushwa? Jiggery-pokery? Lay off, Jackson. Not in this book, fella! The colloquialisms in this book are the real thing. They're jake. Hipper-dipper! Dig me? They've got the goods, see? I know my onions, and if you don't believe it you can go chase yourself, have a kitten, you heel. You drip! You must be some of Hitler's work. This book is the cat's meow, the cat's pajamas and the cat's whiskers, all at the same time. The bee's knees, too! So be a swell guy and amscray before I get sore! Shove in your clutch, buddy, jitterbug on out of here. Dry up! Go cut out paper dolls! Boy, oh, boy, that gripes my middle kidney!

Now isn't that the drooliest, smoothest, dreamiest slang you ever heard? Hubba hubba! Hot dog! Sure is swell! O Lord and butter!

And so, dear reader, get hep. Here is but a microcosm of America's colloquialisms and slang from the 1920s, 1930s and 1940s, some from the upper class, some from the lower, and much from the strata in between.

---

all reet, all root: a fad pronunciation of "all right," mostly by students, in the 1940s. Also, "reet."

all six, hit on: to hit on all six cylinders; to perform 100 percent. From at least the 1920s on.

1920: "The man who was going strong in the old premotor days was said to be exerting himself to the top of his bent. . . . Now we say, 'He's sure hittin' on all six.' " Literary Digest, *May 22.*

all wet: mistaken; wrong; full of it. Originating in the 1930s.

amscray: get out; leave; beat it. From the 1940s.

and how!: emphatic response similar to "You said it!" From 1920 on.
1930: "I am so tired of hearing sap, oh boy, and how, sez you, guts and dirty bum that I could almost leave for the Fiji Islands to escape them." *"The Great American Slanguage," Outlook, November 12.*

applesauce: baloney; bullshit; foolishness; nonsense. From the 1920s on.

attaboy!: way to go; well done! Also, attagirl! From 1910 on.

babe: an attractive female.
1930s: "We got two nice babes, respectable, and the party set me back around seventy dollars." *John O'Hara,* Hope of Heaven.
1943: "I remembered the babe who threw the drink in his face." *Chandler, 'Lady in Lake.'*

baby: one's sweetheart. Also used to denote something of value or something highly esteemed. "Step on the accelerator and that baby flies." From the 1920s on.

baby vamp: an attractive or popular female, used by college males in 1927.

balled up: messed up; confused; mixed up. From the 1920s.

barb: a college student unaffiliated with a fraternity. From 1900 through the 1940s.

barney: a fixed contest. "The fight was an obvious barney." From the 1930s through the 1940s.

bat one's gums: to talk idly; to chat; to shoot the breeze. From the 1940s.

battle: an ugly female. From the 1930s and 1940s.

bearcat: an attractive, hot-blooded or fiery girl. From the 1920s.

beat one's gums: to talk idly. Also, "beat up the chops."

beat it: common term for scram or get lost; leave. From 1905 on.

beef: a complaint. Also, as a verb, to complain. From the 1920s on.

bee's knees: a common fad expression of the 1920s, similar to the "cat's meow," designating something or someone excellent, first-rate, dreamy. "He's the bee's knees."

beeswax: business, as in "None of your beeswax;" child and student use from 1920 on.

bent: drunk. From the 1920s.

B-girl: a prostitute or promiscuous female who picks men up in bars. The "B" designated bar and the quality of being "second choice" among soldiers. From 1938 on.

bimbo: a loose or promiscuous woman from the 1930s on. In the 1920s, a bimbo was a tough guy.

bird: a man, woman or, sometimes, an odd person. "What a funny old bird he was." Among college students, a popular female. From the late 1920s.

bird dog: a chaperon at a school dance. Student use from 1935 on.

bitch: as a noun, a complaint or gripe. As a verb, to complain or gripe, used throughout the World War II period.

bitch kitty: a difficult, irritable, complaining woman. From the 1930s.

blotto: drunk. From the 1920s.

bobby-soxer: A teenage girl from the early 1940s, named after the white bobby socks she wore as part of a widespread fashion trend.

bohunk: a derogatory name for a central European immigrant. From 1900 to 1930.

boing!: a fad expression used mainly by males in the 1940s. The word, spoken to sound like a spring popping loose, was used whenever a sexually attractive female entered the area, and suggested either the eyes popping out of one's head or the penis becoming suddenly erect. Very popular among students and World War II soldiers.

bombshell: a very attractive female, especially "blonde bombshell." From the mid-1930s through the 1940s.

boogie-woogie: any jazz, swing or fast blues. From 1935 on.

bootleg: bootleg liquor. From 1920 on. See Prohibition.

breezer: an automobile with an open or convertible top. From 1925.

broad: a woman or girl. Also, a prostitute or a promiscuous woman. From the 1930s on.
1940s: "One-eyed Solly Abrahams . . . refers to Miss Billy Perry as a broad, meaning no harm whatever, for this is the way many of the boys speak of the dolls." *Damon Runyan*, Romance in the Roaring Forties.

browned off: commonly used in place of "fed up." From late 1930s on.

brown-nose: a kiss-up; an apple-polisher; an ass-kisser. Popular among students and soldiers from 1940 on. Sometimes used as a verb.

brush off, give one the: to ignore or snub someone; to reject. From the 1940s on.

bubs: a woman's breasts, especially if large. From 1900 on.

bucket: a big, worn-out car. A rust bucket. From the 1930s on.

bug-eyed Betty: an unattractive or unpopular female, used by male college students in 1927.

bughouse: an insane asylum. From the 1940s.

bull: any type of policeman, including an FBI man or a railroad cop, from the late 1800s to 1930. Also, bullshit, nonsense, exaggeration, etc., as used today. As a verb, to shoot the breeze or to exaggerate. From the 1920s on.

bum's rush, the: ejection from a place by force; being thrown out or kicked out.
1922: "Dey gimme de bum's rush." *Eugene O'Neill*, The Hairy Ape.

bunny: a term of sympathy and endearment for someone who is lost, confused, hurt, etc., and frequently preceded by "poor little" or "poor lost." From 1925 on.

bus: any old, worn out, large car. From 1915 on.

bushwa: a softer equivalent of "bullshit" or "horseshit," popular since 1920. Also spelled, booshwah.
1938: "There has been a lot of bushwa tossed around about how moving pictures aren't worthy of their audience."
Otis Ferguson, New Republic, *August 31.*

business, the: a working-over; a beating; a thrashing; murder. "Give 'em the business, boys." From the 1940s.

butterfly's boots, the: designating anyone or anything that is excellent, wonderful, or dreamy. See also the cat's meow. From the 1920s.

buzz: a charge, a kick; a thrill. From 1935 on.

cake-eater: a ladies' man. From the 1920s.

canary: a female jazz vocalist. As a verb, to sing professionally. "Chirp" was used as well. From the 1940s.
1944: "She had to go back to canarying." Collier's Magazine, *September 23.*

can house: a brothel. From at least 1930 on.

canned: drunk. Also, "canned up,"; "get a can on." From the 1920s on.
1928: "So the old man give them a drink of some hard cider, and they got canned up a little more." *J.M. Cain,* American Mercury.

caper: a robbery or other criminal act, from 1925 on. In the mid-1940s, students used the word to denote any hijinks, pranks or fun time.

cast a kitten: also, "have kittens." To have a fit. This term was used either humorously (as when laughing hysterically) or negatively (as when violently angry). "Stop tickling me or I'll cast a kitten!" "He was so mad I thought he was going to cast a kitten." From the 1920s.

cat: a jazz musician. From 1940 on.

STUDENT SLANG OF THE 1920S

girlfriend: Sheba. A fad name of affection begun after Rudolph Valentino's movie, "The Sheik."

boyfriend: Shiek. From Valentino's movie, "The Sheik."

>   1928: "We soon became the best of friends and, though I'm far removed from the sheik type, I think she liked me from the start." *"On the Lam,"* American Mercury, *August.*

unpopular or unattractive girl: pig's coattail; washout; mess; flat tire; bug-eyed Betty.

popular or attractive girl: angel; thrill; bird; live one; baby vamp; peach; choice bit of calico; sweet patootie; panic; red-hot witch.

stupid person: dumb Dora (dumdora); dumbbell.

stupid, idiotic, ridiculous, unsophisticated: wet.

>   1925: "A term which has puzzled most laymen who have never visited a modern college atmosphere is 'wet.' . . . Being wet implies the lack of a sense of humor and proportion, the absence of a sense of sophistication and good breeding . . . " Literary Digest, *March 14.*

college dance: drag. "We went to the drag last night."

one who is perfectly or fashionably dressed: Joe Brooks. "You're a regular Joe Brooks with that ascot, Peter."

cat's meow: a very popular phrase describing someone or something excellent, wonderful or dreamy. From the 1920s, with wide variations. See also bee's knees.

cat's pajamas: a very popular variation of the cat's meow. From the 1920s.

cat's whiskers: a variation of the cat's meow. From the 1920s.

1926: "I leave the stage, but I know that, in America at least, I am the cat's whiskers. The elevator boy said as much, and I surely have no reason to doubt him." *Cyril Maude quoted in* Golden Book Magazine, *July.*

1926: "The Charleston is next. Cat's whisker (La moustache du chat)." Living Age Magazine.

charity girl: a sexually promiscuous woman. 1940s.

chase yourself, go: get lost; beat it; scram. From 1900 on.
1930: STRANGER: "Is the Skyhigh Hotel a first class place?"
  TAXI DRIVER: ". . . it's a swell dump."
  STRANGER: "I beg pardon. A dump? You mean it will not do?"
  TAXI DRIVER: "Say, how do you get that way? I said it's hot."
  STRANGER: "Too hot, you say? Can you tell me of a cooler one?"
  TAXI DRIVER: "Aw, go chase yerself."
  "The Great American Slanguage," Outlook, *November 12.*

chassis: the body, especially the female body. From at least 1930 on.

chatterbox: a car radio. From 1940 on.

cheesecake: photos and pinups of attractive women, especially in sexually provocative poses and clothing. Also, the women themselves. A widely used term throughout the 1940s.

chewing gum: double talk; any ambiguous or confusing talk. From the 1920s.

chew out: to scold or bawl out. Very common term, especially among soldiers in the 1940s.

Chicago: used as an adjective to describe someone who looks rough or like a gangster. "He's got that Chicago look about 'em, know what I mean?" 1930s. See Section Five: Crime.

chips are down, the: describing a negative or troublesome situation. 1940s.

choice bit of calico: an attractive or popular female, used by college males in the late 1920s.

chug-a-lug: to drink down a beer in one gulp without stopping for breath, a college test of manhood from 1940 on.

chunk of lead: an unattractive or unpopular female, used by male college students in 1927.

clam: a dollar.
1939: "I hit a crap game for about 80 clams. . . ." *John O'Hara,* Pal Joey.

C-note: a $100 bill. From at least 1939 on.

come clean: tell the truth, tell all. From at least 1930 on.

come on like gangbusters: to enter the scene in a big way or in a loud or blatant manner, after the "Gangbusters" radio show that opened with loud machine gun fire and sirens. From 1936 on.

cooking with gas, now you're: to be up to date, fashionable. From 1940 on.

crumb: an unattractive or unpopular girl, used by male college students in 1927.

cut a rug: to dance, especially jitterbug. From the 1940s.
1943: "Are you a secret jitterbug, unable to resist the temptation to cut rugs to tatters on the sly even at the price of hiding your head in polite society?" New York Times Magazine, *November 7.*

cutting out paper dolls: insane; crazy. After a recreational activity in an insane asylum. 1940s.

cuzzy: sexual intercourse. 1930s.

daddy: a young woman's boyfriend or lover, especially one with money. 1912 on.

dame: a girl or a woman. This word had a wide variety of connotations, positive and negative. It was employed as early as 1900 but didn't gain widespread use until the 1930s and 1940s.
1940s: "Maybe I could go for a dame like you if you ditched the dopes you run around with." *"The Green Hornet" radio program.*
1940: "The male has to believe that he dominates the female, because if he doesn't . . . he'll hunt around until he finds a dame or dames he does dominate."
   V. Faulkner, *"A Smattering of Bliss,"* Saturday Evening Post.

Daniel Boone, pull a: high school and college students' humorous term, meaning to throw up, so-called because in stories, Boone always went out and "shot his supper." From 1910-1935.

darb: any great person or thing. "That car's a darb." 1920s on.

date bait: any desirable member of the opposite sex. 1940 on.

dead soldier: an empty beer or whiskey bottle. 1920s on.

deb: a debutant. During the 1940s, girls aged thirteen to eighteen were more often called debs than teenagers. See Section Five: Crime.

dick: a private detective. In use from 1900 on, with more widespread use from the 1920s on. See Section Five: Crime.
1929: "Listen," said the proprietor, "you look a lot like a lady dick and we don't want none of your kind round here."
Outlook, *March 13.*

dig: to understand; to comprehend. "Dig me?" From 1941 on. Even earlier among hip, jazz circles.
1941: "Dig me?" Life, *December 15.*
1942: ". . . tailors prophesied last week that quality, not quantity, would set the style. Detail will be wackier and colors louder. In other words, the zoot will still be solid, if you dig me."
Newsweek, *September 7.*

Dillinger: Cab Calloway's "Hepster's Dictionary" gives this definition: "a killer-diller, too hot to handle." Among criminals of the 1930s, to pull a Dillinger was to pull off an outrageous or bold crime, so-named after the nervy exploits of John Dillinger.

dinge: a derogatory term for a Negro. From pre-1900 to the 1930s.

dish: an attractive girl or woman. From the 1930s on.

doll: an attractive girl or woman. From 1920 on.
1928: "Tall, well-proportioned, with beautiful gray-blue eyes, golden bobbed hair, and a cool, haughty carriage, she seemed out of place among the painted dolls and the course-spoken, drunken racketeers. . . ." American Mercury, *August.*

doll up: to dress up; to fix oneself up to look one's best. From the 1920s on.
1940s: "Say, Mary, how do you like my full dress suit? I'm kind of dolled up, ain't I?" *Jack Benny radio program.*

dope: drugs, especially cocaine or opium, in general use since 1920.

doublecross: to cheat or betray someone. From about 1900 on.

dough: money. 1920s on.
1932: "We didn't have much dough. I took only enough to buy gas on the way over. . . ." American Mercury, *May.*
1940s: "I don't like this situation on account of there is a couple of guys back in camp what owe me dough from last pay day. . . ." Yank, the Army Weekly.

drip: an unappealing person, especially male. Someone who is not popular, fashionable or interesting, etc. "He's such a drip." Student use from 1935 on.

drone: a boring, uninteresting person. Used by students from 1940 on.

drooly: a nice-looking or popular boy. Any object that makes one drool. Used among teen girls from 1940 on.
1944: ". . . as a special big date, a drive to a wayside inn about three miles out of Nyack for 'pizza pie', an Italian dish . . . described by Robin as a 'wonderfully drooly concoction.'
Ladies Home Journal, *December.*

dry up: to shut up; to drop dead; go jump in a lake. "Why don't you just dry up?" Used throughout the period and before.

dumdora (dumb Dora): a dumbbell; a person without much intelligence, especially a woman. A word popularized by flappers.
1924: "Much credit goes to the flapper . . . as the coiner of words. . . . Dumbbell and dumdora seem to belong to her by inherent right; at all events, she has been the chief agency giving them currency." Literary Digest, *November 1.*

dummy up: shut up; clam up; act like a dummy; don't say anything. From the 1940s.

eating you, what's: what's the matter with you?; what's bothering you? From at least 1916.
1940s: "Brecker, what's eatin' you?" *"The Shadow" radio program.*
1940s: "What's eatin' you, sarge?" "What's eatin' me, you say? Plenty!" *The "Green Hornet" radio program.*

14

edge: intoxication; a buzz. "He had an edge on." From 1920 on.

eel's hips: a variation on the cat's meow. 1920s.

elephant's eyebrows: a variation of the cat's meow. 1920s.

Ethel: an effeminate male. From 1920.

fag: before 1920, a cigaret. After 1920, a cigaret or a homosexual or an effeminate male.

1944: "Most of us never even tried a cigarette before we were 16. . . . Actually, we think 18 is about the right age to begin; that is, if a person wants to begin. Some of us feel it's kind of cheapish for a girl always to be dragging a fag; for a young girl, anyway." Ladies Home Journal, *December.*

fella: fellow. Although rarely heard today (mostly spoken by the older generation), "fella" was as commonly used in the 1920s, 1930s and 1940s, as "guy" is today. "A nice sort of fella, John is." "Round up the fellas for a baseball game."

1937: "The cops on this beat know us all since we were kids. They know we're not fellows to do anything wrong. We don't allow gambling. We made it a rule because some fellows haven't got the control they ought." Literary Digest, *July 17.*

1930s: "We had to get a colored fella to clean the place up after the way we left it." *John O'Hara,* Hope of Heaven.

finger: to accuse one of a crime; to lay blame on; point the finger at. 1930s.

fish: a college freshmen, from 1900 through the 1940s. Also, from 1915 on, a prison term denoting one arrested or thrown in jail for the first time.

flapper: any progressive, free-spirited young woman (usually under 20) who was openly interested in sex and wore such bold fashions as short dresses with stockings rolled to the knee, heavy makeup and bobbed hair. The flapper was also known to drink and smoke openly. Many young women copied flapper fashions, but did not necessarily adopt the smoking, drinking or sex. In the early 1920s, anything associated with flappers was considered indecent and elicited widespread moral outrage. See also Section Seven: Clothing and Fashion.

1922: "Who was this wild and winsome coot

That made poor Adam pull the boot

And taste of that forbidden fruit?

A flapper.

This Cleopatra maiden fair

For whom great Caesar tore his hair.

Who was this vamp so debonair?

A flapper.

Who is it now that flashes by

With scanty clothes and dropping eye,

For whom some sap would gladly die?

A flapper.

Who is it spends their hard-earned kale

Who makes this plant a woeful tale.

Who is more deadly than the male?

A flapper." *"The Collegiate World"*

1922: "More girls are smoking cigarets and are aspiring to be vamps and flappers." Literary Digest, *June.*

1922: "To bring the flapper to terms, approve of her. Then she'll stop it." Outlook, *October.*

1922: "From many sources come testimonies that "flapperism" has passed the peak." Outlook, *October.*

flivver: originally, a Ford Model T. After 1928, any old, broken-down automobile.

1928: "A traffic cop performed about sixty feet to the south, and a Police Department flivver, with a uniformed cop at the wheel, rested at the curb near him. . . ." American Mercury, *August.*

floozy: an unrefined and not sharply intelligent girl or woman who is fun and charming and often promiscuous; a good-time girl. Variations: floozie, floogy, flugie. As in the 1940 song title: "The Flat-Floot Floogy with the Floy Floy."

flub the dub: to slack off or be lazy. Also, to screw up; to flub. 1940s.

fluff, a bit of: a young woman or girl. Also, a piece of fluff. From the 1930s.

flugie: see floozy.

fly boy: a glamorous term for an aviator, either civilian or military. From the 1920s on.

fog: to move quickly. Also, to kill. 1930s on.

footsie: caressing the feet of a member of the opposite sex with one's own feet, usually under a table. Also known as footy-footy. From the 1940s on.

for crying out loud: popular acceptable euphemism for, "for Christ's sake." 1930s on.

four-flusher: one who pretends to have money but sponges off of others. 1900 on.

frame-up: a set-up; getting an innocent person in trouble by providing false evidence against him.
1930: "I'll prove to you it's a frame-up." *W. Weeks,* All in the Racket.

fried: drunk. 1920s.

frosh: first-year high school or college student. From the 1920s on.

fuck: although rarely seen in print and never heard in the movies or over the airwaves, this word was used as a noun, verb or adjective, with all the same connotations we know today. It was widely used by members of all the armed forces, especially during battle, in World War II. In fact, the word became much more openly used in general society when those soldiers returned home.

futz: a euphemism for "fuck." "Don't futz around with that."

gams: legs. Although sometimes denoting a man's legs, the word more often was taken to mean a woman's legs, especially if they were shapely. From the 1930s and 1940s.
1939: "Yes that is how good this Melba was. Gams and a pair of maracas that will haunt me in my dreams. . . ." *John O'Hara,* Pal Joey.

gay: happy, lively. A much-used word in the 1920s, with no connection to homosexuality.

1921: "For the students with money the homes of "society" are open, but to be acceptable to most of those girls the boys must be gayer than would be allowed in many old-fashioned homes, liquor and dancing being the custom in most of them." Literary Digest, *July*.

1926: "If he knew all as he had against him, Miss, he wouldn't be so gay." Golden Book Magazine, *July*.

get-up: an outfit or uniform. 1930 on.

ginger: vitality; liveliness; effervescence. She had a lot of ginger. From the 1940s.

gin mill: a cheap drinking establishment or speakeasy. 1920s on.

glad rags: the fancy clothes one wears when going out on the town. From 1900 on.

glamour puss: a nice-looking young man or woman. Students used from 1940 on.

gnat's eyebrows: a variation of the cat's meow. See the cat's meow.

gnat's whistle: a variation of the cat's meow. See the cat's meow.

gold brick: as a noun, one who tries to shirk responsibilities or to loaf. As a verb, to shirk responsibility, try to get out of work. From the 1930s, and most common during World War II.

gold-digger: a woman who courts a wealthy man solely for his money. From 1925 on.

goods, the: the right stuff; the desired material. Also, a person having the right stuff. "She's got the goods." Also, the facts, the truth; evidence against someone involved in a crime. "The cops had the goods on me, so I ran." 1920s on.

goof: a stupid, bumbling person. Widely used in the 1920s, especially among flappers; again widely used during World War II.

goon: originally, a hoodlum, thug, or muscular person who beat up people to intimidate them for criminal purposes. From the 1930s. The word eventually evolved from 1935 to mean any unattractive, geek-like person, especially among teenagers and college students.

Gordon Water: popular term for Gordon's gin. 1925.

got your boots on: According to Cab Calloway's *Hepster's Dictionary,* "you know what it's all about."

gowed up: under the influence of drugs, especially opium or marijuana.
1940: "Some gowed-up runt they took along for a gun-holder lost his
   head." *R. Chandler,* Farewell, My Lovely.

greeby: a short-lived teen word for "terrible." 1945.

gripes my cookies: irritates, disgusts me. Many variations. 1940s.

gripes my middle kidney: a common phrase of the mid-1940s meaning to give a pain or irritate; the equivalent to "pain in the neck."

gripes my soul: a common phrase of the 1930s meaning to give a pain or irritate.

groove, in the: a term widely used by swing musicians and jazz band listeners to describe music that "cooks," that moves the listeners to tap their feet, snap their fingers, etc. The phrase suggests a phonograph stylus fitting perfectly between a record's grooves. "In the Groove" was the title of a popular song in 1938. The phrase was used throughout the 1930s and 1940s and eventually branched into an additional meaning of thinking or acting in the correct fashion.
1943: "There will be nothing left of the uncouth jive jamming, but all
   the basic steps will be there, carefully lifted out of the groove. . . ."
   New York Times Magazine, *November 7.*

groovy: evolving from "in the groove," a state of mind in which one feels as one or in tune with the music being played, especially swing music. Also, music that is "in the groove." Used among swing musicians and music lovers from as early as the 1930s. In the 1940s it also described someone who was "hep" to swing music.

hair of the dog: a drink of alcohol. Since 1925.

half cocked: unprepared or inexperienced in what one is about to do. "Going off half cocked."

half seas over: thoroughly drunk. Also, "half under" and "half the bay over." From the 1920s and again during World War II.

harp: an Irishman. 1920s.

have it, let: to hit, beat up or shoot someone. 1930s on.

hay: a piddling amount of money, usually used in the phrase, "and that ain't hay." 1939 on.

hayburner: an automobile that uses a lot of gas and oil or is expensive to run. 1920 on. Also, a money-losing race horse.

headlights: a woman's breasts, especially if large. So named after the auto headlights of the cars of the 1940s.

heave: popular high school and college student term for vomit. 1940s.

heavy sugar: a lot of money. 1929 on.

heebie-jeebies: the willies; the creeps; fright; anxiety. After the title of a 1926 song.

heel: a scoundrel; a rat; an SOB; a bastard. 1920s on.

he-man: a masculine man; a macho man. Since at least 1920.

hep: hip; savvy; in the know; aware and up on fashions and trends. As early as 1915, but more common from 1935 on. Cab Calloway's *Hepster's Dictionary* was published in 1938.
1924: "Unless some of you wake up and, as you would say, 'get hep to yourselves,' you are never going to be anything."
P. *Marks*, The Plastic Age.

hep cat: a hip, aware, fashionable person; a savvy person.
1938: "A hep cat is a guy who knows what it's all about.
Cab Calloway's Catalogue: A Hepster's Dictionary.

high hat: a snob. Also, to act like a snob. 1920s on.

high pillow: a big shot; an important person. 1940.

hinge: a glance. "I took a quick hinge at her eyes." 1939.

hip: same as hep. From at least 1915, but used more often than hep after 1945.

hipper-dipper: excellent; super. Since at least 1940.

hoary-eyed: drunk. Throughout the period.

hoist: to rob, steal or hold up. "To hoist a place." Since 1935.

hokey-pokey: cheap candy or ice cream for kids. Also, the seller of such items—a "hokey-pokey" man. Also, a "hokey-pokey" counter. Since at least 1900.

holding the bag, left: to be left without or cheated out of one's due share of something, suggesting an unfilled bag. Also, to be blamed for something. Since at least 1906.

homework: high school and college students' sneaky word for sex. "Homework" was a popular song in 1949.

hooch: during Prohibition, homemade or bootleg whiskey. After Prohibition, any cheap whiskey. Also spelled "Hootch."

hood: very common word evolving from "hoodlum" in the late 20s.

hooey: baloney; bullshit; nonsense. A very popular word from 1925 to 1930 and used somewhat thereafter.
1930s: "Next year, according to Wiston, is a presidential year, and
    we're going to have a revolution."
      "Oh, hooey." *John O'Hara,* Butterfield 8.
1933: ". . . I fell for you in a big way and if you'll be on the level I'll
    give everybody the go by for you and that isn't a lot of hooey either."
    John Dillinger in letter to girlfriend.
1938: "This death threat may sound like a lot of hooey to you, but I've
    been assigned to guard you. . . ." *"The Shadow" radio program.*

hoofer: a stage dancer, especially vaudevillian. From the 1920s on.

Hooverville: a community of ramshackle shacks, usually near a dump, where unemployed workers took residence in search of scraps. Named after Herbert Hoover, President at the dawn of the Depression. 1930s.

hop: cocaine, opium or marijuana, used throughout the period. Also, a teen dance or dance party. Also used throughout the period.

hopped up: under the influence of drugs; high. Used throughout the period.

hop up: to take drugs, get high. Used throughout the period.

horsefeathers: a very popular euphemism for "horseshit." In vogue in the 1920s.

hotcha/hot cha cha: sexy; hot; attractive. 1930s.

1932: "Even these tabloids suggest the thing, with a sort of hot cha-cha leer at the private lives of cows. . . . 'Hot cha-cha' struck us as an unlikely addition to Aunt Agatha's vocabulary."
Harper's Monthly, *October.*

1937: "The cellar social club (is) where city youngsters of America have hung out a shingle and become practicing physicians intent on relieving their own ills. The shingle is not graced by a chaste M.D. . . . 'Manhattan Nut Club,' it is apt to read, or 'Hotcha Debutantes.' " Literary Digest, *July 17.*

1939: "He run Sternwood's hotcha daughter, the young one, off to Yuma." *R. Chandler,* Big Sleep.

hot dog!: an exclamation of excitement or delight. Similar to, "Oh, boy!" Since at least 1930.

hot patootie: a sexually attractive female. Since 1930.

hots, the: sexual desire. From as early as the 1940s.

hotsie-totsie: hunky-dory. After a 1926 song title.

hot sketch: a character; a card. 1920s.

hubba hubba: an expression used by a male or group of males upon seeing an attractive female; similar to whistling at a woman. Very popular during World War II.

hurdy-gurdy: a hand organ, often played on the streets during the 1920s and 1930s.

TEEN SLANG OF THE 1940S

attractive guy: drooly; heaven sent; swoony; mellow man; hunk of heartbreak; glad lad; Jackson; groovy; twangie boy; sugarpuss; glamourpuss; doll; Casanova; he-pal.

attractive girl: slick chick; whistle bait; rare dish; solid sender; dilly; dream puss; zazz girl; destroyer; 20-20; able Grable; blackout girl; wolfess.

unattractive guy: some of Hitler's work, no doubt; dogface; void coupon (after the rationing coupons of the war); stupor man; sad Sam; droop; drool; goon; toad; Joe Corn; drip.

unattractive girl: some of Hitler's work, no doubt; sad sack; goon; rusty hen; spook; scrag; dog biscuit; crate; seaweed; zombie.

girl who necks with everyone: toujour la clinch; goo ball; smooch date; hot cake; share crop; neckerchief.

fast boy: B.T.O. (Big Time Operator); wolf; active duty; educated fox.

girl crazy: doll dizzy; lap happy; dame dazed.

boy crazy: slack happy; khaki wacky.

prude: Mona Lizard; Percy Pants.

jilted: shot down in flames; defrosted; robot bombed.

good dancer: pepper shaker; rhythm rocker; cloud walker; ducky shincracker; jive bomber.

strict parent: crab patch; curfew keeper; egg beater.

good: smooth; divine; dreamy; super; priceless; luscious; simply, too perfectly.

terrible: sub zero; salty; greeby; icky; loathsome; deadly; grim; foul.

hello: Hey, devil, what say?; Hi, there, playmate.

exclamations: Holy Joe!; O Lord and butter!; Patch my pantywaist!; Oolie droolie!

gross!: Oh, nausea!

you're kidding!: Honestly!; It's devastating!; Well, cut off my leg and call me Shorty; I'm perfectly panic-stricken!

making out: necking, smooching; monking; boodling; mugging.

icky: sappy, corny, sentimental or old fashioned. Teen slang from the 1930s and 1940s.

in like Flynn: Success, sexual or otherwise. The term was coined after the reputation of actor Errol Flynn, who was known to have his way with women. Popular in the 1940s, especially among soldiers.

iron: among motorcycle enthusiasts, a motorcycle. From 1925.

ish kabibble: a widely used retort, meaning, "I should care," "I don't care," or "I'm not worried." Since 1925.

"It": sex appeal. The movie actress, Clara Bow, was nicknamed the "It Girl," beginning in 1925, for her natural sexiness, and for her starring role in the movie, *It.* The word, usually appearing in quotations, was used through the 1940s.
> 1942: "Do you believe in dieting for beauty?"
> "Absolutely. A girl can't eat her cake and have *it* too."
> *"Club Matinee" radio program.*

jack: money. Common from 1920 on.
> 1945: "He had lived long enough to realize that a young feller with a sudden success and a pile of jack can have good reason for woe."
> *Bill Mauldin,* Back Home.

Jackson: a popular direct address, normally only used with someone hep or popular, but not always. "Hey, Jackson." It originated in Harlem in 1935 and gained wide use among students and soldiers during the 1940s. Phil Harris frequently addressed Jack Benny as "Jackson" on Benny's radio show.
> 1940s: "Oh, hello, Phil, what's new?" "Hi, ya, Jackson, what's new?"
> *Jack Benny and Phil Harris, "Jack Benny" radio program.*

jake: an adjective, meaning "everything is just fine"; okay; everything is cool. 1920s on.
> 1929: "It's one of the nicest little stores downtown, right on the corner of Maxwell and Dane," said one of them. "The alley runs up to the back door and we can unload easy. Everything will be jake."
> Outlook, *March 13.*

Jane: any female. Also a man's sweetheart. From 1915 on.

let George do it: a popular work-evading phrase, in the 1920s and again in the 1940s.

pull a Jap: to pull any kind of surprise on someone, especially an attack. After the Japanese surprise assault on Pearl Harbor. 1940s.

java: popular term for coffee, since before World War I.

jeepers creepers!: euphemism for Jesus Christ! An expression of surprise. "Jeepers Creepers" was a popular song in 1939.

jerk soda: to dispense sodas and ice cream at a soda fountain. To be a soda jerk. Used throughout the period.

jig: a derogatory term for a Negro, short for "jigaboo." From at least the 1930s.

jigaboo: derogatory term for a Negro. Since at least 1910.

jiggery pokery: trickery; deception. 1940s.

jingle: a phone call. Similar to "buzz" or "ring." "Give me a jingle." 1940s.

jitney: any car employed as a private bus, usually charging five cents. Also, a nickel. 1920s.

jitterbug: an enthusiast of swing music, especially those who like to dance to swing. As a verb, to dance in wild, swing fashion. Late 1930s through the 1940s. See Section Nine: Music and Dance.
1938: "Jitterbugs are the extreme swing addicts who get so excited by its music that they cannot stand or be still . . . They must prance around in wild, exhibitionist dances or yell and scream."
Life, *August 8.*
1945: "This is a suit for hep cats and jitterbugs. I wouldn't wear this thing!" *George Burns, "Burns and Allen" radio show.*

jive: baloney; bullshit; insincerity. "Don't give me any of that jive." Also, fast-tempo swing music. As a verb to deceive or bullshit. Also, to fit; to go together or match. 1940s.

joe: coffee. Used throughout the period.

Joe Brooks: anyone who dresses or is dressed to perfection. Used by college students from the 1920s.

Joe Zilsh: any male college student. Also known as Joe College or Joe Yale. From at least 1920.

john: toilet; bathroom. Used throughout the period.

joint: a place; a bar, nightclub, home, business establishment, etc., sometimes, but not always, with a negative connotation.
1930s: ". . . the third day I got all duked up and went out and ate a sandwich at some joint over on Third Avenue. . . ."
John O'Hara, Hope of Heaven.
1943: "He . . . called up a couple of his friends . . . and they came, and before long the joint was jumpin."
H.A. Smith, Life in a Putty Knife Factory.

juice joint: a speakeasy. From 1920.

kale: money. From 1900 on.

keen: fond of. "He wasn't at all keen about the idea." From 1915 on. Also, swell, beautiful.

keep company: dating; going steady. "Mary has been keeping company with Joe." From 1935 on.

kick: please. 1940 on. As a verb, to complain, bitch. Used throughout the period.

kike: a derogatory term for a Jew. From at least 1920 on.

killer-diller: a humdinger; a beaut. From the 1930s and 1940s.

kisser: the mouth. From the 1930s and 1940s.

knockout: an extremely good-looking female, but sometimes a male. From 1936 on.

knock up: to make pregnant. From 1920 on.

know one's onions: to know one's business; to know what one is talking about. 1920s on.

knucklehead: popular term for a stupid person; an idiot. 1940s.

lamb pie: a charming person. 1940s.

lam, on the: fleeing from the police. 1920s on.

lather, get in a: get angry; get upset, worked up. Used throughout the period.

lay off: cut it out; cut the crap; knock it off. "Aw, lay off that wise-guy stuff." 1920s on.

legit: legitimate; legal; on the level. Also, on the legit. 1940s.

lettuce: money. From at least the 1930s on.

level, on the: above-board; legitimate; honest; straight. Used throughout the period.

level with: be honest; tell it straight. "Level with me." Used throughout the period.

lid: one's hat. 1930s.

limey: a British sailor or citizen, a carryover from World War I. 1920s.

live wire: a wild or lively person. 1920s on.

lollapalooza: a humdinger; a beaut; someone or something out of the ordinary. 1930s on.

loot: money. From 1945 on.

louse up: to ruin; screw up; spoil. 1930s on.

lug: a stupid man, especially a big one. 1930s on.

maracas: a woman's breasts. 1930s on.

mazuma: money. From 1915 on.

meatball: popular term for an idiot or a jerk. From the 1940s.

Mick: derogatory term for an Irishman. Used throughout the period.

milquetoast: a very timid or mild person, so named after Caspar Milquetoast, the cartoon character created by H.T. Webster in 1924.

mind your own potatoes: mind your own business. 1920s on.

Mockie: a derogatory term for a Jew. 1930s on.

moll: a female; one's sweetheart, especially a gangster's. From the 1930s on. See gun moll, Section Five: Crime.

moola: money. From the 1930s on.

moon: a verb that had a much different definition in the 1930s and 1940s than it does today. It didn't mean to bare one's buttocks, but to daydream or to be "off in a cloud," as when one is in love.
1937: "They listen incessantly to the swing bands on the air. They dance. They play ping pong. Or they simply moon and talk about life from the depths of a deep chair." Literary Digest, *July 17.*

moonshine: homemade, bootleg whiskey. Since 1920. See Section Two: Prohibition.

moxie: guts; nerve; balls. From the 1930s on.
1943: "You're young and tough and got the moxie and can hit."
   D. Hammett, His Brother's Keeper.

neck: very common term meaning to kiss, cuddle and generally make out. From the 1920s on.
1937: "Once upon a time you 'spooned,' then you 'petted,' after that you 'necked'—still the most widely used term—but now you may 'smooch' or 'perch,' or, reaching the heights of college argot, you may 'pitch and fling woo.' " *E. Eldridge,* Saturday Evening Post, *February 20.*

nifty: great; neat; excellent; cool. "A nifty pair of shoes." Used throughout the period.

nookie: sex. Used throughout, but especially during World War II.

nothing, don't know from: don't know anything; don't have any information. "He don't know from nothing about that." Used throughout the period.

number, hot little: a very attractive female. From at least the 1930s on.

nut, off one's: crazy; nuts. Throughout the period.

ofay: black's commonly used term for a white person. Since the 1920s.

old boy: a male term of address, used with other males. "Jonathan, how are you, old boy?" Commonly used from 1925 to 1940.

old man: same as "old boy."

on the make: seeking a sexual partner. Also, ambitiously or aggressively seeking success in one's business. Both from the 1930s on.

oomph: sex appeal. From about 1939 on.

oomph girl: any woman, but especially a movie star, with sex appeal. From at least 1939 on.

palooka: an average or below average boxer, from the 1920s and 1930s. From 1940 on, any big, stupid lug.

panic: to lay them in the aisles; to produce a big reaction from one's audience. "She panics them with her dog routine." An entertainment term from the 1920s on.

panther sweat: whiskey. Also, panther piss. From 1925 on.

pantywaist: a wimp; a sissy. Widely used from 1930 on.

pantywaisted: wimpy; effeminate. From 1930 on.

passion pit: a drive-in movie theater. From 1940 on.

patsy: a fall guy; a pushover; one who, though innocent, gets the blame.

pebble on the beach, not the only: "not the only fish in the sea;" there are others to choose from and I don't need you. "You're not the only pebble on the beach." Throughout the period.

peddle one's papers: go away; leave; get out of here. "Go peddle your papers elsewhere, Jack." From the 1940s.

percolate: originally, to boil over, as overheated automobile engines frequently did in the early days. In 1925, the word gained a new meaning, "to run well or smoothly." The word was frequently shortened to "perk."

Percy pants: a sissy; a wimp; a prudish male. From at least the 1940s.

pet: to make out; to kiss and fondle or caress. This was the dominant make-out word until about 1925, when the term "necking" gained popularity.

petting party: one or more couples making out together in a room or automobile. The term was very popular throughout the 1920s, especially by those who were morally outraged by the practice.

1922: "Flappers were common and petting parties expected occurrences long before their piquant names brought them notoriety." Literary Digest, *June 17.*

1922: "To the girl of today petting parties, cigaret smoking, and in many cases drinking, are accepted as ordinary parts of existence." University of Pennsylvania Punch Bowl.

1926: "WARNING! Automobile Petting Parties Must Cease. . . . Automobiles containing men and women, boys and girls, and parking on side streets, by-roads, dark roads, etc. both in the city and surrounding country, where petting parties and other obnoxious conduct are indulged in by the occupants, must cease. . . . Parents are warned that their girls are in grave danger—and unless something is done to stop this thing, disgrace and shame will be the result. . . . All petting parties are hereby warned that such practice must cease in this section—heed this warning before strenuous action is taken. We mean this thing must stop." *Yocona Klan No. 98, Knights of the Klu Klux Klan, Water Valley, Mississippi, Ad in* North Mississippi Herald, *January.*

phonus bolonus: phoney baloney. From the 1930s and 1940s.

1940s: "Of course this message is nothing but the phonus bolonus, but Waldo drops in for it and gets in the car." *Damon Runyan,* Romance in the Roaring Forties.

piffle: baloney; nonsense; bullshit. Throughout the period.

pig's eye, in a: never; not likely; when hell freezes over. Spoken sarcastically. "Yeah, we'll win all right—in a pig's eye." 1930s on.

piker: a cheapskate; one who is overly cautious with his money. Also, a coward. Used throughout the period.

1940: "If I were a secret explosives storer, I wouldn't be a piker about it. They'd be all over the place." *C. Jameson,* Saturday Evening Post.

pin: to announce one's engagement or intention to "go steady" by giving or accepting one's sweetheart's fraternity pin. A common student practice until the mid 1930s.

pinch: to arrest. Pinched: to be arrested. Used throughout the period. "The cops pinched us for speeding."

pinko: liberal. 1920s on.

pip: an outstanding or extraordinary person or thing, sometimes said sarcastically. 1920s on.

pot: an unattractive girl. Used by students in the mid-1930s.

powder, take a: to run away; leave. From at least the 1930s on.

prom-trotter: a gregarious student who attends all school social functions and especially dances. From the 1920s.

quiff: a cheap prostitute. Any female who is easy to persuade to have sex. 1925 on.

race music: jazz or blues. Jazz and blues records were sold primarily to blacks in the 1930s and 1940s.

rain pitchforks: to rain very hard. Used throughout the period.

rat on: to tell on; to turn someone in for a wrongdoing. From at least 1930 on.

razz: to give someone the raspberry; to criticize, put down or heckle someone. To razz or give someone the razz. 1920s on.

Red: a communist, after the red communist flag. 1940 on.

reefer: a marijuana cigaret; a joint. From at least 1930 on.

regular: normal; typical; average, in the sense of a "regular fellah." Throughout the period.

rent party: see Section Three: The Great Depression.

Reuben: a hick; an unsophisticated or naive person from the country. Also, Rube. Used throughout the period.

ride, take someone for a: to take someone to a deserted location and murder them. Also, "take someone for a one-way ride." From the gangster shootings of the 1920s.

rips: students' fad word for pants or trousers from 1945. Shorts were called "clipped rips."

ritz, putting on the: after the luxurious Ritz Hotel in Paris, doing something up luxuriously or in high style. Used throughout the period.

ritzy: after the luxurious Ritz Hotel in Paris, luxurious, elegant or classy. Used throughout the period.

rub: a student dance party. 1920s. Also, the act of necking or making out, 1930s.

rube: a hick; an unsophisticated person from the country. Also, Reuben. Used throughout the period.

rummy: a drunkard; a drunken bum; an alcoholic. Throughout the period.

rush: to court one for membership in a fraternity. Also, to aggressively court a member of the opposite sex. 1920s on.

sad sack: an unpopular or depressed person; a loner; one who is no fun to be with. Student usage from the 1930s. Military use for a miserable soldier throughout the 1940s.

sap: a fool; an idiot. Very common from the 1920s on.
1930: "He doesn't know what it's all about. A regular Christer, that sap." Outlook, *November 12.*
1940s: "You, Judge Wilson and Sloan, the prosecuting attorney, and those twelve good and true saps on the jury . . . for everyday I sit in the death house, one of you will be killed."
"The Shadow" radio program.
1940s: " 'You are nothing but a little sap,' Miss Missouri Martin tells Miss Billy Perry." *Damon Runyan, Romance in the Roaring Forties.*
1940s: "Hungry? I'm starved. I shoulda ate alone but I always wait for you like a sap." *S. Blau,* Yank, The Army Weekly.

shove in your clutch: get moving; get out of here; beat it. 1930s and 1940s.

sauce: whiskey; alcohol. 1930s on.

says you: a reaction of disbelief or irritation. "Yeah, says you, buddy." 1920s on.

scram: beat it; get lost; get out of here; leave. "Get your things and scram." 1930 on.

scratch: money. Throughout the period.

scream, a: something or someone hilarious. From 1930 on.

screaming meemies: the shakes; the heebie-jeebies. 1920s on.

screwball: a loony person; a nut; a weirdo. 1930s on.

see a man about a dog, have to: originally an expression meaning, "I've got to leave now," often referring to going out and buying bootleg whiskey. From the 1920s. From 1940 on, said humorously when one had to go to the bathroom.

send: to thrill or excite; to "get off" on. At least late 1930s through the 1940s.

> 1943: (Jitterbugging) "is a state of mind; it is induced by . . . listening to the blowing of the swing trumpet . . . the sweet ecstasies of the tenor sax. If that does not send you, you are a plain failure. . . . "
> New York Times Magazine, *November 7.*

shag: with a date. To go out shag, is to go with a date or an escort. Student usage from 1940 on.

shamus: a policeman or detective. Later, a security guard. Also called a sham. 1930s on.

> 1940: "Not a real copper at that. Just a cheap shamus."
> R. *Chandler,* Farewell, My Lovely.

sheba: one's girlfriend or an attractive female. 1920s.

sheik: a boyfriend or an attractive male. After the Rudolph Valentino movie by the same name. 1920s.

shiv: a knife. Used throughout the period.

simoleon: a dollar. "He hit me up for fifty simoleons." Used throughout the period.

sinker: popular name for a doughnut from 1920 on.

sitting pretty: in a prime position. 1920s on.

skag: a homely or ugly female. From the 1930s on.

skirt: any female. Throughout the period.

slick chick: an attractive, sharp-dressed female. Also, a female who is hep. Very popular during the 1940s.

smooch: kiss. 1930s on.

SNAFU: Situation Normal, All Fucked Up. A popular acronym originating in the military in 1940 and quickly spreading to the civilian population.

the snake's hips: the equivalent to the cat's whiskers or the bee's knees, 1920s. Also, the snake's toenails.

snoot full, have a: to be drunk. 1920 on.

snuggle pup: a teen term for a sweetheart who likes to cuddle. 1920s.

sockdollager: a knockout punch; a successful blow; any action having great impact. 1920s on.

soda jerk: one who dispenses soda at a drugstore soda fountain. Used throughout the period.

sore: angry; irritated; resentful. Very common throughout the 1930s and 1940s.
1931: "Well, I'm on my way to do eleven years. I've got to do it, that's all. I'm not sore at anybody. Some people are lucky. I wasn't."
   Al Capone to Elliot Ness, November.
1938: "Although I'm not going to sue anybody, I'm still good and sore." New Republic, *August 17.*
1944: "The colonel will get sore if he sees a lot of guys together."
   Yank, The Army Weekly.
1945: "I don't think I would have been allowed to keep it up if there hadn't been two officers who were amused for every one who got sore." *B. Mauldin,* Back Home.

so's your old man: a reply of irritation. From 1915 on.

spade: a derogatory term for a Negro. 1920 on.

spook: student slang for a creep. 1945.

spoon: to neck; to kiss. Early 1920s and before.

1921: "Say, Mary, do you remember how we used to spoon and kiss in the automobile in the dark corner of the park summer nights?" Literary Digest, *July 9.*

squirrel fever: sex drive; horniness. 1930s and 1940s.

stinker: a rotten person; a real jerk. From at least 1930 on.

sugar daddy: a rich older man who showers a younger woman with gifts or money in return for sexual favors. 1920s on.

1932: "You have been running true to the form of your sisters. . . . Just a poor weak fool of a girl with a couple of sugar papas." The American Mercury, *May.*

swell: good; great; fine; excellent; nice. A very popular word, used by virtually everyone, from hoboes to presidents. The sampling of excerpts below only hints at the word's pervasiveness throughout society in the 1930s and 1940s.

1938: "I worked on a Broadway paper where the managing editor used to say, "Broun, Mr. Eddie X has just given us a big ad for Sunday. See that he gets a swell notice when you write your vaudeville review." New Republic, *August 17.*

1938: "You are a toothbrush manufacturer and when you hear that your biggest competitor has doubled his sales . . . since going on the air, you decide that what you need is a radio program. You talk it over with your executives and they say it's a swell idea. . . ." Fortune, *May.*

1941: "It's a shame about Sarah. . . . She's such a swell girl otherwise!" *Ad for Listerine toothpaste, December.*

1944: "Boy, oh boy, chocolate flavored Bosco sure makes milk taste swell." *Advertisement,* Good Housekeeping.

1945: "George and Gracie will be right back. . . . I want to remind you that Swan is swell for everything, for baby, for you, for dishes. . . ." *Ad, "Burns and Allen" radio program.*

stuck on: infatuated with; in love with. "You're really stuck on her, aren't you?" Popular among students in the 1920s.

sweater girl: a girl who wears tight sweaters and uplifting bras to accentuate her breasts, a style popularized by Jane Russell in the 1940s.

swish: a male homosexual. From at least the 1940s.

talkies: movies with sound, used widely from 1928 to mid-1930s. Also called "talkers."

teenager: a word not commonly used until 1930. Previously, a teenager was called a young adult. In the 1940s, teen girls were often referred to as debs, short for debutantes.

tell it to Sweeney: go tell it to someone who will believe it. 1920.

three-letter-man: student's jocular term for F-A-G, a homosexual or effeminate male, popular from 1935 on.

tin Lizzy: see Section Six: Transportation.

Tin Pan Alley: in the 1920s, the music industry, specifically the offices of music publishers, agents and composers in New York between 48th and 52nd Streets.

tomato: a sexually attractive or "ripe" female. 1920 on.

toot, on a: on a drinking spree. "He's been on a toot for days." From 1920s on.

toots: a girl or a woman. The female equivalent of "pal" or "buddy." Derived from tootsy. "Hand me that hammer, will ya toots?" From at least 1930 on.
1940s: "Nevermind the wisecracks, toots, we're troubleshooters for the phone company." *"Three Sappy People," Three Stooges.*

tootsy: friendly term for a female that quickly evolved into "toots."

up and up, on the: on the level, legitimate. 1920s on.

vamp: a seducer of men; an aggressive female flirt. Also, to flirt or seduce. 1920s.

HARLEM SLANG, 1930s AND 1940s

air out: to leave; to take a walk.

astorperious: haughty; superior-acting.

> 1930s: "You over-sports your hand your own self. Too blamed as-tor-perious. I just don't pay you no mind."
>
> *"Story in Harlem Slang,"* American Mercury.

Aunt Hagar's chillun: Negroes collectively; the black race.

balling: having a good time.

bam: down south.

big apple: New York City. Also, the big red apple.

biggity: haughty; superior-acting. "Why are you acting so biggity?"

bull-skating: bragging; talking big.

coal scuttle blonde: a black woman.

cruising: parading down the avenue. Also known as percolating.

Diddy-wah-diddy: a suburb of hell or a faraway place.

dig: get it; understand.

draped down: sharply dressed, usually referring to a zoot suit.

dumb to the fact: ignorant of what one is talking about.

gator-faced: a long face with a big mouth.

gimme some skin!: shake hands.

Ginny Gall: a suburb of hell or a faraway place.

ground rations: sex.

home boy: a neighborhood boy or young man.

> 1930s: "Me, I knocks de pad with them cack-broads up on Sugar Hill, and fills 'em full of melody. Man, I'm quick death and easy judgement. Youse just a home boy, Jelly. Don't try to follow me."
>
> *"Story in Harlem Slang,"* American Mercury.

inky dink: a very black person.

jelly: sex.

juice: liquor.

July jam: anything very hot. "That woman is hotter than July jam!"

jump salty: to get angry.

Miss Anne: a white woman.

Mister Charlie: a white man.

ofay: white person.

peckerwood: poor southern white person.

pe-ola: a very light-complexioned Negro girl.

pimp: outside of Harlem, a procurer of prostitutes. Inside Harlem, a male who sold his love talents to a woman in exchange for a place to live or other considerations.

playing the dozens: a verbal duel in which two people trade insults about each other's parents or ancestors.

reefer: a marijuana cigaret.

rug-cutter: a good dancer. Also, someone who frequented house-rent parties.

scrap iron: cheap booze.

sender: a person with the right stuff, the goods; a solid sender.

Sugar Hill: northwest portion of Harlem, near Washington Heights, where professional people lived.

the man: the law; the boss.

trucking: strolling. Also, a dance step.

woofing: casual conversation, as dogs barking at each other from across yards.

zigaboo: Negro. *"Glossary of Harlem Slang,"* American Mercury.

V-girl: Originally, a woman who worked in a defense plant during World War II. The *V* stood for Victory. The name evolved, however, to describe any female willing to do sexual favors for any man in uniform, in order to "aid the war effort."

weenie, get the: to be cheated or given the short end of the stick; to be ripped off. From 1940 on.

wet, all: wrong; stupid; full of beans. "Ah, you're all wet, Frank." From 1930 on.

wet smack: a wet blanket; a killjoy. 1930s on.

whistle bait: an attractive female, one a man on the street is likely to whistle at. 1945.

wife: college student's affectionate term for a dormitory roomate. 1920s.

wiggle on, get a: get moving, get going, get a move on. Used through-out the period.

wolf: a shirt-chasing man; a sexually aggressive man or a ladies' man. Very popular term from 1930 on.

wolf whistle: a whistle, usually made by a male when a sexy female walked by. In vogue during World War II.

wooden nickels, don't take any: a fad expression of 1920, meaning "take care of yourself, don't do anything stupid."

Prohibition

L obbying by the powerful Anti-Saloon League and the Women's Christian Temperance Union led to passage of the 18th Amendment in 1919, which made it illegal to manufacture, transport or sell any beverage containing one-half percent or more of alcohol. The Volstead Act, or National Prohibition Act, which provided enforcement for the 18th Amendment, was passed by Congress on October 28, 1919 and went into effect on January 16, 1920. In what would prove a kind of dooming loophole, however, the *buying* and *consuming* of alcohol remained legal throughout the United States.

Millions of drinkers scoffed at Prohibition. With its legitimate manufacture eliminated, liquor in the form of "moonshine" and "bathtub gin" were simply produced in thousands of homemade stills across the country. Between 1921 and 1925 alone, the government seized some 696,933 such stills. One area of Chicago, the most notorious booze-hustling city in the country, was estimated to have an average of one hundred stills per city block.

Indeed, thirsty Americans could find liquor just about anywhere. In Canada, per capita liquor sales soared from 9 gallons to 102 gallons per year as Americans crossed the border to imbibe legally or to smuggle booze back to the states. And those who couldn't go to Canada had alternatives in Bermuda, the Bahamas and Mexico.

Closer to home, alcohol could readily be purchased from boats offshore; from local speakeasies; from neighborhood pharmacists, (prescriptions for alcohol fell conveniently within the legal realm, and thus ten million prescriptions for alcohol were written annually during Prohibition); and even from innocent-looking drugstores and ice cream parlours, which frequently served as fronts for illicit liquor businesses.

Even though prohibition agents made more than 500,000 arrests for liquor violations between 1920 and 1930, the illegal flow of alcohol continued unabated. And no wonder, as thousands of policemen were themselves involved in the trade. "Sixty percent of my police are in the bootleg business," Chicago Police Chief Charles Fitzmorris admitted during the height of Prohibition.

To prove how easily booze could be bought, one Prohibition agent in 1923 clocked how long it took him to make an illegal purchase after arriving in various cities. The results:

New Orleans	35 seconds
Detroit	3 minutes
New York	3 minutes, 10 seconds
Boston	11 minutes
Atlanta	17 minutes
Baltimore	18 minutes, 20 seconds
Chicago	21 minutes
St. Louis	21 minutes
Cleveland	29 minutes
Minneapolis	31 minutes
Washington	2 hours, 8 minutes

Surveys showed, in fact, that the Prohibition Bureau's agents were managing to stop only 5 percent of rum runners and just 10 percent of stills, much like drug trafficking statistics of today.

Unforeseen by many, Prohibition actually glamourized alcohol and *increased* its abuse in some places. In Chicago in 1927, arrests for drunken driving skyrocketed 476 percent while deaths from alcoholism rose 600 percent.

Prohibition also spurred the growth of organized crime and gang warfare and was the direct cause of hundreds of murders (Chicago alone had over seven hundred gang murders directly related to the liquor trade). Worst of all, it gave rise to such notorious criminals as George Bugs Moran, Dion O'Bannion and Al Capone, who in 1927 alone, raked in an estimated $105 million from bootlegging and other illegal enterprises.

A national poll taken in 1926 revealed the nation's attitude toward Prohibition: 49.8 percent thought the law should be modified; 31.3 percent called for a complete repeal; only 18.9 percent were satisfied with the law as it was.

By 1929 it became increasingly clear that Prohibition was largely unenforceable. The public was either opposed to it, apathetic, or profiting too highly from it. By then, five states were refusing to enforce Prohibition altogether, leaving the job to Federal authorities.

"All that the Prohibitionists have accomplished by their holy crusade," wrote H.L. Mencken in 1932, "is to augment vastly the number of boozers in the United States, and to convert the trade in alcohol, once a lawful business, into a criminal racket."

The nation agreed. Finally, what Herbert Hoover would call "the great experiment, noble in motive," was over, and in December of 1933, Prohibition was finally repealed. Many Americans celebrated, of course, by getting falling-down drunk.

⸺➤•○•◄⸺

Anti-Saloon League: One of the major organizations advocating for Prohibition and the most powerful lobby in Washington in the years leading up to Prohibition.

arrests, trivial and overzealous: Trivial arrests for liquor violations tied up the courts for years. Even children and little old ladies were arrested and put on trial, usually with great protest from the public. One of the most outrageous cases of Dry zeal occurred on April 8, 1929, when Deputy Sheriff Roy Smith went with a search warrant to the home of suspected bootlegger Joseph DeKing in Aurora, Illinois. When DeKing refused to let the deputy sheriff in, three more deputies were called in and stormed the house with mustard bombs. They knocked DeKing out with a club, and shot DeKing's wife dead with a shotgun blast to the abdomen (she had been screaming "help!" into the telephone). In horror, the DeKing's 12-year-old son grabbed a revolver and shot the Deputy Sheriff in the leg. Later one gallon of wine was found.

From his hospital bed, Smith stated, "I wish there was no such thing as Prohibition. I'm through with it. Try to enforce the law and see what happens."

1929: "It is the sentence of this court that from and after this day you shall be confined in the Detroit House of Corrections for the remainder of your life." Judge Charles Collingwood sentencing Mrs. Etta Mae Miller, mother of ten, for selling two pints of liquor, her fourth offense as a "bootlegger." Dr. Clarence True Wilson, General Secretary of the Board of Temperance, Prohibition and Public Morals, said of the stiff sentence: "Our only regret is that the woman was not sentenced to life imprisonment before her ten children were born. When one has violated the Constitution four times, he or she should be segregated from society to prevent the production of subnormal offsprings." *January 14,* Time.

1930: "Mrs. Sallie Glassgow, sixty-two years old, who stood trial for selling one pint of liquor and four quarts of beer. Convicted. . . . Mrs. P.P. Ridley, seventy-two years old, who confessed she had sold a quart of blackberry wine. . . . Clyde Cox, eleven years old, who pleaded guilty to selling liquor. His father had run a barbecue stand, and Clyde made the deliveries. . . . Such absurd trials go on daily throughout the country with preliminary hearings being conducted even on Sunday in New York in futile efforts to clear up congested calendars." Outlook.

Barleycorn, John: popular personification of bootleg liquor or moonshine, used throughout Prohibition.

1920s: "One result of the demise of the genial John Barleycorn will be that one-third of all saloons in the metropolitan area . . . will close." *News story quoted in* Daddy Danced the Charleston.

1924: "When John Barleycorn, hamstrung and a fugitive, was driven to adopt the covert existence he now leads in this great moral Republic, the forces of Christian purity looked about them for new enemies to conquer." American Mercury, *March.*

barrel house: an illegal alcohol distillation plant.

blind pig: a drinking establishment, similar to a speakeasy—and sometimes called such—with a deceptive or blank facade. Blind pigs were located in basements, behind peepholed doors, at the back of legitimate shops, and even in tenement buildings. The most common type of blind pig had a false front to make it look like a tobacco shop, tool manufacturer, launderette, lamp company, barbershop, photographer's studio, wallpaper store, funeral parlor or any one of a hundred other innocent-appearing establishments. A lookout would commonly be stationed at the front of the enterprise to let into a back room or bar, patrons who wanted drinks. The lookout weeded out the occasional naive customer who "didn't know the score and wanted only to buy a lamp." The larger cities had thousands of these establishments. Detroit alone had an estimated ten thousand to twenty thousand blind pigs, according to *Outlook.*

1929: "Within a half mile of my home I have run across more than twenty speakeasies wholly by accident. They operate under an engaging variety of disguises; a bakery where one may obtain a superb glass of lager, a dry cleaner and pressing establishment where a solid phalanx of garments in the window effectively conceals the festivities within, a dozen or so cigar shops where cigars are grudgingly sold, a vegetarian restaurant, and a real estate office."

F. Smith, *'Look Behind the Front,'* Outlook, *March 13.*

1929: "A certain blind pig proprietor in my own city . . . rented several small shops in the downtown area and fitted them out to resemble laundry agencies; a tiny office in front with a counter and shelves where the 'lookout' was stationed, and in the rear a commodious bar screened from the public's gaze by deal paneling. The windows were decorated with broad bands of blue, bearing a hand laundry sign, and so realistic was the general effect that unsuspecting customers proved a source of considerable embarrassment. It became necessary to accept laundry as a regular adjunct of bootlegging. . . ." *Ibid.*

blocker: A Southern slang term for a moonshiner. Also blockader.

1920: "Every blocker has his own method of construction . . . and we know the designs so well by this time that when we find a still we can tell just who made it." New Republic, *May 26.*

bootlegger: one who manufactures and sells alcohol illegally. Also, a booze smuggler.

1921: "The trouble about defeating Prohibition now is that we would
have to beat the combined vote of the Prohibitionists and the bootleggers." Columbia Record.

bootlegging: the illegal manufacture or sale of alcohol. Also, the smuggling of alcohol. The term originally referred to hiding a bottle of
booze in one's high boot.

booze-making shops: many shops opened during Prohibition that specialized in selling everything needed to manufacture one's own alcohol: hops, yeasts, malt, cornmeal, grains, copper tubing, kettles, etc.
Ostensibly, such shops sold the goods to "enable the housewife to
make catsup or rootbeer." The stills themselves were also available
anywhere in the nation.

1930: "As for the small still in a private home, the problem was Hercu-
lean. Not only could a portable one-gallon still be purchased on the
open market for as low a price as six or seven dollars . . . the public
libraries carried on their shelves many books and magazines which
discussed the art of distilling liquor with such commonplace utensils
as washboilers, steam cookers and even coffee percolators. The government itself had contributed to the existing literature on this
subject (Department of Agriculture Bulletin No. 182 published in
1915, and others), describing in detail the manufacture of alcohol
from apples, oats, bananas, barley, sorghum, sugar beets, potato
culls. . . . " Outlook, *October 15.*

brown: bootlegger's slang for whiskey.

brown plaid: bootlegger's slang for Scotch.

busthead: popular nickname for bootleg or homemade alcohol.

Capone, Al: Also known as "Scarface," a Chicago-based, Italian gangster, easily the most successful and most violent of all the bootleggers,
having ordered dozens of murders throughout Prohibition. He was
known to have scores of policemen, judges and other public officials
and as many as one thousand gunmen on his payroll. His illegal enter-
prises, especially bootlegging, brought a huge fortune, a reported $105
million in 1927 alone. His headquarters was comprised of two whole
floors at the Metropole Hotel on South Michigan Avenue. He was

ultimately convicted of tax evasion in October of 1931 and sentenced to eleven years in prison. He died of syphilis after being let out of prison in 1939.

1930: "They call Capone a bootlegger. Yes. It's bootleg while it's on the trucks, but when your host at the club, in the locker room or on the Gold coast hands it to you on a silver platter, it's hospitality. What's Al done, then? He's supplied a legitimate demand. Some call it bootlegging. Some call it racketeering. I call it business. They say I violate the prohibition law. Who doesn't?" *Al Capone.*

Carry Nation: staunch Prohibitionist who from 1901 to her death in 1911, carried a hatchet into Kansas saloons and split open beer kegs, smashed bottles and wrecked bars. She was arrested thirty times, but managed to pay her fines by selling souvenir hatchets.

coffin varnish: popular nickname for bootleg or homemade alcohol.

cost of alcohol during Prohibition: a shot of good bourbon, scotch, gin, rye or brandy went for seventy-five cents to a dollar at the better establishments, twice as much as before Prohibition. Draft beer was sold for twenty-five cents a glass and bottled beer as high as seventy-five cents. Gangs sold speakeasies a barrel of beer for $55 and a case of good hard liquor for $50-90. "Gallon goods," raw alcohol with extracts and coloring thrown in to make it look like genuine liquor, typically sold for fifty cents a shot; this was sold at 85 percent of New York speakeasies, often under the pretext that it was genuine. Moonshine typically sold for $6-15 per gallon, providing the moonshiner with an excellent profit; a gallon of the stuff cost as little as fifteen cents to make in a still.

counterfeit liquor: redistilled, denatured alcohol mixed with artificial flavorings and placed in bottles with the exact labels used by authentic liquor manufacturers. Sophisticated bootleggers had virtually every type of bottle and label available and thus frequently passed off their homemade concoctions for the real stuff.

1924: "I am convinced that there is a great deal of counterfeiting of liquor labels going on. Agents have brought in . . . large batches of such spurious labels, together with Government stamps and so forth." *William Mayward, U.S. Attorney, Southern District of New York.*

1924: "As we ascend to the top floor other armed sentinels confront us, and never for a moment are we out of range of their eyes or their guns. On the top floor one might imagine himself in the Bureau of Printing and Engraving at Washington. . . . Here are dies and plates galore, and presses printing counterfeit Internal Revenue stamps by the tens of thousands, and counterfeit liquor labels, American and foreign, in all the hues of the rainbow by the millions. . . . On other floors machines and workmen are busy washing bottles, filling, corking, sealing, labeling and packing them in cases."
Harper's Monthly.

cutterized: a rum-running or smuggling term meaning, "to be followed and hounded by a Coast Guard cutter." The Coast Guard could not arrest a captain for carrying liquor in his boat unless and until it was unloaded in the U.S. Cutters sometimes followed vessels for days waiting for such a discharge to take place. The Coast Guard, often frustrated by smugglers' elusive maneuvers, were notoriously over-zealous with the use of their firepower in stopping vessels, and sometimes injured or nearly injured innocent bystanders onshore.

1932: "Of course when you are loading, you must not mind one of the Coast Guard cutters coming alongside, checking the brands and asking you questions, none of which you are obliged to answer. The cutters are always at Rum Row (four and one-half miles off the west coast of Mexico), ready to follow the smaller boats when they leave. This is called cutterizing, and when one of the boats has been cutterized for weeks and her captain has become frantic, he is said to have cutteritis. At the time I write, one small boat has been off the coast for three months, loaded with 800 cases and unable to discharge them, due to a cutter lying close by all the time. The rum-runner's captain has cutteritis; but he is holding on, hoping to slip away finally in a fog." *R. Frisbie, "Rum Row,"* American Mercury, *May.*

cutting: bootlegger's term for manufacturing counterfeit liquor.

drive-by shootings: See Section Five: Crime.

drunkenness, terms for: In March of 1927, *New Republic Magazine* took a survey of all the words and phrases popularly in use at the time to describe a state of drunkenness. A partial list follows:

lit	squiffy
oiled	lubricated
owled	edged
jingled	piffed
piped	sloppy
woozy	happy
half-screwed	half-cocked
half-shot	half-seas-over
fried	stewed
boiled	bent
sprung	jazzed
canned	corked
corned	potted
slopped	tanked
tight	full
wet	high
pickled	liquored
ginned	primed
pie-eyed	wall-eyed
bleary-eyed	hoary-eyed
over the bay	four sheets in the wind
crocked	loaded
lathered	plastered
soused	polluted
saturated	stinko
blind	stiff
under the table	paralyzed
ossified	embalmed
blotto	lit up like the commonwealth
lit up like a Christmas tree	lit up like a store window
boiled as an owl	loaded for bear
loaded to the muzzle	burning with a blue flame

dry: as a noun, a person who is against drinking alcohol and is for Prohibition. As an adjective, not having or allowing any liquor to be sold.

1926: "A genuine dry is always dry, but a genuine wet has mornings when he has his doubts.'' Vallejo *(California)* Chronicle, *June.*

1928: "Congress and the country are full of drinking drys. If you are going in for suppression, suppress the millions of citizens who are the ultimate consumers of the goods."

"Crime and the Bootlegger," Literary Digest, *August 25.*

1928: "Apparently the wet-dry psychology is the offspring of congenital inability to think clearly and the evangelical prohibition movement. The state of feeling which causes a Middle Westerner to vote dry and drink wet is the same that causes him to stamp his ballot under the Republican emblem. . . ." New Republic.

goat whiskey: Indiana moonshine.

hip flask: a small container for booze, carried concealed at the hip, or in a large pocket, a fad item of the 1920s.

1926: "Hip flasks have never become a fad at Harvard."

Literary Digest, *July 17.*

1926: "Before Prohibition there was a very healthy public sentiment against drink. This is not true today. It is quite the proper thing for the young man of today to carry a flask and to offer it to his young friends. . . ." *Rev. Joseph Burke, President of St. Edwards University.*

hooch/hootch: bootleg liquor.

1926: "The youthful drinker takes to hootch on the same principle that his smaller brother takes the pie in mother's pantry."

Literary Digest, *July 17.*

horse liniment: popular nickname for bootleg or homemade alcohol.

jackass brandy: Virginia moonshine made of peaches, noted for producing internal bleeding.

jake: Jamaican ginger, a legal medicine comprised of almost pure alcohol, sold in drugstores. It was commonly used in the midwest to make one drunk but often caused paralysis that lasted for months and sometimes permanently.

ladylegger: a female bootlegger.

monkey rum: moonshine made from molasses.

moonshine: homemade alcohol. It was notorious for poisoning drinkers because amateur distillers often neglected or were unable to separate the heavier alcohol components. Also known as shine.

1924: "The other source for 'hooch de luxe' is the 'moonshine' still. . . . Scientific distillation eliminates the 'heads and the tails' of the distilled product, and thus produces a reasonably pure ethyl alcohol; but this is impossible with the amateur process, which carries into the distillate the heavier alcohols, such as propyl, amyl, and butyl . . . dangerous poisons. . . ." Outlook, *July 23.*

moonshiner: one who makes moonshine.

1928: "Sam told me of thirty moonshiners in a radius of five miles . . . . Moonshiners in my neighborhood brewed batches of beer for fortnightly orgies. These functions were community events, each guest contributing a nominal sum to cover the cost of hops, malt syrup and incidentals."

"Moonshine on the Mississippi," New Republic, *Nov. 7.*

Moran, George "Bugs": notorious Chicago bootlegger who took control of a large portion of the waterfront liquor trade after Dion O'Bannion was killed. Moran's gang was most famous for hijacking Al Capone's liquor trucks and for ultimately being brutally gunned down for the same in the famous St. Valentine's Day Massacre of 1929. Moran narrowly missed being killed himself. See St. Valentine's Day Massacre.

near beer: a legal form of beer with either no or very low alcohol content. Near beers were sometimes injected with wood alcohol by bartenders with syringes. A bartender might ask a patron cryptically, "Do you want a lollipop on the side with that?" meaning, "Do you want your near beer spiked?"

O'Bannion, Dion: notorious baby-faced Chicago florist/bootlegger who liked to arrange flowers and murders and typically carried three guns in his suit. After killing an estimated twenty-five bootlegging rivals, O'Bannion was himself gunned down in his own flower shop on November 10, 1924.

one-way ride: gangster term for being picked up, driven to a remote locale and murdered, popularized during the 1920s.

panther piss: popular nickname for bootleg or homemade alcohol.

poisonings: thirty-five thousand people died from drinking homemade liquor spiked with such poisnonous substances as wood alcohol. The alcohol, intended for industrial use only, permanently damaged the stomachs and nervous systems of thousands more. Some even went blind. Three drinks cut with just 4 percent wood alcohol were enough to cause blindness, according to a report by Bellevue Hospital.

panther whiskey: Maryland homemade booze, noted for its heavy content of esters and fusel oil.

Prohibition agent: paid as much as forty dollars per week. Of the 3,000 serving nationwide, 500 were killed by gangs. Between 1920 and 1928, 706 agents were fired and 257 others prosecuted for taking bribes, according to a Treasury Department report. The most famous agent was Izzy Einstein, who with his partner Moe Smith, donned dozens of disguises and costumes to outwit the bootleggers. Over a five-year span they made a record 4,392 arrests. Feared and hated by bootleggers, Einstein was widely known to be "incorruptible." Mysteriously, both were fired by the Prohibition Bureau in 1925 "for the good of the service," possibly because they had become too recognizable. Einstein wrote about his experiences in a book called *Prohibition Agent No. 1.*

protection money: fees paid by bootleggers and owners of speakeasies and blind pigs to the local police, to prohibition agents and sometimes to local politicians to avoid arrest, a common practice throughout Prohibition. Federal Prohibition agents were the toughest to bribe, while the local police frequently required only a free drink or two to make them "look the other way." Protection money was often referred to as "ice" by the police, prohibition agents and gangsters.

1928: "The neighbor not only manufactured a poor product, but rashly neglected to pay his pro rata for protection. When he was raided and sent to prison, Sam, now having a little capital of his own, set up an independent establishment."
"Moonshine on the Mississippi," New Republic, Nov. 7.

1932: "Now about protection. You'll no sooner get started than some plainclothes representative of the police captain in whose precinct your joint is situated will call on you. You don't have to see him.

He'll see you. You'll find him very reasonable and pleasant to deal with. All these tales about the cops sucking the life's blood out of the speakeasies are absurd. The police realize that a man has got to live; and that if they shake down a joint too much they are killing a golden goose. Twenty or twenty-five bucks a month will be ample and if you aren't doing so good you can always get a reduction. A few beers on a hot day or a couple of quick shots on a cold night will more than satisfy the cops on the beat. Once in awhile you can slip them a couple of bucks or a pint of rye. If they become objectionable you can get tough with them and report them to the captain. It's good to keep in with the cops; they often hear about Federal raids and will tip you off if they consider you their friends. . . ." *J. Sayre, "How to Run a Speakeasy," Outlook, April.*

raids: a raid by the police or Federal Prohibition agents on a speakeasy, blind pig or other establishment, in order to make arrests. Thousands of raids were made on establishments each year nationwide, but with little effect on the liquor trade.

1932: "It must not be concluded . . . that all prohibition agents are venal, or that no speakeasies are ever dealt with according to the law. . . . In the district which includes Manhattan—and extends over several counties to the north—3,227 speakeasies were raided in 1931. Enforcement is being carried on."

J. Hilder, "New York Speakeasy," Harpers Monthly, April 1932.

real McCoy, the: popular term describing quality liquor, as smuggled from Rum Row by Bill McCoy, the nation's most famous rum runner.

rot gut: popular nickname for bootleg or homemade alcohol.

Rum Row: the U.S. offshore waters, initially at least three miles from either U.S. coast, later increased to twelve miles, where the Coast Guard lacked the authority to make arrests, and where large vessels loaded with liquor sold their wares to smaller, smuggling speedboats. See cutterized.

rum runner: a liquor smuggler. In most cases, a boat captain who uses his vessel as a floating wholesale liquor outlet offshore, or one who shuttles booze from such a vessel onto shore. Also, the boat itself.

1930: "Cruising off Newport, R.I. one night last week, a coast guard patrol boat leveled its searchlight on a dark, low hull bearing the number C-5677. Guardsmen, recognizing the liquor-runner-suspect 'Black Duck,' shouted stop orders. When the 'Black Duck' veered to speed away, guardsmen opened fire, killed three suspected smugglers, wounded a fourth." Time, *January 6.*

run: to smuggle liquor into the U.S. Also, to run liquor in a truck or automobile to a speakeasy or other drinking establishment in order to make a sale. In automobiles, liquor was sometimes concealed in spare tires, false ceilings and double-gasoline-tanks. One shrewd bootlegger bought a tank truck, filled it with whiskey, and labeled the tank "Standard Oil." Bootleggers caught running alcohol commonly had their vehicles seized by the government.

1927: "It is usual in automobile running to send out two or more cars together. The front car carries the liquor, the covering car blocks the road in case of pursuit. Women are very effective in this work, especially as drivers of the covering car. They can put on such an air of helpless innocence and ignorance that it is impossible to connect them with the getaway car ahead."
"Women Bootleggers," Literary Digest, *February 5.*

1932: "I went on board the five-master in the morning and met Captain Rockwell—as I shall call him—a man responsible for running more than 1,000,000 cases of liquor into the States."
R. Frisbie, "Rum Row," American Mercury, *May.*

rye sap: midwestern term for rye whiskey.

scatter: a speakeasy.

see someone about a dog, got to: a cryptic remark made by someone intending to go out and purchase bootleg whiskey.

soda pop moon: homemade booze containing a heavy content of isopropyl alcohol, made in Philadelphia.

speakeasy: an Irish word for an undercover bar; a bar or club located in a mansion, penthouse or other private home, behind or in the basement of a legitimate restaurant or in back of a phony retail establishment. See blind pig.

New York alone had an estimated 32,000 speakeasies, all of which sold booze and beer illegally. Speaks were immensely popular, but not just anyone was allowed in. To screen out Prohibition agents speaks gave their trusted patrons their own keys or, more commonly, their own membership cards. A membership card from a prominent speak was often all that was needed to gain entry into other speaks. Sometimes patrons needed only to ring a bell or knock on a door at the front where a lookout gave suspicious "once-overs" through a sliding peephole. If a patron was known or if he spoke the right code phrase, such as "Joe sent me," he was promptly let in. A Prohibition agent with a search warrant, of course, was stalled at the door until any illegal hooch inside could be hidden or destroyed.

Many speaks ran first-class restaurants, where patrons sometimes drank from tea or coffee cups to finish out the facade. If the drinking was done from a back room the patrons might be asked to "speak easy" so as not to be heard from the adjoining establishment.

1929: "The intricate and mysterious rites observed before patrons are allowed to enter seem to be chiefly intended to add romantic excitement to the adventure, since the authorities are not likely to remain long unaware of their existence. Introduction by someone who has been there before is usually required. Then there is the business of registering the new patron's name and perhaps the issuing of a card of admittance to be presented on the next visit. It is sometimes made even more important looking by a signature or a cabalistic sign on the back of the card. Many persons about town carry a dozen or more such cards.

"The devious means employed to protect the entrances to speakeasies probably adds to the general mystification. Bells are to be rung in a special way. A sliding panel behind an iron grill opens to reveal a cautious face examining the arrivals. . . ." New York Times.

1932: "Though people are entering Tony's by the dozen, they are being sharply scrutinized at the door. Those not being immediately recognized must produce membership cards in order to gain admittance. Technically, the place is a club with the right inherent in all clubs to exclude non-members from its premises."
"New York Speakeasy," Harper's Monthly, April.

1932: "The cooking here is every bit as good as the best you find in

Paris. As a matter of fact it's good in most of the better speakeasies. That's why, in New York at any rate, the hotels are losing money on their restaurants. Speakeasies have run away with the cream of the dinner trade. . . ." *Ibid.*

1932: "When the Eighteenth Amendment was passed I earnestly hoped that it would be generally supported by public opinion. . . . That this has not been the result, but rather that drinking generally has increased; that the speakeasy has replaced the saloon, not only unit for unit, but probably twofold if not threefold; that a vast army of lawbreakers has been recruited and financed on a colossal scale; that many of our best citizens . . . have openly and unabashed disregard for the Eighteenth Amendment; that crime has increased to an unprecedented degree–I have slowly and reluctantly come to believe. . . . " *John D. Rockefeller Jr.*

still: a contrivance for distilling alcohol.

1928: "One youth in the vicinity was earning enough from occasional distillation during the summer to keep him handsomely at a university for a current session. It was his still I had discovered by chance, on my trip to the dam." New Republic, *November 7.*

1928: "Early and late he toiled at his still, his mash barrels and his coils." *Ibid.*

strike me dead: popular nickname for bootleg or homemade alcohol.

stuff: bootleg whiskey.

St. Valentine's Day Massacre: the most famous of all gangland murders during Prohibition. Suspecting that the rival "Bugs" Moran gang was hijacking his liquor trucks, Al Capone allegedly ordered a massive hit. At 10:50 A.M. on February 14, 1929, a black Packard pulled up to the S.M.C. Cartage Company, Moran's booze-running depot on Clark Street in Chicago. Of the five men who emerged, three were dressed in police uniforms; the other two in overcoats. The men nonchalantly entered the depot and quickly and efficiently gunned down, with machine guns and a shotgun, seven of Moran's men, all of whom perished. To give the appearance of a police raid, the Capone "police officers" emerged from the building with guns trained on the two overcoated men, then drove off. Moran himself avoided being shot by sheer luck. He had seen the Packard pull up and wisely snuck away from the premises. He told the police angrily later that, "Only the Capone gang kills like that."

sugar moon: homemade beet-sugar whiskey, made primarily in the west.

tarantula juice: popular nickname for bootleg or homemade alcohol.

3.2 beer: beer comprised of 3.2 percent alcohol, the first alcoholic beverage allowed by the government after Prohibition was repealed.

Untouchables, the: a group of federal agents, headed by Eliot Ness, who raided and destroyed several breweries run by Al Capone.
1931: "(Ness) remembered that the appellations employed to describe his group had been used in the caste history of India to describe the 'untouchables.' . . . And now that word has come to designate the kind of government agent, grown up out of prohibition enforcement, who cannot be 'touched' by the bribes of gangsters and liquor syndicates." New York Times, *June 18.*

wet: as a noun, one who is against Prohibition and for the free consumption of liquor. As an adjective, pro-liquor or having liquor available.
1926: "To win a primary these days a candidate must be a chameleon that looks wet to the wets, dry to the drys. . . ."
Cincinnati Enquirer, *June.*
1932: "The majorities in Congress were annoyed by several test votes. They complained that valuable time was being taken up by the extreme wets while the nation was waiting for action on the Depression."

VOTE IN THE UNITED STATES SENATE:
Aug. 1, 1917—18th Amendment	65 Dry	20 Wet
May 18, 1932—2.75 Beer	61 Dry	24 Wet

E. *Hill,* The American Scene.

whisper sister: a woman proprietor of a speakeasy.
1927: "The female speakeasy proprietor is neither rare nor romantic. She is strictly commonplace and businesslike. She is legion in

number—and the hardest thing in the bootleg world to catch or convict. . . . The ladylegger who runs a speakeasy is known in the trade as a 'whisper sister' in a tea shop or a restaurant or a hotel. It may be, and not unfrequently is, the woman's own house. The apartment speakeasy is spreading throughout the big cities. . . ."
"*Women Bootleggers,*" Literary Digest, *February 5.*

white lightning: bootleg or homemade whiskey. More specifically, a dangerous form of Virginia moonshine.

white mule: bootleg or homemade whiskey.

Women's Christian Temperance Union: a major driving force, along with the Anti-Saloon League, in getting Prohibition passed.

yack yack bourbon: Chicago moonshine made of iodine and burnt sugar.

THE GREAT DEPRESSION

D riven by the possibility of making huge and effortless profits, hundreds of thousands of amateur and professional
investors poured their hard-earned savings into the booming bull stock market of 1928. Scores of businesses did the
same, gambling on Wall Street speculation instead of
their own products to bring them income. These businesses, amateur investors and others often bought their shares "on
margin," that is, through credit, a dangerous situation that soon grew
out of control.

The stock market finally hit an all-time high on September 3, 1929.
But in the following weeks it declined, sometimes precipitously. The
big drops caused widespread panic-selling and stock prices tumbled
still further. A massive drop came on October 24, Black Thursday,
when security values lost six billion dollars. A guard at the New York
Stock Exchange described the scene on the floor: "They roared like
a lot of lions and tigers. They hollered and screamed, they clawed at
one another's collars. It was like a bunch of crazy men. Every once in
awhile, when Radio or Steel or Auburn would take another tumble,
you'd see some poor devil collapse on the floor." The market plunged
again the following Monday, and on Tuesday it plunged the furthest
of all. "Stock prices virtually collapsed yesterday," said the *New York
Times*, "swept downwind with gigantic losses in the most disastrous
trading day in stock market history."

Prices eventually bottomed out in November and recovered by the
end of the year, but the damage was done. What did it all mean?

Everyone wanted to know. What would the repercussions be? Did the Crash mean anything at all?

The answers came all too soon.

Within six months, four million Americans were out of work. By winter of 1931, eight million Americans were unemployed. By the end of 1931, 13.5 million.

In 1932, 56 percent of blacks and 40 percent of whites were without jobs. Many of the jobless remained that way throughout the Depression. But even those who were lucky enough to keep their jobs saw their incomes plummet by as much as 50 percent or more.

Behind these shocking statistics lie untold suffering: The breakup of thousands of families. The dropping out of school by millions of children. Hunger. Mental depression. Humiliation. Suicide.

For the average Joe, the Depression began with a simple cut in pay. Then a cut in the work week, from six days to three. As companies across the country experienced a sharp drop-off in business, the inevitable layoffs followed.

Many of those laid off applied for local relief funds, a bare subsistence of three or four dollars per week when such funding was available at all. (The number of families on relief in New York from October 1929 to Spring 1930 jumped 200 percent. Relief there amounted to $2.39 per family per week.)

At the employment agency, men stood in a line that stretched around the block, only to be told at the end that there was no work. So they knocked on the doors of every business in town and offered to work the first month for free. They were told, again, no work.

That unlucky average Joe probably took out a line of credit at the local grocery store. Beans replaced meat on the dinner table. His pantry, and his children, grew lean. If he was especially hard-hit, the electricity and gas were shut off in his home.

With growing desperation, these men and their wives pawned their valuables, including their wedding rings. If they were burdened with several children, they resorted to outright begging. They sold apples on the streets, or packed up the family in the car and searched from state to state for work.

A lot of families doubled up with other families in a single apartment. Some built shacks around dumps and ate garbage. Others smashed store windows at night and looted them for food. Many men lost their families altogether.

Throughout America, the desperate and humiliated stood in bread-lines sponsored by the Salvation Army or some other charity. They waited for a bowl of cabbage soup and a crust of bread. It was better than the weeds and dandelions some had resorted to eating.

The most desperate pleaded directly with their political officials to help them personally, as this letter to Pennsylvania governor Gifford Pinchot attests: "I am sending this letter to you and your wife to ask you won't you please help me. I have six little children to take care of. I have been out of work for over a year and a half. Am back almost thirteen months and the landlord says if I don't pay up before the 1 of 1932 out I must go, and where am I to go in the cold winter with my children? If you can help me please for God's sake and the children's sakes and lives please do what you can and send me some help, will you? I cannot find any work. I am willing to take any kind of work. . . . Thanksgiven [sic) dinner was black coffee and bread and was very glad to get it. My wife is in the hospital now. We have no shoes to wear; no clothes, hardly. Of what will I do I sure will thank you."

Six months of unemployment stretched to a year, two years, three. And all the time, the economists insisted it would all soon blow over. President Hoover, meanwhile, refused to deliver Federal aid. He was convinced that such action would sap the initiative of the middle class and make them lazy.

Many in the working class were puzzled. They had worked hard in the past. Most had had nothing to do with the dizzy stock speculation that caused the stock market crash that helped bring on the present situation. So why were *they* suffering? Who's fault was all this, anyway?

"There is not an unemployed man in the country that hasn't con-tributed to the wealth of every millionaire in America," Will Rogers said in the midst of the Depression. "The working classes didn't bring this on, it was the big boys that thought the financial drunk was going to last forever, and overbought, overmerged and overcapitalized. . . . We got more wheat, more corn, more food, more cotton, more money in the banks, more everything in the world than any nation that ever lived ever had, yet we are starving to death. We are the first nation in the history of the world to go to the poorhouse in an automobile."

And so it was that a hit song, "Brother, Can You Spare a Dime?" defined the period and became the lament of a nation. For most, the agony wouldn't end until close to the end of the decade. A poll by *Fortune* in 1937 showed that only one quarter of the population thought the Depression was over that year, while 50 percent thought it was in the process of getting over. Only with the massive economic demands of World War II was the Depression finally vanquished completely.

——➤·◦·◄——

amateur investors: housewives, cabdrivers, farmers and many other neophytes—hearing stories of the incredible profits being made through stock market speculation—flooded the stock market in 1928 and risked their life savings, often with disastrous losses.

1928: "These amateurs were not schooled in markets that had seen stringent, panicky drops in prices. They came in on a rising tide. They speculated on tips, on hunches, on 'follow-the-leader' principles. When a stock rose sharply they all jumped for it—and frequently were left holding the bag of higher prices."
The Nation, *August 15.*

apple sellers: Northwest apple growers had a bumper crop in 1930 and the surplus was sold on credit to the unemployed to sell on the streets, usually for five cents each, but sometimes for "whatever the buyer was willing to give." The apple sellers and their crates were a common sight in cities around the nation. New York alone had some six thousand apple vendors, but these were declared a public nuisance in 1931 and ultimately removed from the streets.

1931: (A sign seen over an apple vendor's stand in Manhattan in January)

FINANCIAL STATEMENT 30 DAYS
THE PUBLIC APPLE INSTITUTE
Limited Partnership Grant
Gross Sales $240.00
Wholesale Cost $133.50
$106.50

Overhead—

- A lot of rotten apples secreted in boxes
- Frozen apples while idling for buyers
- Losses due to bums while giving information to pedestrians
- Feeding my pet—a worthy horse every morning about 9:30.
- Colds in the chest, cough-drops from exposure
- Hot coffee during stormy days, occasional appetite to consume an apple.
- Feeding beloved children passing by me to the Children's Protective Association of East 45th Street.

Total $28.50
Net Profit $78.00

Loss of earnings as during normal times $77 per week: $308
Expenses for self and boy $132.00

Total $78.00
                        -132.00
                        ???????

bank closings: over one thousand banks failed and closed in 1930 alone. Such closings panicked depositors. Rumor of impending closings frequently brought out mobs of depositors and investors, who made "runs" on their institutions to withdraw their money before the doors closed and left them penniless.

bank holidays: the deliberate, temporary closing of banks to prevent "runs" from panicky depositors.
1931: "RUNS CLOSE TWO BANKS: Union Town, PA. The National Bank of Fayette County was closed tonight by a board of directors following heavy withdrawals. . . . Spencer, W. Virginia. The Roane County Bank was closed today by the board of directors because of recent heavy withdrawals." New York Times, *Oct. 11.*

bank night: a gimmick used by movie theaters to draw a larger audience during the Depression. One night per week, a designated amount of money was given away to the lucky person or family whose name or number were drawn. Some movie theaters gave away dishes.

1930s: "My father's name was called at bank night once. I remember he had these milk bottles sticking out of his pockets that he was going to turn in for cash to the milk company. He walked up on the stage and got his money and it didn't bother him a bit. But the bottles mortified my mother, because a lot of people already thought we were poor and she was embarrassed. The bank night money didn't amount to much, but my father was ecstatic." *Mary McCutcheon.*

bank run: a mob of depositors making panicked withdrawals, often forcing the bank to close for a "holiday."

1931: "When the debris of the market-break was cleared last December, I had $2,000 left of an original $7,000. I asked my broker to send me a check for the balance, which was subsequently deposited in the Manufacturer's Trust. . . . Well sir, there was a run on that bank last week. I stood in line seven hours before I got my money—$1,300. Upon entering my home, I was held up in the doorway at the front of two guns (one would have been enough) and the money taken away. . . . And so it goes, Mr. Editor. What between the brokers, bankers and burglars, what chance has John Citizen got?" *letter by Robert Ellison to* Time, *January 5.*

barter: grew in popularity throughout the Depression. At Madison Square Garden, men could buy tickets at some boxing matches with canned goods or a pair of shoes. An Oklahoma hotel accepted eggs, chickens and fresh vegetables in exchange for a room. One midwest newspaper even offered a one-year subscription for ten bushels of wheat.

breakups: crumbs, broken bread crusts and bread that failed to rise, sold cheaply in bags by bakeries to the poor.

cellar clubs: social clubs formed by youths in the cellars of tenement buildings in large cities across the country. The clubs in New York were attended regularly by an estimated 250,000 youths, aged eighteen to twenty-five, many of whom were jobless, and because of the Depression, could afford to go nowhere else for entertainment. One Brooklyn block had a reported forty-odd cellar clubs, attesting to their popularity among the poor. Furnishings usually amounted to no more than a few chairs, a radio, a piano and a Ping-Pong table. For a dues payment of thirty cents a week, members (mostly men) could talk, listen to music, smooch with their girlfriends away from the watchful eyes of a chaperon, or organize various community activities. Some clubs invariably attracted "toughs" and gangmembers who smoked marijuana, drank, gambled, and committed "sex crimes," but at least an equal number of members were chaste conservatives who performed various charity drives and other humanitarian work for their neighborhoods.

1937: "What are the dire crimes perpetuated by the cellar clubs and their memberships? Opponents have their answers pat: all sorts of laws are broken, sex crimes 'originate' in the clubs, gambling goes on, boys and girls spend evenings in the dimly lit rooms without chaperons of any sort." Literary Digest, July 17.

Civilian Conservation Corps: an organization initiated as part of the New Deal to put 500,000 youths to work in national forests and parks.

drought and dust bowl: the midwest drought and dust bowl that began in 1930 added severely to the nation's depression woes. Thousands of farmers saw their topsoil dry up and actually blow away. Many of these were forced to pack everything they owned and look for more fertile ground in the west, especially California. See farms and oakies. See also Chronologies: History, Events, Innovations and Fads for a description of the dust bowl disaster.

1931: "City dwellers last week were sharply reminded of the Drought when 500 half-starved farmers and their wives raided the food stores of England, Arkansas (pop. 2,408). Most of the hungry citizens . . . had been fairly prosperous husbandmen until last year. Their crops had been ruined. Their provisions were gone. . . . With guns tucked in their clothes they demanded Red Cross relief. When this was not forthcoming, they threatened to loot the stores. 'We want food and we want it now! We're not beggars, we're not going to let our children starve!' they shouted. . . . England's merchants, hard-pressed by the Depression themselves, began to dole out food. More than 300 were each supplied with a ration worth $2.75." Time, Jan. 12.

evictions: thousands of families were evicted from their homes, unable to pay their rent or mortgages, and ended up doubling up with other families to split expenses. See landlords.

1932: "The evictions in Philadelphia are frequently accompanied not only by the ghastly placing of a family's furniture on the street, but the actual sale of the family's household goods by the constable. . . . Only the other day a case came to my attention in which a family of ten had just moved in with a family of five in a three-room apartment. However shocking that may be to members of this committee, it is almost an everyday occurrence in our midst."
Relief official, Philadelphia, February.

farms: farmers saw prices for their products plummet during the Depression. As a result, thousands upon thousands of farms were unable to make a profit or break even and were foreclosed upon by the banks. Many farmers in the midwest banded together at foreclosure sales by scaring off prospective bidders, buying up all of a fellow farmer's valuables for cheap prices, and then giving them back to the farmer the next day. As part of the New Deal, the government paid some farmers not to grow certain crops or to leave their fields unplanted. With fewer crops glutting the market, prices rose sharply in 1933.

free food dump: any open spot near a Hooverville or other location where food was dumped, free for the taking, by restaurants, organizations and private citizens, for the benefit of the poor and homeless.

gardens: cooperative gardens fostered by the states, by relief agencies, by universities and by corporations to provide work and sustenance to the unemployed. Thousands of these gardens sprung up all over the country in donated fields, yards and vacant lots. Gardens in the Calumet district of Michigan alone supplied some twenty thousand kitchens with produce in 1932.

Hoover blankets: newspapers. Because many slept in the streets after being unemployed for months; a derogatory reference to President Herbert Hoover.

Hoovercarts: old automobiles pulled by mules, originating among North Carolina farmers who were too poor to buy gasoline and spare parts. Also known as Hoover wagons.

Hoover flags: empty pockets, a disparaging reference to President Herbert Hoover.

Hoover, Herbert: the president in office when the Depression began, he was unable to raise the country's morale because of his lackluster personality and was, in fact, widely blamed for the nation's economic woes. Despite evidence to the contrary, throughout his term he insisted that nobody in America was starving. (The New York City Welfare Council tallied 139 starvation or malnutrition-related deaths in 1933 alone.) He also stuck doggedly to the belief that local charities could handle the nation's relief load, even though surveys showed they were grossly inadequate.

Hooverville: any makeshift community of shanties, shacks and packing crates, usually set up near a dump, where the residents could pick over garbage. 1930s.

landlords and shopkeepers: much of a community's financial burden throughout the Depression fell on local shopkeepers and landlords. Shopkeepers often gave hungry families a line of credit that all too frequently went unpaid. Some angelic shopowners went as far as erasing all debts. Landlords sometimes carried a family's rent for months before puting anyone on the streets. Often it came down to issuing an eviction notice only when one's own family faced destitution.

1932: "In Philadelphia, as in most other cities . . . thousands of small, independent shopkeepers are going bankrupt trying to help their neighbors. The *Philadelphia Record* found any number of these corner grocers, butchers and bakers, heavily in debt themselves, who had on their books unpaid accounts of customers running in some cases into hundreds of dollars. . . . [One] shopkeeper, pointing to a bill of $200 that was owed him, said: 'Eleven children in that house. They've got no shoes, no pants. In the house, no chairs. My God, you go in there, you cry, that's all. What can you do? Let them go hungry?' . . . So, too, with many landlords . . . [Some] allow their tenants to live on for months without paying any rent. In one small area covering a few city blocks I found more than two hundred families who were back in their rent anywhere from six to eighteen months." The Nation, *March 9.*

1932: "When Mr. and Mrs. James Hennum announced that they had canceled all the debts on the books of their general store in Sloan, Iowa, some debtors came and offered to pay. But in each instance the Hennums refused. 'My wife and I believe in forgiving and forget-ting,' Mr. Hennum said. 'This depression has been hitting folks pretty hard.' Their debtors numbered several hundred, and the debts ranged from a few cents to $1,000, some of them having been owed for fourteen years." Associated Press, *July 9.*

New Deal: Franklin Delano Roosevelt's program for combating the Depression. It included the creation of dozens of government agen-cies, including the Securities and Exchange Commission to regulate the Stock Exchange, The Federal Deposit Insurance Corporation to protect bank depositors, the Social Security system to ensure Ameri-cans' financial security, and the Work Projects Administration to create jobs, to counter all the forces that came together to create the Depres-sion. The agencies were put in place from 1933 on.

NRA: the National Recovery Administration, a government agency cre-ated as part of the New Deal in 1933, to legislate prices and wages and to administer codes of fair practice as a means of countering effects of the Depression. The Supreme Court declared the agency illegal in 1935.

oakies: refugees from the midwest dust bowl disaster who packed up their belongings by the thousands and headed west in search of a better life in California and elsewhere, adding to the nation's Depres-sion woes.

relief: subsistence funding provided for food and fuel to needy families by cities and local charities. No national relief program existed during the Depression. New York funding dropped to $2.39 per family per week in 1932, but many who qualified could not even get this small amount because funding was so scarce. Detroit's relief dropped as low as fifteen cents per day per person at one point. But some cities and towns had no relief at all and others limited their assistance to families with three or more children. All told, only one-fourth of the nation's unemployed qualified for relief or had relief funds available to them.

rent party: a dance party held at one's home, provided for a small contribution by one's neighbors, in order to collect enough money to pay the rent. Originating and most popular in Harlem throughout the 1930s, but known elsewhere. The music was jive or swing.

Roosevelt, Franklin Delano: popular, morale-building president who is credited with helping to vanquish the Depression. In his inaugural address he spoke the now famous words of the Depression: "Let me first assert my firm belief that the only thing we have to fear is fear itself—nameless, unreasoning, unjustified terror which paralyzes needed efforts to convert retreat into advance." Once in office, he took immediate action and, consulting with a Brain Trust of college professors, launched a huge program called the New Deal, which centered around the creation of dozens of new agencies, to counter the nation's economic woes.

skiffle: a rent party.

Unemployment Relief, President's Organization On: the government agency that tried to boost the nation's morale and encouraged cities and neighbors to help each other through the crisis during the Depression. It was charged by critics as being all talk and no action.

1931: "OF COURSE WE CAN DO IT! *We dug the Panama Canal, didn't we? And they said we couldn't do that. *We put an army in France four months after we entered the World War, didn't we? And surprised the world. *Now we've got a tough one to crack right here in our own back yard. Men are out of work. Our men. Our neighbors. Our citizens. Honest, hard-working folk. They want jobs. They're eager to work. But there aren't jobs enough to go around. Somebody's got to tide them over. Who's going to do it? The people who dug that ditch. The people who went to France, or bought Liberty Bonds, or went without sugar—Mr. and Mrs. John K. American. That means you—and you—and YOU!—every one of us who is lucky enough to have a job. We're going to share our luck with the folks out of work, aren't we? Remember—there's no national fund they can turn to for relief. It's up to us! And we've got to dig deeper than we did last winter. But if we all dig deep enough we can keep a roof over every head, food in every pantry, fuel on every fire, and warm clothing on every needy man, woman and child. . . . That will beat Old Man Depression and lead the way to better days. Can we do it? Of course we can do it. Give . . . and give generously."

The President's Organization on Unemployment Relief, Literary Digest, *November 21.*

Will Rogers: A hugely popular humorist who is widely credited with boosting national morale during the Depression. His down-home wit cut politicians down to size and elevated the hard-working little guy. 1931: "Now everybody has got a scheme to relieve unemployment. There is just one way to do it and that's for everybody to go to work. Where? Why, right where you are, look around and you will see a lot of things to do, weeds to cut, fences to be fixed, lawns to be mowed, filling stations to be robbed, gangsters to be catered to. There is a million little odds and ends right under your eye that an idle man can turn his hand to every day. Course he won't get paid for it, but he won't get paid for not doing it. My theory is that it will keep him in practice in case something does show, you can keep practicing so work won't be a novelty when it does come." *Radio broadcast, October 18.*

Snapshots of the Depression

- The number of unemployed transients caught illegally hopping rides on the Missouri Pacific Railroad jumped from 13,745 in 1929 to 186,028 by 1931. In 1932, the Southern Pacific Railroad kicked 700,000 vagrants from its trains.
- According to the Children's Bureau, more than 200,000 children were roaming the country as drifters at the height of the Depression.
- On March 19, 1930, eleven hundred men waiting in a breadline in New York mobbed two trucks headed for a nearby hotel and made off with their deliveries of bread and rolls.
- In 1931, reporters found Pennsylvania miners and their families "huddled on the mountainsides, crowded three or four families together in one-room shacks, living on dandelions and wild weed-roots . . . many were dying of those providential diseases which enable welfare authorities to claim that no one has starved."
- In the Spring of 1932 in Chicago, a group of fifty desperate men were seen at the back of a restaurant fighting over a barrel of garbage.
- In Detroit, two families who shot their landlord in order to prevent eviction were acquitted by soft-hearted jurors.

- The five-day work week was adopted. Millions of people who had previously worked six days per week, increasingly had Saturdays off.
  1937: "While five years ago the five day week was exceptional, it has now become quite general." *National Industrial Conference Board.*
- The rate of marriage dropped from 10.14 (per thousand population) in 1929 to 7.87 in 1932. The birthrate also dropped, from 18.9 in 1929 to 16.5 in 1933.
- Emigration outpaced immigration by a significant margin. Many Americans actually sought jobs in Russia.
- The most popular slogan of 1930: "Prosperity is just around the corner."
- Suicide peaked. According to the *Spectator,* an insurance weekly, the average suicide rate for the previous thirty years had been 17.8 per 100,000 people. That rate rose to 20.5 in 1931, with a total of 20,000 suicides for the year.
- The rate of arrests in New York rose 33 percent in 1930. Lootings increased sharply in Detroit, with desperate men smashing store windows at night to make off with food or other necessary items.
  1931: "Unemployment has the inevitable tendency to make men take things into their own hands. Few men have criminal tendencies, but every man must eat. . . . Deprive him of the means of feeding his family and you at once expose him to peculiar temptation, which is pretty hard to withstand."
  Arthur Woods, former Police Commissioner of New York, October 11.

WORLD WAR II

n the dance floor, Americans jitterbugged to the beat of the "Chattanooga Choo Choo." At the movies they chuckled over the antics of Abbott and Costello in *Buck Privates*. On the baseball field they cheered Ted Williams's .406 batting average, and the Brooklyn Dodgers-New York Yankees rivalry in the World Series.

The Great Depression of the 1930s was over. Men's suits were going for $30. Road-hogging cars for $1,500. Americans were working. They were productive. They were making $40 a week on average and, barring the rumors of joining the war in Europe, they were more secure than they had been in years.

But at noon on December 8, 1941, the day after the bombing of Pearl Harbor, America's new-found security all but evaporated. A record sixty million Americans stared in horror at their radios as President Roosevelt spoke these grave words:

> Yesterday, December 7, 1941—a date which will live in infamy—the United States of America was suddenly and deliberately attacked by naval and air forces of the Empire of Japan.
>
> The United States was at peace with that nation, and, at the solicitation of Japan, was still in conversation with its government and its Emperor looking toward the maintenance of peace in the Pacific. . . .
>
> The attack yesterday on the Hawaiian Islands has caused severe damage to American naval and military forces. Very

many American lives have been lost. In addition, American ships have been reported torpedoed on the high seas between San Francisco and Honolulu.

Yesterday the Japanese government also launched an attack against Malaya.

Last night Japanese forces attacked Hong Kong.

Last night Japanese forces attacked Guam.

Last night Japanese forces attacked the Philippine Islands.

Last night the Japanese attacked Wake Island.

This morning the Japanese attacked Midway Island.

Japan has, therefore, undertaken a surprise offensive extending throughout the Pacific area. The facts of yesterday speak for themselves. The people of the United States have already formed their opinions and well understand the implications to the very safety and life of their nation. . . .

I believe I interpret the will of the Congress and the people when I assert that we will not only defend ourselves to the uttermost, but will make very certain that this form of treachery shall never endanger us again.

Hostilities exist. There is no blinking at the fact that our people, our territory, and our interests are in grave danger.

With confidence in our armed forces—with the unbounded determination of our people—we will gain the inevitable triumph—so help us God.

I ask that the Congress declare that since the unprovoked and dastardly attack by Japan on Sunday, December 7, a state of war has existed between the United States and the Japanese Empire.''

Three days later the horror was redoubled when Germany and Italy declared war on the U.S. Suddenly freedom was threatened by the expansionist visions of not one, but two sets of enemies on opposite sides of the world.

American men between the ages of twenty-one and thirty-six had already registered for the draft a year before and, with over sixteen million men to draw from, in addition to a standing regular army of 375,000, it seemed America would add an invincible muscle to an

already large Allied force; certainly they could overcome any new onslaught the Japanese or Germans might launch.

But the Japanese quickly took a devastating toll on forces in the
Pacific. The U.S. and Great Britain had been caught flat-footed and
reeled with defeat after defeat. The resource-hungry Japanese readily
secured Hong Kong, Singapore, Malaya, Burma and Thailand, and
soon set their sights on Australia. Meanwhile, the German forces were
threatening to take over the Soviet Union, and, in the Atlantic and
elsewhere, were sinking hundreds of Allied ships and tankers, ultimately producing a gas shortage in the U.S.

The picture grew increasingly grim until Major James Doolittle,
leading a squadron of B-25s, managed to infiltrate Japan and bomb
Tokyo in broad daylight on April 18, 1942. Soon after, in May, the
American navy sank its first Japanese aircraft carrier, a major morale
booster. The battle of Midway followed in June and, working with a
smaller fleet, the Americans destroyed four Japanese carriers and 332
aircraft, handing the enemy its first humiliating defeat. On August 7,
the first U.S. Marines landed on Guadalcanal, the start of an extended
series of battles that escalated to a brutal test of resolve from which
the Americans ultimately emerged victorious.

On the homefront, Americans came together in a mass effort of
camaraderie. Civilians helped the military watch the skies for approaching enemy airplanes. Civilians watched the shores for submarines. They conducted air raid drills, blackouts and dimouts. They rationed. They salvaged. They conserved. They worked overtime. They
planted Victory gardens, wrote morale-boosting letters to the troops.
They bought war bonds. They bought even more war bonds. They did
everything their government asked them to do and then some. Women
literally put on pants and got down and dirty in war plants across the
country. When they came home, they cooked the meals *and* fixed the
broken furnace. Unlike lesser wars since, Americans knew exactly what
was at stake. The enemies, bent on world domination, were clear and
horrible and had to be stopped at all costs.

"More than any other war in history," said Dwight Eisenhower
after the defeat of Germany, "this war has been an array of the forces
of evil against those of righteousness. It had to have its leaders and it
had to be won–but no matter what the sacrifice, no matter what the

suffering of populations, no matter the cost, the war had to be won.''

The press and the government worked in tandem to sanitize the war. Frequently, news stories of battles were heavily slanted in favor of America's military competency, with losses downplayed. Barely mentioned or not mentioned at all, were the thousands of Allied deaths that came not from the enemy, but from "friendly fire.'' Poorly or too-quickly trained, Allied troops frequently misidentified their own planes and ground forces, with tragic results.

With time and experience, however, Allied forces grew in competence and, in battle after battle, increasingly edged out the enemy.

Finally, after having being driven from Russia, France and Belgium, Adolph Hitler committed suicide on April 30, 1945, and German hostilities ceased.

The dropping of atomic bombs on Hiroshima and Nagasaki on August 6 and 9, 1945, killed 170,000 Japanese. On August 15, following a devastating defeat of Japanese forces by the Soviets in Manchuria, Emperor Hirohito told his citizens in a radio broadcast they should "Bear the unbearable'' and accept unconditional surrender to the Allies.

The war was over. The long road of recovery lay ahead. Every nation playing a major role in the war came out weakened and vulnerable except one: the U.S. It emerged a booming superpower. "We came out with the most unbelievable machinery, tools, manpower, money,'' noted Paul Edwards in Studs Terkel's, *The Good War.* "And the rest of the world was bleeding and in pain.''

⟫•◦•⟪

ON THE HOMEFRONT

air raid warden: tens of thousands of ordinary citizens volunteered to act as wardens during air raid alerts and blackouts. Wardens were trained in first aid, fire prevention, the use of gas masks, and the handling of incendiary bombs. Their chief responsibility, however, was to get lights turned off. Because not everyone complied, shouts of "dim those lights!'' became a common evening cry throughout the war.

air raid warnings and blackouts: Some cities in the U.S. began conducting air raid alerts and blackouts the day after the attack on Pearl Harbor. On December 8, 1941, San Francisco went black after receiving a report, later learned to be false, of approaching enemy aircraft. On December 9, New York City had its first alert (no air raid sirens were in place then, so police cars and fire trucks simply blew their sirens simultaneously) with the report of enemy aircraft off the East Coast. The alarm sounded at 1:25 P.M., and school let out not only in New York but on up through the New England states as well. New York had its second alert the next day at 8:41 A.M.

Blackouts continued to be conducted periodically in various cities (San Francisco had seven by January 1942) throughout the war. Sometimes "dim outs" were ordered and only lights facing the sea were shut down. Virginia and Maryland shores were dimmed out in March of 1942. Automobile drivers failing to dim their lights as they approached coastal areas were subject to one-year jail terms and $5,000 fines. New York was dimmed out in June. The *Herald Tribune* described one scene after all the familiar outdoor advertising lights had been shut off: "The opening night of Ray Bolger's new musical *By Jupiter* saw [theatergoers] completely baffled by the lack of familiar West Side landmarks and feeling their way from Sardi's to the Shubert Theater and back by an elaborate system of navigation based on the Braille system and dead reckoning. . . ."

Despite, or perhaps because of the elaborate precautions, only one Japanese aircraft ever reached U.S. shores. In November 1942, Officer Nobuo Fujita of the Imperial Japanese Navy managed to drop several incendiary bombs over an Oregon forest in a bizarre attempt to start a conflagration. The plane, equipped with pontoons, had been transported to U.S. shores inside a Japanese submarine. See spotters.

1941: "Two formations of 'many planes,' described as undoubtedly enemy aircraft, flew over the San Francisco Bay area tonight, it was announced officially by Brigadier General William O. Ryan, commander of the Fourth Interceptor Command, after a progressive blackout had blotted out naval and military establishments and whole cities along the Pacific Coast. . . . Conflicting reports spread, contributing to the 'war of nerves,' as the sirens wailed and broadcasting were silenced." New York Times, *December 8.*

baseball: 4,000 of the 5,700 players in the minor and major leagues eventually served in the war. The most sorely missed were, among others, Joe DiMaggio, Ted Williams, Hank Greenberg, Stan Musial,

Warren Spahn, Yogi Berra, Jackie Robinson and Phil Rizzuto. Most of the minor leagues discontinued play, while the majors brought up old players out of retirement or adopted very young players. All night games were banned until 1944. Football suffered similar shortages.

1942: "Should an air raid siren sound while you're watching a major-league baseball game, don't leave the ballpark. A sticker on the back of your seat will tell you what to do. If you are not to move at all, red and green arrows will direct you beneath the stands. You'll probably be sitting in the best bomb shelter in the neighborhood."
Notice broadcast by big league baseball clubs in the spring of 1942.

blackout shades and curtains: light-blocking shades or curtains, used by apartment and homeowners to keep their lights from shining outside during blackouts and dim outs. Some made their own by "seaming together two pieces of fabric, one black and one to match [interior decor]" as advised by *House and Garden* magazine. Others simply purchased opaque shades from the store.

1942: "Provision must be made to darken every window, glass door, skylight and exterior opening wherever lights are used after dark, using dark blinds, window shades, thick curtains, special screens or other heavy material. Any material which allows a glow to be seen outside will not do. . . ."
Blackout instructions, Appalachian Electric Power Company.

civil air patrol: launched in December 1941, an organization of civilian flyers who patrolled the air spaces around coastlines (as far out as 150 miles) in search of enemy submarines. Within months, some of the civilian planes were equipped with small bombs and depth charges, some of which were actually dropped on a total of fifty-seven German submarines, two of which were heavily damaged. By the end of the war, some ninety airplanes were lost and twenty-six civilian flyers killed in the line of duty.

defense plant workers: tens of thousands of women worked in defense plants during the war. They riveted, welded and soldered right along with the men. Because these women often worked long or late shifts, and their husbands were frequently away at war, their children were sometimes left to fend for themselves at home. The result: juvenile delinquency rose 56 percent during the war.

1942: "The demand for women in war plants is taking thousands of household servants, and eventually nearly all housewives will be doing their own work. Many of them will be in the industry as well."
P. McNutt, The American Magazine.

favorite entertainments of wartime: Due to gas rationing, blackouts, shortages and other inconveniences of wartime, Americans entertained themselves at home more than ever. Books sold in record numbers. The sale of playing cards rose 1,000 percent. Radio listening grew by 20 percent. Among America's favorite radio entertainers, Harry James, Tommy Dorsey, Glen Miller, Bing Crosby, Frank Sinatra, Dinah Shore, Bob Hope, Red Skelton, Arthur Godfrey and Burns and Allen ranked at the top. At the movies, Van Johnson, Gary Cooper, Bette Davis, Greer Garson and Ingrid Bergman led in popularity.

gas shortage: exacerbating an already difficult situation with national gas rationing, a gas *shortage* brought on by tanker sinkings in the Atlantic caused most gas stations along the East Coast in the summer of 1942 to close down. The few that remained open sometimes had lines of three hundred cars waiting to tank up. Many drivers became stranded on the sides of roads. Tanker trucks became like pied pipers, with long strings of fuel-hungry cars following them wherever they went. See rationing.

letter-writing: letters from home were big morale boosters to "the boys overseas." Family members wrote often, but even those without a soldier in the family were urged to drop a line to at least one lonely man, as attested by this full-page magazine advertisement sponsored by Dole in 1944:

> CAN YOU PASS A MAILBOX
> WITH A CLEAR CONSCIENCE?
> Just suppose that instead of this mailbox you came face-to-face with the boy in uniform you've neglected to write! . . . After all, writing a letter is such a *little* thing to do . . . and yet to those in the Service it is the most important thing in the world. From the Southwest Pacific, a Dole employee who is now in the Service writes as follows: "Mail is a great thing. It is a

barometer on a ship. When we don't have mail for long periods, the morale becomes very low . . . but just as soon as mail is brought aboard, the entire ship brightens and the change in atmosphere is certainly surprising.''

Even if you have no one of your own in the Armed Forces, drop a cheery line to a neighbor's son or daughter, a former business associate, or, perhaps, one of the servicemen you've entertained in your home. To speed your letters and to save valuable shipping space, use V-Mail.

rationing: At one time or another during the war, the government rationed nearly everything in order to preserve resources for the military. Rationing and restrictions were carried out in a number of ways. Most notable was a series of stamp books, issued through schools to every man, woman and child in the U.S., starting in May 1942 with "War Ration Book One." The books dictated how much any one person could buy of any item and, though triggering black market sales and hoarding, ultimately proved effective.

The first food item to be rationed was sugar, beginning in April 1942. It remained in short supply throughout the duration of the war. Coffee followed in November, although it returned to store shelves the following July. Sale of canned meats and fish were frozen in February of 1943, which like many other restricted items, produced a panicked run on supermarkets throughout the U.S.

"War Ration Book Two," released that February, contained blue and red stamps, each worth ten "points." The red stamps were allocated for meats and cheese; the blue, processed foods. Individual rations amounted to twenty to twenty-five pounds of canned vegetables (fresh foods were not rationed) and about ninety pounds of meat and thirteen pounds of cheese per year. A one-pound can of beans or a pound of pork chops could be purchased for eight points plus whatever the store charged, for example.

The first non-food item to be restricted was rubber. (The Japanese had seized Malaya and the Dutch East Indies, the source of more than 90 percent of the U.S. rubber supply.) To conserve this precious resource, all "idle" tires not in use had to be relinquished under the government's "Idle Tire Purchase Plan."

To cut down on tire use, the government rationed gasoline and issued ration stickers, which were placed on vehicles to show how much gas could be purchased. An "A" sticker was good for four gallons (later changed to three), per week, providing about sixty miles of driving, according to government estimates; a "T" sticker (for truckers) was good for unlimited gas; "B" and "C" stickers denoted "limited to essential driving." (C coupons, allocated to doctors, ministers, mail carriers and others provided the largest ration of gas and were thus widely counterfeited and sold on the black market; four thousand service stations lost their business licenses for being accomplices in the counterfeit market.)

In December 1942, when national gas rationing went into effect, traffic thinned out visibly everywhere, sometimes dramatically so. With families unable to take their ritual Sunday drives or their long-distance vacations, many parks and tourist attractions closed down.

In January 1943, the government went even further; they banned "pleasure driving" altogether. Drivers with A stickers caught going anywhere for "pleasure" were penalized by losing their gas rations. However, enforcement was almost impossible, and the ban was subsequently lifted in September.

If there was anything as tightly restricted as rubber and gasoline, it was metal. The War Production Board banned the use of metals in dozens of nonessential items, including dogtags, spittoons, hair curlers, lobster forks, bird cages, cocktail shakers, asparagus tongs and many more.

Among the most sorely missed items of all were cigarets and booze, which grew extremely scarce in 1944.

1942: "The first stamps in War Ration Book One will be used for the purchase of sugar. When this book was issued, the registrar asked you, or the person who applied for your book, how much sugar you owned on that date. If you had any sugar, you were allowed to keep it, but stamps representing this quantity were torn from your book (except for a small amount which you were allowed to keep without losing any stamps). Book One was issued to you on application by a member of your family, the number of stamps torn from the books of the family was based on the amount of sugar owned by the family, and was divided as equally as possible among all these books."
War Ration Book One, May.

1942: "Your first War Ration Book has been issued to you, originally containing twenty-eight War Ration Stamps. Other books may be issued at later dates. The following instructions apply to your first book and will apply to any later books, unless otherwise ordered by the Office of Price Administration. In order to obtain a later book, the first book must be turned in. You should preserve your War Ration Books with the greatest possible care. . . ."

". . . . When you buy any rationed product, the proper stamp must be detached in the presence of the storekeeper, his employee, or the person making delivery on his behalf. If a stamp is torn out of the War Ration Book in any other way than above indicated, it becomes void. If a stamp is partly torn or mutilated and more than one-half of it remains in the book, it is valid. Otherwise, it becomes void. . . ." *War Ration Book One, May.*

1943: QUESTION: Is it patriotic to take a vacation this summer? ANSWER: It certainly is! In fact, Government officials recommend taking the right kind of vacation.

QUESTION: What is the right kind of vacation? ANSWER: One that minimizes the use of critical materials and vital transportation in reaching vacation spots . . . and the kind of vacation that will build you up and renew your energy for more war work.

QUESTION: What type of transportation shall I use? ANSWER: When the distance is not too great, travel by motor car, if your A card ration permits . . . and use B and C cards only as authorized. Use trains or busses sparingly on week ends. . . . Select a cabin in the woods. Stay put! Fish, canoe, sail and swim in the waters of a Minnesota lake. . . . *Minnesota Tourist Bureau ad,* Time, *July 26, 1943.*

1943: "SONS OF HEAVEN GET A TASTE OF HELL. . . . American torpedoes—swift, sure, deadly—are giving Tojo's 'Sons of Heaven' a taste of hell. The fuel for torpedo propeller turbines is *alcohol* . . . one of many fine chemicals produced by Commercial Solvents for war as well as for peace. . . . Since the best alcohols are serving America's fighting men, your favorite lotion or perfume may be hard to get. After victory, Commercial Solvents' alcohols will again be available for every civilian need."

Advertisement for Commercial Solvents Corp., Time, *July 12.*

1944: "A Gallup poll of what people value most would probably find the all-essential ration book ahead of diamonds on the list. Burglars broke into a suburban home a few weeks ago. In reporting his losses to the police, the owner sighed gratefully, 'Thank God, they took only the silver, my wife's jewelry and my Phi Beta Kappa key. We had our ration books safely hidden in the folds of a sheet in the linen closet!' " *Constance Foster,* Ladies Home Journal, *December.*

1944: Kate Smith "sees red when she hears charges that American housewives are not cooperating with rationing and food-saving programs. And she has interesting proof of how hard they are working at these vital-to-victory jobs. 'I get triumphant letters. Letters from women who say they're using even less than their rations because they want to share and play square. Letters about the hundreds of quarts of vegetables they're planning to can from their Victory Gardens. Letters thanking me for the food-saving ideas I give 'em.' " *Jello Ad, featuring Kate Smith.*

relocation of Japanese citizens: In the spring of 1942, more than 100,000 Japanese-Americans living on the west coast were evacuated to ten internment camps made up of tar-paper barracks surrounded by barbed wire and armed guards in various deserted locations in California, Idaho, Utah, Arizona and elsewhere. The evacuation was thought necessary due to growing paranoia over Japanese enemy sympathizers and the possibilities of sabotage. Many of the internees, however, were given leave to work on their farms or even to fight in the war. Some Japanese fighting units had outstanding combat records. Internment continued until January 1945.

1942: "It seems strange to us that airplane manufacturing plants should be entirely surrounded by Japanese land occupancies. It seems to us that it is more than circumstance that after certain Government air bases were established Japanese undertook farming operations in close proximity to them. You can hardly grow a jackrabbit in some of the places where they presume to be carrying on farming operations close to an Army bombing base. . . . So we believe, gentlemen, that it would be wise for the military to take every protective measure that it believes is necessary to protect this State and this Nation against the possible activities of these people. . . ." *California Attorney-General Earl Warren, Congressional Hearing, February.*

1942: INSTRUCTIONS TO ALL PERSONS OF JAPANESE ANCESTRY LIVING IN THE FOLLOWING AREA: All that portion of the City and County of San Francisco, State of California. . . . All Japanese persons, both alien and non-alien, will be evacuated from the above designated area by 12:00 o'clock noon Tuesday, April 7, 1942. No Japanese person will be permitted to enter or leave the above described area after 8:00 A.M., Thursday, April 2, 1942, without obtaining special permission from the Provost Marshal at the Civil Control Station located at 1701 Van Ness Avenue, San Francisco, California." *Western Defense Command and Fourth Army Wartime Civil Control Administration poster.*

salvaging: On the heels of rationing came rubber drives and scrap metal drives and paper drives and silk drives (silk stockings were reprocessed into parachutes) and, for the construction of explosives, fat drives. All across the nation, children and housewives pitched in alongside small business owners and factories and membership organizations to aid the war effort. Piles of scrap mushroomed over the landscape, and many cities and towns even had scrap parades, with lines of trucks filled with odds and ends rumbling down Main Street, to the cheers of onlookers.

1943: "SAVE YOUR WASTE FATS TO MAKE EXPLOSIVES! 1. *The Need is Urgent.* War in the Pacific has greatly reduced our supply of vegetable fats from the Far East. It is necessary to find substitutes for them. Moreover, fats make glycerine. And glycerine makes explosives for us and our Allies—explosives to down Axis planes, stop their tanks, sink their ships. We need millions of pounds of glycerine and you housewives can help produce them. 2. *Don't* throw away a single drop of used cooking fat—bacon grease, meat drippings, frying fats—every kind you use. After you've got all the cooking good from them, pour them through a kitchen strainer into a clean, wide-mouthed can. Keep in a cool, dark place. Please don't use glass containers or paper bags. 3. *Take them* to your meat dealer when you've saved a pound or more. He is cooperating patriotically. He will pay you for your waste fats and get them started on their way to the war industries. It will help him if you can deliver your fats early in the week." *Government instructions to housewives.*

1940s: "Well, friends, the makers of Swan, the new white floating soap, join George and Gracie in inviting you to tune in to your Columbia station next Monday at the same time. And may we remind you again to turn in waste fat regularly. It's needed for explosives and life-saving medicines. And don't forget the two red points you'll get for every pound. . . ." *Close of "Burns and Allen" radio show.*

1940s: "Official Fat Collecting Station." *Sticker on door.*

1940s: SINK A SUB FROM YOUR FARM . . . BRING IN YOUR SCRAP. "Brave Men Shall Not Die Because I Faltered." NATIONAL SCRAP HARVEST. *Ad showing a sinking enemy ship; sponsored by John Deere Co.*

1940s: THEY'VE GOT MORE IMPORTANT PLACES TO GO THAN YOU . . . SAVE RUBBER. CHECK YOUR TIRES NOW. *Poster showing infantrymen in a jeep.*

1940s: SAVE YOUR CANS . . . Help Pass the Ammunition. *Prepare Your Tin Cans For War.* 1. Remove tops and bottoms. 2. Take off paper labels. 3. Wash thoroughly. 4. Flatten firmly. *Poster of machine-gunner using a round of tin cans as ammunition.*

spotters: civilian ground observers employed by the government to watch the skies for enemy aircraft, in shifts, twenty-four hours a day. Men and women, and even children helped to staff these observation posts which, at first, were often spots of ground out in the open. Later, shelters were built from individual fund drives, or rooftop or top floor spaces were donated. At one point during the war, some 600,000 Americans were working as official ground observers. Many more watched the skies on a casual basis, for the sheer adventure of it.

1943: "Los Angeles volunteering has fallen off badly. Information center clerks complain that plane spotters are so unskilled that they report "every damn blackbird they see as a Messerschmitt." *Time, July 19.*

Rosie the Riveter: national symbol to thousands of American women working in defense plants. Rosie was named after Rosina Bonavita, who, with a coworker, put 3,345 rivets on a fighter wing in only six hours.

stars who served: dozens of movie and TV personalities served in the war. Some were already famous. Some would become famous after the war. A partial list:

AIR FORCE: Gene Autry, Charles Bronson, Jackie Coogan, Clark Gable, George Gobel, Charlton Heston, Alan Ladd, Norman Lear, Walter Matthau, Burgess Meredith, Cameron Mitchell, Tom Poston, Robert Preston, Jimmy Stewart, Dick Van Dyke, Jack Webb.

ARMY: James Arness, Desi Arnaz, Mel Brooks, Art Carney, Hugh Downs, Lorne Greene, Joey Bishop, Hal Holbrook, William Holden, John Huston, George Kennedy, Bert Lancaster, Karl Malden, Robert Mitchum, Bert Parks, Sidney Poitier, Tony Randall, Ronald Reagan, Carl Reiner, Will Rogers, Mickey Rooney, Telly Savalas, Rod Serling, Red Skelton, Eli Wallach, Efrem Zimbalist, Jr.

MARINES: Sterling Hayden, Bob Keeshan, Ed McMahon, Hugh O'Brien, Tyrone Power, George C. Scott, James Whitmore, Jonathan Winters.

NAVY AND COAST GUARD: Eddie Albert, Raymond Burr, Sid Caesar, Tony Curtis, Buddy Ebsen, Henry Fonda, Rock Hudson, Gene Kelly, Jack Lemmon, Victor Mature, Don Rickles, Jason Robards, Soupy Sales, Robert Stack, Rod Steiger, Robert Taylor.

submarines off the coast: a popular civilian pasttime was to search for enemy subs through binoculars from shore. Enemy submarines frequently prowled both coasts of the U.S., with German U-boats coming within three miles of the eastern shore at one point. The first U.S. warship sunk by enemy subs was the USS Jabob Jones, off Cape May, New Jersey on February 28, 1942. Along the Eastern Sea Frontier, from Maine to Georgia, in 1942, over 140 ships were ultimately sunk by the enemy, sometimes with the explosive action clearly witnessed from shore. Vacationers on Virginia Beach saw two freighters attacked in June. Submarine defense tightened dramatically thereafter, however, with the Germans sinking only sixteen additional ships in the next two and one-half years.

On the Pacific coast, a tanker ship was shelled by a Japanese submarine off Santa Cruz on December 19, 1942. Four other ships were also attacked along California, two of them sinking. On February 23, 1942, another Japanese submarine near Santa Barbara shelled an oil installation, with minimal damage. The last submarine action off the west coast was the sinking of two tankers on October 4 and 6, 1942, off the coast of southern Oregon.

V-Homes: American homes that carried out a number of duties to aid the war effort were thus honored with V-home certificates (placed in windows) from the Office of Civilian Defense. The *V* stood for Victory. 1942: "We in this home are fighting. We know this war will be easy to lose and hard to win. We mean to win it. Therefore we solemnly pledge all our energies and all our resources to fight for freedom and against fascism. We serve notice that we are personally carrying the fight to the enemy, in these ways:

I. This home follows the instructions of its air-raid warden, in order to protect itself against attack by air.

II. This home conserves food, clothing, transportation, and health, in order to hasten an unceasing flow of war materials to our men at the front.

III. This home salvages essential materials, in order that they may be converted to immediate war uses.

IV. This home refuses to spread rumors designed to divide our Nation.

V. This home buys War Savings Stamps and Bonds regularly.

We are doing these things because we know we must to Win This War." *V-Home certificate, Office of Civilian Defense.*

Victory Gardens: to help supply America's food demand, the government urged citizens to conserve food and to grow their own vegetables in backyard "Victory Gardens." At the height of the war, some twenty million such Victory Gardens sprouted up not only in backyards, but in vacant lots, dirt parking lots, city parks, practically wherever the soil could be tilled, ultimately supplying 40 percent of the country's produce. Thus, throughout the war, two of the most common family weekend activities were gardening and home canning.

war bonds: purchased by American citizens to help finance the war, government-backed savings bonds initially costing $18.75 each (bonds with larger denominations were available) grew in value to $25 in ten years. Through the course of the war, hundreds of different ads appeared in magazines, newspapers, posters and billboards urging America to "Buy War Bonds" and to "Keep on Buying." The ads were not only published by the government but by numerous businesses as well. Millions of Americans bought the bonds during "War Loan

Drives," often at makeshift bond booths at schools, street corners, movie theaters, etc.; it was widely viewed as one's patriotic duty to do so. Indeed, with a final price tag of $350,500,000,000, America's effort in the war could never have been financed without them.

1943: BACK THE ATTACK! BUY WAR BONDS. *Government poster.*

1940s: "So We'll Meet Again. . . ." (Soldier waving goodbye from airplane) BUY MORE WAR BONDS." *Poster.*

1943: "SCARED, KID? [Young soldier holding rifle] Hell, no. I don't scare easy. But I'm no fool, either. I know where I'm going . . . and it's not to a church social. But I'm an American, and all my buddies are Americans. We've got a messy job on our hands, and we're doing it. Because we know it's got to be done. You folks back home have a job, too. Like buying War Bonds. And I don't mean War Bonds you can afford, either . . . I mean War Bonds you *can't* afford. War Bonds that mean being inconvenienced . . . one-thousandth as much as those guys who haven't had their wet, stinking clothes off in three weeks of crawling through the jungle, killing Japs. War Bonds that mean being uncomfortable . . . one-thousandth as much as those kids lying out in the desert, waiting for the medical boys to give them a hypodermic. . . . So forget that 10% stuff. Buy War Bonds until you can look at the guys who come back with one arm or one leg or no eyes, without a guilty feeling in your heart."

Full page ad, Felt and Tarrant Manufacturing Co., Time, *July 12.*

1943: "WARNING: Be on the Lookout for Optimistic Olivers. These Men Are Dangerous Citizens. They're American citizens, it's true . . . but they're worth a million dollars apiece to our enemies. This 'it-won't-be-long-now' talk spreads like wildfire. Rosie the Riveter and her coworkers take an afternoon off for a permanent. . . . Mrs. Jones isn't so careful about saving her tin cans. . . . Joe Zilch guesses he doesn't have to put so much of his paycheck into War Bonds. That's what a few Optimistic Olivers can do to our 'all out' war effort. It's up to you to button your lips. . . . There's no short cut to victory . . . it's a long road—an expensive trip! Let's not kid ourselves . . . nobody's going to win this war for us. We can drag it out, or we can wind it up with a terrific wallop. The sooner those War Bond dollars pile up in Uncle Sam's pockets, the sooner we can give those guys that double shellacking. . . . What's your score? Would you care to match it with that of a Marine just back from Guadalcanal? 10% is only the beginning . . . WE'VE GOT TO WIN! BUY BONDS . . . AND KEEP ON BUYING.''

Full page ad, Pepsodent Co., Time, *July.*

SLANG, COLLOQUIALISMS AND EVERYDAY SPEECH

Army

Anastasie: A term for censorship, used widely in France. Named after St. Anastasie, who was unable to speak after having her tongue cut out, by orders of Emperor Diocletian.

ack-ack: antiaircraft gun. The term is thought to be derived from the British Army's old telephone alphabet in which "A" was pronounced "Ack." "A.A." for antiaircraft was thus "ack-ack."
1940s: "My squadron came in with the second wave of ships, so the ack-ack boys had plenty of time to find their range."
   Mike Beaudoin, *"Jump for the Wing,"* Combat.

archies: antiaircraft guns.

armchair general: one who gives his opinion on everything, even when he is completely uninformed; a Monday morning quarterback.

armored cow: canned milk. Also called "city cow."

army banjo: shovel.

army strawberries: prunes.

asparagus beds: Tank traps.

Aussies: Australian soldiers.

AWOL: absent without leave.
1940s: "From this moment on you're under the tightest possible security. No leaves. No mail. . . . Any man attempting to go AWOL will be shot." *"Kill Mr. X, If Necessary,"* Ray Adams, Combat.

B-19: any fat female, named after the airplane.

BRITISH AIR RAID PRECAUTIONS

The U.S. had little to fear compared with Britain, whose air raid warnings were usually for real. Here's how a typical English family coped with and prepared for nightly bombing runs by the Germans.

> 1940: "We all three sleep downstairs in our own beds, which are in the dining room, and that room has heavy wooden shutters inside to stop flying glass, and the corner where Janet sleeps is splinter-proofed outside with Tate sugar boxes filled with earth and piled up five feet high.
>
> "At the foot of my bed at night is a pair of flannel trousers, slippers and warm windjammer. Mary has warm trousers and woolen cardigan ready, so that we are all prepared for a rapid exit or to go to the assistance of neighbors if need arises.
>
> "In case of sustained bombings locally, there are ear plugs and rubber mouth grips ready. Just inside the front door is a large suitcase packed with clothing for each of us in case of rapid exits. . . .
>
> "When I am in town I am always equipped with a haversack containing gas mask, brandy, emergency rations of chocolate, Horlick's tablets and chewing gum, bandages and first aid kit and a rubber air cushion. . . .
>
> "Janet always takes her gas mask to school, and every child there has a tin with emergency rations in case they are delayed during a prolonged warning, as they are not allowed to come home until 'all clear' sounds. . . ."
>
> *Englishman to brother in New York, letter published in* New York Times, *November 3*

baby food: cereal.

barker: a large artillery gun.

barracks: shelter or lodging for soldiers.

barracks lawyer: a know-it-all complainer who argues about military regulations. Also known as a guardhouse lawyer.

1941: "Melvin Piel, guardhouse lawyer for Company A, explained it all on the way downstairs. We were going to be assigned to our permanent stations." *Marion Hargrove,* See Here, Private Hargrove.

battalion: three companies.

battery acid: army coffee.

beans: nickname for a cook.

bear grease: general issue soap.

bedpan commando: a nurse or other medical assistant.

being shit on from a great height: catching hell from a commanding officer, more frequently a British term.

blackout: army coffee.

blackstrap: army coffee.

blanket drill: sleep.

blitz: a bombing or an all-out attack.

blow joe: an enlisted man. A reverse of "Joe Blow."

bobtail: a dishonorable discharge.

brass hat: a staff officer.

brig: jail. Also known as the "clink," the "stockade," and the "hoose-gow."

brown bombers: laxatives.

bubble dancer: a dishwasher.

bucking for a section eight: trying to get discharged through various means, such as faking insanity or a physical ailment.

bulldog: military police.

bunky: a buddy or friend.

burp gun: a German automatic gun, so-called because of the burping sound it made when fired.

Butch: nickname for a commanding officer.

cackle jelly: eggs.

camel corps: infantry.

camp happy: a little crazy or touched in the head.

can: bathroom or toilet.

canteen: any army retail store.

cat stabber: a bayonet.

CB: confined to barracks.

chairborne: designating officers or other soldiers who worked in offices.

cheese toaster: a bayonet.

chest hardware: medals.

chicken: a very young recruit.

chili bowl: an army haircut.

chop chop: hurry up; on the double.

chow: food.

civvies: civilian clothes.

Clara: all clear air raid signal.

combat fatigue: also known as shell shock, a nervous condition brought on by combat, with symptoms including jumpiness, insomnia, irrationality.
1940s: "He was no longer considered fit to command men. But until he was judged a victim of combat fatigue, we had suffered under his neurotic despotism for a miserable six months."
Jules Archer, "Lieutenant, You're Crazy, Sir," Combat.

C.O.: commanding officer
1942: "The commanding officer is always referred to as the C.O., until the rank of general is reached, and then he may be called the C.G., the commanding general." *Ralph Ingersoll, The Battle is the Pay-off.*

company: three platoons.

94

corpuscle: corporal.

corps: two or more divisions. Two or more corps make an army.

cowboy: a tank driver.

C-rations: tinned food or meals, used when an army is on the move and a kitchen truck or station cannot be set up.
1943: "The C-ration is a set of six small cans, the contents of which is different. Two of the cans provide one man with breakfast, two are the staples of midday dinner and two are for supper. The best-liked C-ration can is the one with baked beans and hunks of meat and vegetables. One of the cans contains candy and crackers."
    Ralph Ingersoll, The Battle is the Payoff.

cream on a shingle: creamed beef on toast.

croot: a recruit. Also known as a "rookie."

crowbar hotel: a jail.

crumb hunt: kitchen inspection.

court-martial: a trial for a crime.

day the eagle shits, the: pay day.

Dear John letter: a letter from a sweetheart back home, informing the soldier that she has found someone else to date or marry, or that she wants a divorce. Usually referred to simply as a "Dear John."

devil's piano: a machine gun.

didie bag: a bag for keeping valuables in.

division: three regiments.

dog fat: butter.

dog house: a guardhouse.

dog tag: the metal identification tag worn around a soldier's neck.
1940s: "But the sand was red, and his rifle stuck in the ground at his head, and had his dog tag and helmet on it, to tell the grave crew who he was." *"Night Jump," Rone Lowe,* Combat.

D-ration: blocks of chocolate filled with vitamins.

drive it in the hangar: shut up.

dud: a shell that fails to explode.

elephant trap: a large hole dug for dumping garbage in.

enfilade: a sweeping line of gunfire.

faint wagon: an ambulance.

fall in: form up and come to attention.

flak: enemy antiaircraft fire.

flap: a state of anxiety or tension following an air raid alert or other danger. Also, the warning itself.

4-F: government designation for those who, after examination, were found to be unfit for military service, due to either mental or physical disability. The 4-F designation was widely viewed as a badge of shame. However, it was hardly rare. Over four million men were ultimately rejected and designated 4-F by the military by the end of the war.

foxhole: a pit or hole dug to protect oneself from enemy fire.

fuck: one of the most widely used swear words of the war, although never seen in print or heard in the war movies of the day. (A bizarre form of censorship: books might readily describe someone's head being blown off, but a witness to this horror could only say, "Oh, F---," as if readers might faint if they saw the word spelled out.)
1943: "The sergeant translated the order into his own lingo. 'You f-----g eight balls get the f--- off this God-damn hill before I wrap this rifle-barrel around your neck!''
Richard Tregaskis, Invasion Diary.

frat: to fraternize, especially sexually, with the women of the enemy country.

FUBAR: Fucked Up Beyond All Recognition.

general's car: any wheelbarrow.

GI: general issue or government issue. Although World War I soldiers were universally known as "doughboys," World War II soldiers, and especially infantry men, were called GIs, with only occasional references to doughboys.

GI can: In official army inventory terms, a galvanized iron can. In army slang, a bomb as big as a garbage can.

GI Jesus: the chaplain.

GI Joe: popular World War II term for the typical infantry soldier.

GI shits: diarrhea, especially that caused by dysentery.

goldbrick: to shirk one's responsibility or loaf.

goldfish: canned salmon.

goof burner: one who smokes marijuana.

goofy discharge: a discharge given due to mental illness.

go over the hill: to desert or go AWOL.

grandma: low gear in any jeep or truck.

hay: sauerkraut.

Heine: derogatory term for a German.
1943: "While La Bue was bickering with him, Lieutenant O'Leary shouted, 'Here come some Heine scout cars! Get off the road!' "
"One Man's War," Saturday Evening Post.

Hershey bar: the famous chocolate bar was actually used by soldiers as a medium of exchange in parts of Europe. Thus, a prostitute with low rates was called a "Hershey Bar."

hitch: an enlistment.

hot box: a tank.

housewife: a sewing kit.

HQ: Headquarters.

jack: money.

Jap: a Japanese soldier.

jazzbo: derogatory term for a black soldier.

Jerries: German soldiers. Very common term for German aircraft as well.

1943: "Jerries! One o'clock high! A damn zillion of 'em!"
Mike Beaudoin, "Jump for the Wing," Combat.

1940s: "At exactly one o'clock . . . someone wondered out loud why the Jerries hadn't shelled the town, and 15 minutes later they did."
W. Bernstein, Yank, The Army Weekly.

1940s: "Jerry fires lots of tracers," said Bill Weber. "He has a trick with tracers. Jerry has one gun shootin' tracers up high. Then he has other guns shootin' grazing fire."
Sergeant Burtt Evans, Yank, The Army Weekly.

jumping Jesus: a chaplain in a paratrooper unit.

jungle juice: homemade alcoholic beverage. By units fighting in or near jungles.

Kendall did it: a widely used buck-passing line.

kennel rations: hash or meatloaf.

Kilroy Was Here: A line of graffiti that appeared everywhere, from bathroom walls to bulletin boards to the sides of dirty trucks, beginning in 1940. The more inaccesible or unbelievable the location of the inscription, the better the soldiers liked it. Although Sergeant Francis J. Kilroy of the U.S. Air Corps claimed to have started it all, many believed Kilroy was anyone and everyone and no one in particular.

KP duty: kitchen police duty. Assisting the cook in meal preparation and cleanup.

1941: "It was no fault of mine that I was a kitchen policeman on my sixth day. The whole barracks got the grind. And it was duty, not punishment." *Marion Hargrove, See Here, Private Hargrove.*

Krauts: derogatory term for Germans.

1942: "Obviously, the raid's purpose was to gather data on just how advanced the Krauts were in their process."
Ray Adams, "Kill Mr. X, if Necessary," Combat.

1940s: "The Nazis had caught eighty-eight of us in a ditch; caught us kneeling in a trench, hands in the air, while a big German tank with a long 88 waggled at us. Prisoners were one thing that Krauts couldn't be bothered with, for the Americans were hot."
Duane Miller, "Spies in the Bulge," Combat.

lacy: referring to a soldier with an effeminate manner.

lead poisoning: death or injury from a bullet.

leatherneck: a marine.

liberate: popular soldier's euphemism meaning, to loot or steal from an enemy building. Also, to have relations with a female from an enemy country.

Li'l Abners: army shoes.

louie: lieutenant.

Mae West: a vest-like life jacket.

maneuvers: flirting or making out with a woman.

meat wagon: an ambulance.

mess gear/kit: a self-contained kit comprised of a plate and eating utensils.

mess hall: an eating or dining facility.

molotov breadbasket: a box or bin full of incendiary bombs that scatter when hit.

mopping up: finishing off an enemy after a winning battle.

MP: military police.

Nip: a widely used derogatory term for a Japanese soldier. From "Nippon" the Japanese name for Japan.
1940s: "When I get up there I find that I can reach out and touch the Nip on account of there is a hole in the tree."
L.A. Brodsky, Yank, The Army Weekly.

noncom: a noncommissioned officer.

padre: chaplain.

paint remover: army coffee.

pantywaist: a sissy.

pea shoooter: a rifle.

P.C.: Post of command.

pecker checker: a doctor or medical assistant charged with checking soldiers for venereal disease. Also known as a "pricksmith" and a "penis machinist."

peep: a jeep. General Patton himself tried to popularize the use of this word. Although it was never universally adopted, it was used by some units.
1943: "When the peeps, whose drivers don't believe any terrain can stop them, tried to ford the streams, as often as not they would be washed downstream. . . ." *Ralph Ingersoll,* The Battle is the Pay-off.

pill rollers: medical corps.

pineapple: a grenade.

pin-up: a sexy publicity shot of a female movie star, pinned up in tents, barracks lockers, etc. Very popular with the GIs. Betty Grable and Rita Hayworth were favorites.
1940s: "I have that picture (of Irene Manning) over my locker and like it very much. I suggest Sergeant O'Hara go out and learn the facts of life from someone who has been around. Also, the boys in my platoon agree with me that he should be examined for Section 8. Keep the pin-up pictures coming. We like them."
Letter to Yank, The Army Weekly.

pipped: getting shot. "He got pipped."

platoon: three squads. See squad.

police the grounds: pick up or clean up. Also, police up.

poop: information; the facts.

POW: prisoner of war.

prang: an airplane crash.

pro-pack: an envelope containing a condom, soap and an astringent, for protection against venereal disease.

propeller wash: bullshit.

ptomaine domain: the mess hall.

pull rank: to inform another of one's higher rank.

purge: one or more new arrivals in a German prisoner of war camp, a term used by other prisoners of war.

purple heart: medal for heroism or wounds received.

PX: post exchange; an army merchandise store.

roll out: get up and get out of bed.

quiff: a female.

rabbit food: lettuce or carrots.

Rachel: high gear in a jeep or truck.

R and R: rest and rotation or rest and relaxation. A leave from a fighting unit to a base, camp or town away from the action.

regiment: three battalions.

sack: bed.

sack time: sleep time.

sack drill: sleep. Also, sack duty.

sad sack: an inept, unlucky or generally miserable soldier, from the comic strip by the same name.

salvo: simultaneous fire from more than one gun.

sawbones: an army doctor or surgeon.

screaming meemie: a rocket notorious for its sound and destructive power.

see the chaplain: shutup, don't tell me your troubles.

shack up: to form a long-term sexual relationship with a woman near a military base.

shit on a shingle: creamed chipped beef on toast.

shit, shower and shave: To get ready for duty or a night out. Also, shit, shower, shave and shine.

sidearms: salt and pepper or other condiments.

short-arm inspection: a medical inspection of the penis for venereal disease. Also, small-arm inspection.

skirt patrol: looking for women.

SNAFU: a popular acronym; Situation Normal, All Fucked Up.
1940s: "They worked hard and steadily, with a minimum of snafu, and while they were rarely in a position of great danger they were never entirely out of danger." *Sergeant W. Bernstein,* Yank, The Army Weekly.

snowdrop: an MP, or military police officer, from their white helmets, gloves and belts.

softening up: bombing of an enemy position to weaken them for a later attack.

S.O.P.: popular term for Standard Operation Procedure.

soup: a sky raining with bombs and bits of antiaircraft shells.

squad: twelve men.

stateside: the United States; to the U.S. soldier, home.

stocks and bonds: toilet paper.

strangers: Nazi airmen. Also known as "visitors."

sugar report: a letter from one's sweetheart.

suit, put on the: to be drafted or to join the armed forces.

swampseed: rice.

TARFU: An acronym almost as popular as SNAFU, Things Are Really Fucked Up.

tell it to the chaplain: go tell someone else your tales of woe cause I basically don't give a shit. Common retort.
1940s: "Look," said the first sergeant. "Why don't you just tell it to the chaplain?" Yank, The Army Weekly.

tin can: a tank.

tin titty: canned milk.

tommy gun: a Thompson submachine gun.
1942: "Each had a tommy gun slung over his shoulder and there were extra rifles in the back. . . ." *Ralph Ingersoll,* The Battle is the Pay-off.
1940s: "You could separate a commando from his wife or mistress, but taking away his tommy gun—that was cutting off his right arm." Combat.

Navy
admiral's watch: a good night's sleep.

airedale: a naval aviation recruit.

alligator: an amphibious tank.

ashcan: a depth charge, used to destroy submarines.

AWOL: absent without leave.

baffle painting: special camouflage painting of a ship.

battlewagon: a battleship.

belay: shutup. Also, stop what you're doing.

bells: designating the time of day:

1 o'clock	2 bells
2 o'clock	4 bells
3 o'clock	6 bells
4 o'clock	8 bells
5 o'clock	2 bells

6 o'clock	4 bells
7 o'clock	6 bells
8 o'clock	8 bells
9 o'clock	2 bells
10 o'clock	4 bells
11 o'clock	6 bells
12 o'clock	8 bells

bilge: bullshit. Also, bilgewater.

bird boat: an aircraft carrier.

blow: a storm at sea.

blonde and sweet: coffee with cream and sugar.

boot: a newly enlisted sailor.

boot camp: the six-week naval training camp for new sailors.

brig: a jail on a ship.

brown nose: one who kisses up to officers; an apple polisher.

buzzard: any eagle insignia.

can: a destroyer.
1945: "The fire on deck was so hot we couldn't get closer than fifty
feet at first, but there was desperate need to get it under control. . . .
On a can, any hit is near ammo."
"The Aaron Ward Horror," Chief Boatswain's Mate John Oden, Combat.
1943: "The [destroyer] heeled over and capsized in the turn, exploding in a blinding flash of fire as it went down. But the Jap can had
been hit too late. Warhoom! A fish hit us forward."
"Night Ride up the Slot," Commander Paul Anderson, Combat.

canary: a nice-looking female.

canteen: a retail store on a ship.

captain of the head: one charged with cleaning the toilets.

Chicago piano: an antiaircraft gun.

104

cigar box fleet: boats carrying vehicles, such as tanks and landing craft, for a shore attack.

coiled up his ropes: said of one who died.

commissary bullets: beans.

crow: an ugly female.

cut of his jib: a sailor's behavior or appearance.

fish: a torpedo.
1943: "A fish hit us forward. Combat information center went dark, the bulkheads shook like jelly, the steel deck heaved. . . ."
"Night Ride Up the Slot," Commander Paul Anderson, Combat.

flashing one's hash: throwing up.

flying coffin: a PBY navy patrol bomber.

foo foo: perfume.

forecastle lawyer: a know-it-all complainer who argues over military regulations.

Four-O: perfect. An answer to the question, "How are you?" So named after the highest efficiency rating given to navy officers.

four-striper: a captain.

French leave: leaving the ship without permission.

frogman: a scuba diver.

funnels: smokestacks of a ship.

furlough: any liberty lasting over seventy-two hours.

galley: a ship's kitchen.

gangway: get out of the way.

Geechie: a native island girl in the South Pacific.

gig: a captain's private boat.

gilligen hitch: an imaginary knot in a rope.

give it the deep six: to throw something overboard.

gob: sailor.

gone native: getting friendly with the natives on shore leave.

goo goo: a native of the South Pacific islands.

gooks: natives of the South Seas.

gook: any brown-skinned or Oriental native.

haba haba: hurry up; on the double.

holiday: a portion of a ship left unpainted, or any unfinished job, suggesting neglect or slackness.

honey barge: a garbage barge.

hooligan navy: the Coast Guard.

katzenjammers: the "shakes" the day after drinking heavily.

liberty: shore leave of forty-eight hours or less.

limey: a British sailor.

Mae West: an inflatable life jacket.

mess: meals, or any meal hall.

mokers, the: a state of down-heartedness; the blues.

monkey drill: callisthenics.

mosquito boat: a light, fast boat with small guns.

mother: an aircraft carrier, especially among flyers.

muck up or out: clean up.

mud hook: an anchor.

Nip: a Japanese soldier, sailor or airman.
1945: "We were a lot more surprised, though, when two Nips broke away from our boys, and immediately mounted a Kamikaze attack on the *Aaron Ward.*"
"The Aaron Ward Horror," Chief Boatswain's Mate John Oden, in Combat.

old man: affectionate term for the captain.

one striper: an ensign.

pea coat: a sailor's waist-length, blue wool coat.

pig boat: submarine.

ping jockey: one who monitored radar or sonar. From the "ping" sound made by sonar.

pipe one aboard: blowing the boatswain's whistle to welcome a high-ranking official or other dignitary aboard.

plotting room: a mapping room used to plan maneuvers.

pollywog: any sailor who has yet to cross the equator.

rust bucket: a destroyer, especially an old, worn out one.

scrambled eggs: the gold insignia on a cap.

scupper: a cheap prostitute.

seabea: popular term for the initials C.B., or Construction Battalion.

sea gull: an "easy" female who follows sailors from port to port.

sea legs, get one's: to become accustomed to the movements of a ship. Also, to become accustomed mentally to life at sea.

send a fish: to fire a torpedo.

shellback: a veteran sailor.

sick bay: a hospital on board ship.

skibbies: the Japanese.

slop chute: a refuse chute leading to the ocean.

Sparks: nickname for any radio operator.
1944: "I had Sparks open the radio circuit and send the reassuring
   message: *Sighted cruiser! Cruiser joined sub service! Hauling A!*"
   Lt. William Sumpter, "The Night We Killed a Cruiser," Combat.

step off the plank: to get married.

swab: a large mop. Also, to mop the deck.

three sheets to the wind: drunk.

three striper: a commander.

tin can: a destroyer or other warship.

tin fish: a torpedo.

two striper: a lieutenant.

watch: a four-hour sentry or lookout duty.

wicky wicky: hurry up; on the double.

zero: a Japanese airplane.
1943: "Three Zeros came over and dove straight for us." Combat.

Marines
banzai!: a Japanese battle cry, often encountered by the marines in the Pacific.
1943: "The Nips reorganized and again rushed in, shouting "Banzai!" The lines sagged, but held."
   R. Blake, "Battle Without a Name," United States Marine Corps in WWII.

beachhead: a shore foothold, especially in enemy territory.

boogies: Japanese air fighters.

boondockers: field shoes.

boot: a new recruit, fresh from boot camp.

brew: beer.

brig rat: a prisoner.

butcher: a military doctor or surgeon.

cattle boat: a transport boat carrying troops.

collision mats: waffles or pancakes.

dogface: a soldier.
1940s: "One night a few weeks later, he noticed four dogfaces sitting

outside one of the PX windows and drinking their beer.''
J. O'Neill, Yank, The Army Weekly.

dragon back: one who has crossed the 180th meridian.

Dumbo: a rescue seaplane.
1940s: ''They would be radioing Dumbo [the rescue seaplane] like
mad now so all we had to do was wait and stay away from the Japs.''
Capt. John Abney, The United States Marines in World War II.

ear-banger: a kiss-up; a yes man.

FiFi: a girlfriend.

48: a two-day leave.

frog sticker: a bayonet.

fuck: contrary to the conspicuous absence of this word in the popular
war movies and books of the period, *fuck,* with all its modern connotations, was used widely by all of the armed forces, especially in battle.

holy Joe: a chaplain.

gooks: natives, especially of the South Seas.

gyrene: a marine. Actually, a combination of marine and GI.

gunny: a gunnery sergeant.

iron kelly: a steel helmet.

Jackson: a name marines called each other. ''Hey, Jackson.''

jamoke: coffee

Mae West: an inflatable life jacket reminiscent of Mae West's well-
endowed breasts.
1940s: ''The cords on my Mae West were caught or twisted and it
wouldn't blow up.''
Capt. John Abney, The United States Marine Corps in WWII.

padre: chaplain.

pearl diver: a dishwasher. One assigned to wash dishes.

pollywog: any marine who has yet to cross the equator.

pom-pom: sex. Used by men serving in the Pacific, and especially the Philippines.

pungyo: pal

ring tails: gunner's nickname for the Japanese.

scuttlebut: gossip.

shack mammy: a native female of the South Pacific.

sinkers: doughnuts.

swabby: nickname for a sailor.

sweetheart: one's rifle.

tin derby: a helmet

Tojo: derogatory term for a Japanese soldier, after General Tojo.

torpedo juice: home-made liquor, concocted from pure grain alcohol drained from a torpedo.

Air Force
Archie: an automatic pilot setting in an airplane.
1944: "I gave them a minute to secure; then pulled out the Archie
    lever, took my hands off the wheel, and let her fly herself."
    Lt. William Sumpter, "The Night We Killed a Cruiser," Combat.

auger in: to crash, especially nose first.

bamboo juice: rice wine. Term used widely by the Flying Tigers.

bandit: an enemy aircraft.

beam, on the: on the right track or course.

bend the throttle: to accelerate beyond cruising speed.

Black Cat: a PBY patrol aircraft, painted black for night flying stealth.
1940s: "Soon we came to a row of large amphibian patrol planes offi-
    cially designated PBYs, but popularly known as 'Blackcats,' so

110

named for their color and their nocturnal habits.''
Walter Untermeyer, "Night Flight," Combat.

bloomer boys: paratroopers.

coffee grinder: an airplane engine.

Chinese three-point landing: a crash or crash-landing.

eggs: bombs.
1940s: ''The bombers had just laid their eggs and I was sitting up there like a big, fat bird . . . watching the pretty bombs burst. . . .''
Mike Beaudoin, "Jump for the Wing," Combat.

dogfight: air to air combat between two or more planes.
1942: ''Soon vanished was the fancy pants flying of the Italian pilots with their 'till-death-do-us part dogfights.''
Dick Halvorsen, "Dogfight in the Desert," Combat.

flak: antiaircraft fire.

Jerry: a German bomber or fighter plane.

Judy: aircraft and ground radio term for, ''Your aircraft is sighted,'' or ''I have you on radar.''

knuckle-buster: ground crew mechanic. Also known as a grease monkey.

meter-reader: jocular term for a copilot.

milk run: any easy, short or routine flight.

rhubarb: to fly low enough to see the rhubarb growing, and strafe an enemy target. A garden level strafing run.

roger: radio acknowledgement meaning ''yes'' or ''message received.''

roll up your flaps: shutup; be quiet; stop talking.

silk, hit the: make a parachute jump.

skibby: a Japanese prostitute or girlfriend.

splash: to crash into the water.

WACS (Women's Auxiliary Corps, U.S. Army)

The WACS were at first resented by some of their male counterparts fighting at the front, but respect grew with time, as attested by the letters to *Yank, The Army Weekly* magazine below.

1940s: "Why we GIs over here in the Pacific have to read your tripe and drivel about the WACS beats me. Who in the hell cares about these dimpled GIs who are supposed to be soldiers? All I have ever heard of them doing is peeling spuds, clerking in the office, driving a truck or a tractor or puttering around in a photo lab. Yet all the stories written about our dears tell how overworked they are.... Are these janes in the Army for the same reasons we are, or just to see how many dates they can get?"
Seargent's letter to Yank: The Army Weekly.

1940s: "About five months ago, I wrote to your magazine an article about how much I detested the WACS. But now I realize what a first-class heel I was.... My narrow-minded opinion has changed entirely, and I am very proud of those gallant American women.... Please print this, as I got quite a few letters from WACS after they read my last article, and every one of them wrote such nice letters and wished my buddies and me the best of luck. I felt more ashamed than I have ever been before." *Private's letter to* Yank: The Army Weekly.

book rack: a bunk.

canteen cowboy: a man who hangs out at the local canteen to pick up women.

cool: good.

Gabriel: the bugler.

GI Jane: an okay person.

gravy: referring to a nice-looking man. "He's gravy."

gruesome twosome: regulation shoes.

hair warden: the camp hair stylist.

jeep jockeys: women mechanics in the Motor Transport division.

monkey suits: general issue coveralls.

THE DREADED NOTICE OF DEATH

The standard telegram sent to the family of a soldier killed in action:

THE SECRETARY OF WAR DESIRES TO EXPRESS HIS DEEP REGRET THAT YOUR SON PRIVATE JOHN J. DOE WAS KILLED IN ACTION IN DEFENSE OF HIS COUNTRY IN NORTH AFRICAN AREA MAY 6. LETTER FOLLOWS.

The Adjutant General

The follow-up confirming letter provided additional information and a bulletin explaining that, as a named beneficiary, one or both parents would receive six months worth of their son's pay as a gratuity. Telegraph companies were forbidden from delivering a death notice after 10 P.M.

1943: "Often a man's family receives letters from him postmarked after he has become a casualty, inspiring hope that the official report was in error. But letters written at the front cannot always be mailed promptly, and the postmark is never a sure indication of the whereabouts of the writer on that date."
American Legion Magazine, *August.*

night maneuvers: flirting with and fooling around with a man.

scoff: to eat.

WAC shack: the barracks.

Wackery: the WACS barracks.

wolf: a sexy or skirt-chasing male.

wolfing: going out on the prowl for men.

SELECTED WEAPONS AND VEHICLES

Aircraft

Betty: a Mitsubishi, twin engine, Japanese bomber.

1941: "Several people shouted that the attacking planes were Messerschmitts, though they were in fact "Bettys.""
Hunt and Norling, Behind Japanese Lines.

1942: "One day I was sure I was going to die. A Japanese Betty flew over our strip and was hit by our AA guns. The big bomber slipped sideways . . . then moved straight down . . . heading straight for me."
Hunt and Norling, Behind Japanese Lines.

B-17 Flying Fortress: the most common U.S. bomber over Europe throughout the war. It dropped a total of 571,460 tons of bombs over Europe and shot down innumerable German aircraft.

B-24 Liberator: the most common U.S. aircraft of the war, with over 18,000 put into action in Europe, in the Middle East and in the Pacific. It had a crew of up to ten men.

B-29 Superfortress: U.S. long-range bomber, in operation from mid-1944 on. Most famous for its devastating bombing runs on Tokyo and other Japanese cities, and the dropping of atomic bombs over Hiroshima and Nagasaki.

Corsair, Vought, F4U: a carrier-based, single-seat, U.S fighter, capable of speeds exceeding 400 miles per hour. From its production from 1943 on, it was the best fighter plane in the air, boasting a 11:1 kill ratio against comparable Japanese fighters.

Dauntless/A-24: a U.S. carrier-based dive-bomber that gained wide notoriety for bringing heavy destruction to the Japanese fleet in the War in the Pacific, especially at Midway and at the Battle of the Coral Sea.

Hellcat, Grumman F6F: from 1944 on, the U.S. Navy's main carrier-based fighter. It gained superiority over Japanese aircraft from its first flights off the Yorktown in August of 1943. It ultimately shot down some 4,947 Japanese planes, nearly 75 percent of the U.S. Navy's air kills.

Messerschmitt Bf 109: A German single-seat fighter, easily the most common German craft in the air. It was outmaneuvered by British planes but had a longer range cannon. In use throughout the war.

Zero: a fast, extremely maneuverable, Japanese, carrier-based, fighter plane, otherwise known as the Mitsubishi A6M. Its American code name was "Zeke." Zeros outclassed all other planes in the sky and were greatly feared early in the war. They finally met their match in U.S. F4U Corsairs and F6F Hellcats in 1943 and 1944. Kamikaze pilots went down with these planes by the scores late in the war.

1942: "In 1942 . . . the Zero was king of the Far Eastern skies . . . it was light, fast, a marvelous climber and remarkably maneuverable." *Hunt and Norling,* Behind Japanese Lines.

1943: "In the early days of the war, our pilots went up daily in tired, old planes that could barely struggle up to the Nips altitude. Things are different now. . . . Our Lockheed Lightnings and Vought Corsairs can outspeed, outclimb, outshoot and fly higher than the Zero." Air Facts: The Magazine for Pilots, *August.*

Guns, Cannons, etc.
Arisaka: a Japanese rifle.

bazooka: a shoulder-held shell launcher, capable of piercing armor.

1940s: "I picked up a bazooka and crawled among our dead men in the upper floor, looking for bazooka shells. Those shells weighed about four pounds each . . . when I pulled the trigger . . . all the pressure came out of the back end of that tin pipe with a lot of red flame, and the house shook." *"One Man's War,"* Saturday Evening Post.

Beretta Modello 1938A: a 9mm Italian submachine gun.

Beretta 1934: a 9mm, semiautomatic pistol used by the Italians.

booby trap: any antipersonnel mine. These were frequently connected to a larger antitank mine nearby. If a soldier tried to disarm the antitank mine, the antipersonnel mine would blow him to shreds. The German antitank mine was called a Teller mine. It was eighteen inches across, several inches thick, and looked something like a black pie. Its top was fitted with a "spider," that is, a kind of framework on which just the right amount of pressure would detonate the mine. Buried six inches. The German booby trap, or antipersonnel mine, looked something like a flowerpot about six inches high. When detonated, it threw schrapnel balls loaded with TNT four or five feet above the ground, sometimes nearly cutting soldiers in two. Booby traps were sometimes fitted with trip wires across doorways.

Browning Automatic Rifle: popularly known as a BAR, a heavy, semiautomatic rifle, with a magazine holding twenty rounds, and fitted with a bipod for ground firing. Used by the Americans and easily the weapon of choice among experienced fighters.

1944: " 'If you could have only one weapon, what would you take?' asked Taylor. 'The BAR,' three men answered simultaneously. 'But that bipod is useless,' said Moore . . . 'it catches on things on patrols.' " Yank, The Army Weekly.

1943: "I worked that BAR until it began to smoke, as if somebody were cooking it." *"One Man's War,"* Saturday Evening Post.

Colt Pistol: a large, semiautomatic pistol with a magazine holding seven rounds of ammunition, used by the Americans.

Enfield Mark I: a bolt action rifle, with a magazine holding ten rounds, used by the British.

Enfield M 1917: a bolt action rifle, sometimes used by the Americans.

Erma MP-38: a German submachine gun.

Garand: popularly known as the M-1, a semiautomatic rifle, noted for its reliable performance by U.S. soldiers.

1940s: " 'The Germans counterattacked early one morning, and my men came to me and said their M-1 rifles were frozen tighter than a by-god,' said Sgt. Haliburton. 'They asked me what to do. "Hell," I said, "urinate on the sonuvabitches." It didn't smell so good after firing a couple of hours, but it saved our lives.' "
B. Evans, *"Why Old Soldiers Never Die,"* Yank, The Army Weekly.

1940s: "Down the hill below us resounded the 'dat-da dat-da dat-da dat-da' of a machine gun, the 'pow-pow' of M-1s, the 'pha-lot' of 4.2-inch mortars and the hammering 'baa-da-da-banh' of 90 mm guns." *"The Second Battle of Bougainville,"* Yank, The Army Weekly.

grease gun: popular name for the M-3, a submachine gun used by American soldiers.

grenade: various types used by Allied and enemy forces. The U.S. versions were known as the Mark II A1 and the Mark II A2. A phosphorous-filled smoke grenade, also capable of destruction, was called the M-15. Armor-piercing antitank grenades launched from a rifle were also used until the introduction of the bazooka.

howitzer: a short-barreled cannon. The howitzer was larger than a mortar and fired shells in a high arc.

1940s: "They were undoubtedly big guns—probably something around thirty-two centimeters, howitzers judging by the dullness of their rolling echo." *Robert Casey,* I Can't Forget.

machine pistol: a small German machine gun.

1940s: " 'The machine pistol goes "bzt"—like ripping a piece of cloth fast,' said Weber."

B. Evans, "Why Old Soldiers Never Die," Yank, The Army Weekly.

Mauser Karabiner 98K: a bolt-action rifle sometimes used by the Germans.

mortar: a compact, short-barreled cannon, smaller than a howitzer, capable of firing shells 440 to about 6,000 yards (the Germans had one with a range of 7,200 yards) depending on make and size.

1943: "Now we heard a distinct 'ping,' coming from somewhere in the vicinity of Hill 1139. It was a familiar sound—the discharge of a mortar, an enemy mortar. We waited a few seconds, and the shell landed in our midst with a loud 'carrumpp!'

R. Tregaskis, Invasion Diary.

Luger: a 9mm automatic pistol used by the Germans.

Sherman Tank: the British name for the M4, the most common U.S. tank, with over 48,000 in use throughout the war. It was outclassed by German tanks toward the end of the war, but the Germans couldn't compete with the Americans' greater numbers.

Sten: a British submachine gun capable of handling enemy ammunition. The Sten was disliked by troops because it sometimes jammed at critical moments, would sometimes fire if accidentally dropped, and generally appeared poorly constructed. However, the Sten could be quickly dismantled into small pieces for carriage or concealment, which made it a choice weapon for underground forces. Four million Stens were produced during the war.

Sturmgewehr: a German assault rifle.

Taisho 04 Nambu: an 8mm semiautomatic pistol used by the Japanese.

Thompson submachine gun: popularly known as a tommy gun, the standard issue submachine gun until 1942. It could hold twenty-round box magazines or 100-round drum magazines. Known for its reliability among American forces.

V-1 and V-2 Rocket: A German flying bomb and supersonic rocket, respectively, possibly the most terrifying of all German weaponry. The V-1 was first used against the British in the middle of 1944, the V-2 the following September. The V-1 made a loud, house-shaking roar as it passed slowly overhead. It was defended against by fighter planes, antiaircraft artillery and tethered balloons. The V-2 was the first supersonic rocket. Some said the V-2 was the most terrifying because it was undetectable in the air. The first anyone ever knew of it was its explosion. The British nicknamed the weapons "doodlebugs," while the Americans called them "buzz bombs" or "thunderbugs."

CRIME

According to a committee appointed by the American Bar Association, "the criminal situation in the United States so far as crimes of violence are concerned is worse than in any other civilized country."

The committee was speaking not of the 1990s, but of the 1920s and earlier.

Indeed, statistics compiled by Sing Sing Prison reveal that the average homicide rate from 1911-1921 in England and Wales was .76 per 100,000 population; in Canada, .54; in Switzerland, .18; and in the United States, an astonishing 7.20. Robberies were even worse. According to a 1928 issue of *Atlantic Magazine*, "more robberies and assaults with intent to rob are committed in the single city of Cleveland each year than in the whole of England, Scotland and Wales." In fact, Cleveland had 2,327 automobiles stolen in 1927, while London, ten times more populated, had only 290. Liverpool, one and a half times larger than Cleveland, had only ten.

Prohibition increased the crime rate considerably. There were hundreds of gangland murders (some drive-by shootings with machine guns and sawed-off shotguns) in Chicago alone throughout the 1920s. And no criminal doing business today could possibly rival the staggering exploits of Al Capone, who in one year took in a reported $105 million. (That's somewhere around $1 billion in 1990s money.)

There was the Depression, too. Chronic unemployment forced thousands of normally law-abiding men to become looters and petty thieves. "Men who are hungry and whose families are hungry have temptations that are compelling," said one Police Commissioner of New York during the height of the suffering. Indeed, statistics show that in the year 1928-1929, the total number of prisoners admitted to Sing Sing Prison was 1,098. That number rose dramatically in 1930-31 to 1,393, or by 26.8 percent.

At the peak of the Depression came John Dillinger, one of the busiest and most successful robbers ever. He was such a daring criminal, in fact, that his name became synonymous with boldness: to pull a "Dillinger" was to pull off an outrageously nervy crime, which Dillinger was particularly famous for in 1933.

Bonnie Parker and Clyde Barrow. "Pretty Boy" Floyd. "Baby Face" Nelson. Ma and Fred Barker. Alvin "Old Creepy" Karpis. The list of colorful creeps and crooks from the period is a long one. Below is a small sampling of the vernacular they and others like them may have used. Most of the terms were in use during the 1940s. The majority were in use throughout the Prohibition through World War II period.

---

bent rubber: stolen automobile tires. Tires were extremely valuable during the rubber rationing of World War II.

Betsy: affectionate term for any kind of rifle, shotgun or pistol. 1930s and 1940s.

big house: jail; a penitentiary.

big touch: a big robbery that nets a criminal enough money to live off for months or years or possibly the rest of his life.
1928: "It hurt my professional pride to be compelled to operate on so meager a scale. So I drowned my sorrows with rot-gut, and planned and planned for the big touch that would enable me to quit the racket for good. . . ." *"On the Lam," American Mercury, August.*
1928: "We talked incessantly of grands and big touches that would put us on Easy Street. . . ." *Ibid.*

bite on someone, put the: to extort or blackmail.

Bonnie and Clyde: Clyde Barrow and Bonnie Parker, with accomplices, committed numerous murders and robberies throughout the midwest in the early 1930s. Although they were surrounded by police on a number of occasions, they managed to shoot their way out and escape again and again, much to the public's horror and outrage. They killed several police officers during their escapes but were finally ambushed by G-men in Louisiana in 1934.

bleed: to extort or blackmail. To bleed someone dry.

bull: a detective. Sometimes, a uniformed policeman.
1928: "He said that during the past week every traffic and motorcycle cop in the city, as well as a squad of bulls who toured about in fast cars, had received orders to stop and inspect all cars, at all hours, in which there were three or more male passengers."
"*On the Lam,*" American Mercury, *August.*

bump off: to kill.
1930: "Did you hear about Jim getting bumped off?"
'*The Great American Slanguage,*" Outlook, *November 12.*

bunco: a card or pool game swindle, often involving a team of swindlers.

Cadillac: a one-ounce package of cocaine or heroin.

caper: a robbery or other criminal act, from 1925 on.

Capone, Al: see Section Two: Prohibition.

case: to inspect or look over a place with the intention of burglarizing or robbing it. "Go ahead and case the joint, Charlie."

charges for services: some underworld thugs had a standard charge for various criminal services, as attested by the news story below.
1933: "Three ruffians arrested in Philadelphia for threatened assault and battery told the police that the underworld had adopted a sort of blanket code. Under this code, $25 is fixed as the standard price for swinging a sandbag against a head marked for assault, $15 for wielding a blackjack, and $5 for a slap on the jaw. Payment must be made in cash, and must be handed over as soon as the client's victim lands in the hospital." Literary Digest, *November 4.*

Chicago: used as an adjective to describe someone who looks rough or like a gangster. "He's got that Chicago look about him, know what I mean?"

Chicago overcoat: a coffin. Also, a cement overcoat.
1929: A Chicago overcoat is what blasting will get you. . . ."
R. Chandler, The Big Sleep.

Chicago pineapple: a grenade or small bomb, as that associated with Chicago gangsters during Prohibition.

chiseler: a petty swindler or cheater. 1930s on.
1944: "Ration board officials say that the chiseler and the hoarder are an exception, not the rule, and can quickly be spotted."
Ladies Home Journal, December.

chump: a sucker; a dupe; an easy mark for a confidence game. Also, a gang leader's underling.
1932: "Presently one of his gunmen—they don't call them that in their own select circle; rather chumps, slobs or go-guys—drives the machine up to the apartment house door. . . ."
Harper's Monthly, October.
1946: "Our native swindlers define a sucker as 'a fish that will bite on a bare hook.' They call him chump, Mr. Wright, Mr. Goodman, wise guy, easy mark, come-on, flyflat, John, juggins or pigeon."
Life, August.

clink: jail.
1930s: "Jesus, Malloy, I'm giving you all the chance in the world to get me thrown in the clink." John O'Hara, Hope of Heaven.

clip-joint: a nightclub or other drinking establishment where the patrons are intentionally overcharged or even robbed.

coke: widely used term for cocaine, as early as the 1920s.

come clean: to confess what one knows to the police. Also, to produce hidden loot for sharing with other crooks.

Coney Island: any room in a police station where suspects are given the third degree.

convincer: a gun. Any intimidating weapon.

country, take one out to the: to drive someone out to a deserted, rural area and murder them. Sometimes spoken as a veiled threat.

creep joint: a brothel with rooms equipped with closets having secret openings that slide open, so that clothing can be ransacked for money and other valuables while the patron is sexually distracted.

dauber: one who paints stolen cars.

deb: a juvenile delinquent girl or female gang member who is promiscuous and fights. From the 1930s and 1940s.

dick: a detective. Less often, a policeman.

Dillinger: any gutsy, criminal act or prison escape, named after the daring exploits of John Dillinger. To pull a Dillinger.

Dillinger, John: declared public enemy number one by the FBI, easily the busiest and most daring criminal of the early 1930s. In 1933, he and a number of associates (including "Baby Face" Nelson) went on a massive crime spree, robbing banks, supermarkets, drugstores, taverns, company payrolls, and even police stations. Sometimes he pulled off as many as three robberies in a single day. The public was outraged by his exploits, but the police couldn't catch him. Even when they did finally corner him, he would escape—sometimes miraculously—again and again. Dillinger liked to make taunting phone calls to law enforcement officials and sometimes even took photographs of smiling (and oblivious) policemen on the street for amusement. Ultimately responsible for sixteen killings, he was finally cornered and shot to death by the FBI outside a movie theater in Chicago in 1934.
1934: "In a matchless piece of bravado—which eventually assumed both the proportions and the atmosphere of a comic opera—Dillinger escaped from the 'escape-proof' Lake County Jail this morning, after intimidating thirty-three jailers and inmates with a wooden pistol, and locking them in their living quarters, closets and cells. . . . With a colored confederate, also held for murder, he then seized two sub-machine guns from the warden's office of the jail, scaled a wall, commandeered the private car of Lake County's

woman sheriff, and rode past a cordon of fifty guards who had been stationed around the prison especially to keep him safely inside." New York Sunday News, *March 4.*

dirk: a knife.

dope: drugs, especially cocaine or opium. Since 1920.

eel: a slippery character; a weasel.

Federal Bureau of Investigation: The FBI was known as the Division of Investigation until 1935. J. Edgar Hoover headed up the bureau from 1924 on.

fence: one who buys stolen goods.

fence: to sell stolen goods to a criminal purchaser.

finger: to implicate someone in a crime.

fink: to implicate someone in a crime; to play the role of informer; to rat on.

flash dough: any money flashed under the nose of a sucker to gain his confidence in a confidence game.

flatfoot: a policeman.
1930s: "All this time I was expecting some flatfoot to be waiting for me, but I got so I didn't care." *John O'Hara,* Hope of Heaven.

flimflam: to deceive; to rip off by deception. From before 1900 through the 1940s.

fly a kite: to smuggle a letter out of prison and avoid censorship.

fly dick: a detective or policeman in plain clothes. Also known as a fly ball, a fly bull, or a fly cop. From the 1920s and 1930s.

fuzz: a policeman or a detective. As early as 1931.

G: a thousand dollars. Also, G-note. "He's carrying almost ten Gs in his briefcase."
1930s: "There were ten checks, each made out for five hundred dollars . . . Five Gs . . . A lot of money, you know." *John O'Hara,* Hope of Heaven.

ghee: 1940s prison slang for guy. "He's an okay ghee in my book."

G-man: an FBI or Secret Service agent. Any federal agent.
1942: "During his flight he stopped at a tourist camp to burn incriminating documents. The G-men who were trailing him let him burn the papers; later one of them gathered up the ashes, packed them in cotton wool, and shipped them to Washington." Future, Inc., *November.*
1942: "Wrestling holds are taught and blows that disable—tricks that have saved the life of many a G-man." Reader's Digest, *December.*

gong-kicker: a pothead; one who smokes marijuana habitually.

goods, the: evidence against someone in a crime. "The cops had the goods on him, so he bolted."

goon: until 1935, a hired muscleman; a strikebreaking thug. After, a thug or any person looking or acting geeky.

goof-butt: a marijuana cigarette; a joint.

gopher: a young hoodlum. From 1930.

gorilla: a brute hired to act as a bodyguard or to beat up people.

grift: to make small amounts of money by picking pockets, shoplifting, carrying out petty swindles, etc.

grifter: one who makes money through pickpocketing, shoplifting and petty swindles.

guinea football: a small bomb, especially a time bomb.

gumshoe: as a verb, to walk quietly and stealthily, as if stalking someone. Also, to work as a policeman. As a noun, a policeman or a detective. 1920 on.

gun mob: not a mob of gunmen, but a gang of pickpockets. Used throughout the period. Also known as a cannon mob.

gun moll: a gun-toting female, usually the girlfriend or wife of a bank robber or other criminal.

H: Heroin.

happy dust: cocaine.

hatchet man: a hired gun or killer. 1925 on.

heat: police pressure, as from an investigation closing in on criminals. As early as 1925. Also, from the 1940s, a gun. "He was packing heat, so we backed off." To "give someone the heat" was to shoot them.

heater: a revolver.

heel a joint: to steal from a store or bank cash register by means of the heel. See Swindles, Cons and Scams.

hog's leg: a pistol, especially a long-barreled revolver.
1940: "A plainclothesman with his coat off and his hog's leg looking like a fireplug against his ribs." *R. Chandler,* Farewell, My Lovely.

hokus: cocaine, opium or marijuana. From the 1930s.

hood: a hoodlum; a thief.

hooker: a prostitute. The word has been in use since at least the 1930s.

hookshop: a low-grade brothel. 1930s.

hoosegow: the local jail or police station lockup.

hop: cocaine, opium or marijuana, used throughout the period.

hop fiend: a user of cocaine, opium or marijuana, especially an addict. Used throughout the period.

hop head: a user of cocaine, opium or marijuana, especially an addict. Throughout the period.
1932: "The hopheads and the opium smokers known in the rackets as 'the lads who kick the engine around,' are at peace when they have their powders. . . ." Harper's Monthly, *October.*

hop joint: an opium den, the equivalent of today's crack house. Throughout the period.

hopped up: under the influence of drugs. Throughout the period.

hop up: to get high on drugs. Throughout the period.

hot: describing a criminal wanted by the police. Since at least 1932.

hot car farm: a junkyard that serves as a hideout where stolen cars are repainted and motor-block numbers changed.

house dick: a hotel detective.

Indian hay: marijuana. 1930s.

jack: small change, from at least the 1920s on.

jigger man: a lookout at a burglary.

jimmy: a heavy steel bar used to break into houses.

John: a sucker; an easy mark.

John Law: any policeman or law man.

John Roscoe: a pistol; a revolver. Usually shortened to Roscoe. From 1930s on.

jug: bank robber's term for a bank. "We planned to knock off the jug at noon."

juggins: a sucker; an easy mark.

jug hack: a bank guard.

jugman: one who specialized in robbing banks.

juju: a marijuana cigaret; a joint.
1940: "I knew a guy who smoked jujus. Three highballs and three
  sticks of tea and it took a pipewrench to get him off the chandelier."
  R. Chandler, Farewell, My Lovely.

junk: narcotics. Since at least 1920.

junk peddler: a drug dealer.

kite: a letter smuggled in or out of prison.

knock off: kill. Also, to rob.

knock over: to rob.

lay: a place to be robbed. "That shop was a good lay."

Ma Barker gang: Kate "Ma" Barker, Arthur "Doc" Barker, Fred Barker, Alvin Karpis and others made up the Barker gang, who in the late 1920s and early 1930s were gainfully employed as robbers and kidnappers. Ma Barker often counseled her boys on places to rob; her detail work with the National Bank at Fairbury, Nebraska in 1933, for example, netted the gang $151,350. Ma also championed for her boys' early parole whenever they were imprisoned. The gang members were captured and Ma Barker killed (she died with a machine gun in her hands) by the FBI in 1935.

Mary Magdalene: a reformed prostitute.

match game, the: a street hustle in which three matchboxes are shuffled around on a table, with the victim trying to guess which has the matches in it. In reality, the box with the matches is switched with one that has no matches, but the victim is fooled because the hustler secretly has a matchbox taped within his shirt-sleeve which he rattles when he holds up one of the empty boxes.

Michigan bankroll: a roll of green paper with a hundred-dollar bill wrapped over the outside, used to fool pigeons in swindles.

moll-buzz: to steal a woman's pocketbook from a baby carriage. The feat is accomplished when an accomplice accosts the woman on the street and asks for directions. (The directions are such that the woman must completely turn her back.) Once the woman is distracted, a second man approaches the carriage, grabs the purse and drops it into a brown paper shopping bag and nonchalantly continues walking.

mouse: an informer.

oil merchant: a smooth-talking confidence man; one who can swindle someone through charm and fast talk.

on the lam: in flight from justice.

pack a heater: to carry a pistol on one's person.

pack a rod: to carry a pistol on one's person.

Patsy: affectionate term for a revolver or pistol.

piece: a pistol or revolver.

pigeon: a sucker; an easy mark.

pineapple: see Chicago pineapple.

play: to string one along in a swindle; to play one for a sucker.

plug: to shoot. "They plugged him full of holes."

pokey: a county jail.

prowl car: a police car on patrol.

queer: counterfeit money.
1926: "Here in the jungles they turn out their 'sour paper' (bad checks) and their 'queer' (counterfeit money). . . ."
"Thieves Thesaurus," Literary Digest, *December 4.*

racketeering: the practice of extorting money from legitimate businesses by threats of violence. The money paid was called "protection" money. Often paid on a weekly or monthly basis, it "protected" the business establishment from being mysteriously burned down or its owners beaten up in some dark alley. If the fee was high enough, it also bought a measure of intimidation against rival businesses; a new or competing store down the street could easily be put out of business through constant threats of violence or from arson. It was estimated that Chicago alone in 1929 had ninety such rackets, costing employer's a combined $136 million per year. An average of fifty bombings per year throughout Chicago during the 1920s were blamed on racketeers.
1929: "Suppose I happen to be a hoodlum . . . and I choose pretzels as a field. I then 'invite' the pretzel dealers of Chicago to 'join' me. From each of them I demand, say, one hundred dollars per month. For this sum, my men will 'protect' them from competition, since they must raise their prices to pay my one hundred dollars. If any pretzel man refuses to join me I bomb him. I slug his drivers. I cut off his supply. . . ." Harper's Monthly, *October.*

ranked: referring to a burglary or robbery gone wrong.

rat mark: a V-shaped knife wound running from the mouth to the cheekbone, inflicted upon a prison informer as a warning to others.

raus: the act of jostling someone, as if accidently bumping into them, during a pickpocket operation. "We gave him the raus and lifted his wallet."

reefing: a pickpocket's term, meaning to work a mark's pocket lining up with one's fingers in order to get at any cash or wallet that may be there.

rod: a revolver. "Packing a rod." From the 1920s on.
1928: "We sped into the back room, closed the door, and drew out our rods just as the astonished Greek turned. . . ."
American Mercury, *August.*
1928: "The blue-steel barrels of two ugly-looking rods menaced me from over Rose's shoulders." *Ibid.*

rodman: a gunman.
1932: "The average rodman used to get $200 a week, but the depression has hit him just as it has the ordinary forgotten man. Today he gets between $75 and $100 a week, with a little bonus now and then for an extra-fancy bit of homicide." Harper's Monthly, *October*

rub out: to kill or murder someone. Throughout the period.

sap: a club. Also known as a sap stick. As a verb, to club someone.

satch: a form of illicit drugs impregnated in paper or clothing by saturation, used in prison smuggling.

score: a burglary or robbery; money or valuables gotten in a crime. As a verb, to successfully rob or burglarize a place.

scratch: money. Also, a forged signature.

scratch man: a professional or skilled forger.

screw: a prison guard.

sell out: to inform on another; to betray another in order to lessen one's own prison sentence.

shade: a pickpocket's assistant who shields the pickpocket's actions from others.

shadow: a loan shark's muscleman who intimidates borrowers into paying up.

shake down a joint: to extort money from an illegal enterprise, such as a speakeasy during Prohibition, by either impersonating the police and accepting bribes or threatening to go to the police.

Shamus: a policeman. Also, a sham. (Short for Irish shamrock.)
1928: "A wanted thief is conversing with a friend when a policeman comes near. 'Sham—duck!' whispers the friend."
"Language of the Underworld," American Mercury, *May.*

shell game: street game in which a dupe tries to guess under which of three walnut shells a pea is hidden. As the shells are shuffled around on a table, the pea is deftly hidden under the crook of the swindler's small finger.

sing: to tell all to the police; to inform or snitch on another.

sissy rod: any gun fitted with a silencer.

slab, on a: dead; murdered. "If you don't want to end up on a slab you'd better keep your mouth shut."

slug: a bullet.

snow: cocaine.

soup: a rough form of nitroglycerine produced by cooking pieces of stick dynamite in water and skimming off the picric extract. Used for safecracking throughout the period.

spitting on the sidewalk: any trivial offense one is sent to jail for.

square John: a law-abiding citizen.

stall: a pickpocket's assistant whose job is to set up a victim, distract the victim or to get in the way so the pickpocket can escape if discovered.
1928: ". . . among pickpockets, 'putting the duke down' refers to the work of the wire who abstracts the objective from the victim's kick; and 'putting his back up' indicates that the stall is putting the mark, yap, sucker or hoosier into the right position to insure a successful operation. . . ." American Mercury, *May.*

SWINDLES, CONS AND RIP-OFFS

Without the warning voice of television consumer alert programs, the average Joe Blow of the 1920s, 1930s and 1940s was probably more naive about scams and rip-offs than his counterpart of today. Thus smooth-talking swindlers flourished. Some of the confidence games and scams cited here are still in use today. Others, like those involving Prohibition or soldiers returning from war, are unique to the time.

- Badger, the: a blackmailing operation in which a female entices a male dupe into having sex with her and is purposely "caught in the act" by a second man claiming to be the woman's husband. The husband threatens to go to the man's wife and extorts money from the victim to keep things "quiet."
- Prohibition Agent Impersonation: a Prohibition scam in which extortionists act the part of federal Prohibition agents. Wearing fake badges and carrying forged search warrants, they enter a speakeasy or other establishment selling illegal booze and proceed to shake down the joint. The establishment's proprietor, as was common during Prohibition, offers a bribe to the agents. The agents gladly accept and go on their merry way.
- Water in the Gas Tank Scam: a scam in which a man drives up to a busy gas station and orders the attendant to fill his tank, not with gas, but with water. In dismay, the attendant does so, and curious onlookers gather around to watch. When the tank is filled, the man produces a pill and drops it into the gas tank. He tells the onlookers that the pill, developed by a scientist, converts water into gasoline. When the car starts and is driven around, the impressed onlookers purchase a large quantity of the pills. The scam artist then jumps back in his car and drives off to repeat the scam elsewhere. Nobody suspects that a dummy gas tank might be involved until they fill their own tanks with water and discover the pills are worthless. This scam was used several times throughout the 1930s.
- Dead Soldier Mementos Scam: used during war time, a scam in which a hustler writes to the family of a recently killed soldier and tells them that, as a friend and fellow soldier, he has a number of personal effects of the dead soldier and he will send them for a small fee. The family pays the fee and receives either a cheap bible in the mail or nothing.

- Selling Stiffs: a hustler scans obituaries of out-of-town newspapers and sends an express-collect package containing a pen or other cheap item to the address of the dead. Family assumes the deceased ordered the package before his death and feel they must pay the bill, which is outrageously high for such a cheap item. Hustlers with guts sometimes acted out this scam in person, at the deceased family's door, as illustrated below.

  1941: "He cleaned up a comfortable bank roll selling widows fountain pens engraved with the names of their recently deceased husbands. Jimmy's fast sales talk convinced the widows that their husbands had ordered the pens. The obituary columns provided endless leads and the pens, which cost Jimmy fifteen cents each, netted him from $2.50 to five dollars."

  "Portrait of a Punk," The American Mercury, *September.*

- Psychic Card Guesser: a hustler goes into bar and tells patrons he knows a psychic who can, over the telephone, discern which card is picked randomly from a new deck of cards, even from a hundred miles away. Patrons scoff and confidently bet various amounts of money that it can't be done. Patrons either produce their own deck of cards or a new deck is purchased and opened in front of everyone. Patron chooses card at random. Hustler looks for psychic's phone number and calls. The psychic knows almost instantly which card was chosen and patrons lose their bets. How it works: Hustler, seeing the chosen card, pretends to look for psychic's phone number but actually refers to a code list of common words designated to represent the various cards; he utters the secret code word into the phone but the patrons are oblivious because the code may be as cleverly simple as calling the psychic by various names, as in "Good morning, Wanda" (ace of clubs) or "Hello, Mary?" (king of diamonds) and so on. The stunned patrons lose their bets.

- Glim Hustle: a confidence man, posing as an eye specialist, approaches a mark and informs him with great concern that he has noticed a rare disease developing in his eyes and offers to treat him on the spot. After a phony examination, the con man writes a prescription and cooly finagles a fee. The fee may include an advance for future consultation and surgery.

- Heel, the: a rip-off artist approaches a store cashier with a large bill. As the cashier opens the register to make change, a confederate rushes up to the counter and, announcing that he is in a big hurry, asks the cashier for an item behind the counter. While the cashier turns to get the item, the first man reaches into the cash register and takes out a handful of money. The shortage isn't noticed until the next transaction. A variation: confederate female faints dramatically just as the register is opened, diverting cashier so that first confederate can steal a wad of bills. Also known as a hit-and-run play.

- Air Raid Gear: Phony air raid wardens go from house to house selling fire extinguishers. They tell homeowners they are required by the government during wartime.

- Air Raid Furnace Protection: Rip-off artists go from door to door, offering to equip furnaces with safety gadgets that will prevent them from blowing up in the event of an air strike.

- Air Raid Siren Charity: Dishonestly collecting donations for a city or town to buy an air raid siren.

- Government War Recycling Program: phony government men go door to door persuading housewives to donate their household goods to aid the war effort.

- Money-making machine: Con man offers to sell a small press that miraculously produces "undetectable" counterfeit $20, $50 or $100 bills. Inserting one bill produces two bills and, through a clever bit of chicanery, the process can be repeated over and over. The con man risks his own genuine bills in the process and instructs the mark to take them to the bank to assure that they are real. Once convinced, the sucker may fork over several thousand dollars for the bogus machine. A variation produces a five dollar bill for every one dollar bill inserted. 1945: ". . . a grocer of Providence accused Esposito of posing as a doctor and offering 'out of friendship' to triple his investment by inserting bills and blank paper into a pressing device and producing one hundred dollar bills. [The grocer] said he had handed over $15,000 to Esposito and a second man and had received in return a package containing a single one hundred dollar bill bound on top of a packet of plain paper." Life.

136

- Making Citizens: Granting aliens "citizenship" with a phony judge and a large fee. Aliens failing to come up with the cash are threatened with deportation.

AD IN CHICAGO DAILY TRIBUNE, 1932

"Bullet-holes rewoven perfectly in damaged clothes."

stool pigeon: one who informs on others in exchange for police immunity in one's own petty rackets.

sucking the bamboo: smoking opium, 1920s on.

taken for a sleigh ride: swindled; ripped-off; taken for a sucker.

tool: in a pickpocket gang or "gun mob," the most talented pickpocket, and the one who does the actual pickpocketing. Also called the "wire."
1926: "The most skillful one of the gang, usually known as the wire or tool, does the actual stealing while his confederates do the stalling."
"The Thieves Thesaurus," Literary Digest, *December 4.*

touch: a robbery or burglary. Also, the money received from such. See big touch.

typewriter: underworld term for a machine gun, 1920s. The term was revived by soldiers fighting in World War II.

up the river: prison. "Get caught and you'll be sent up the river for good."

violin: a small machine gun.

violin case: a machine gun case.

Walter Winchell: one who "talks too much"; a gossip; an informer. So-named after the radio personality and columnist of the 1930s and 1940s.

DRIVE-BY SHOOTINGS

Drive-by shootings are hardly a new form of violence; they've been around as long as the automobile itself and were particularly prevalent during the gang wars of Prohibition. Then as now, innocent bystanders were sometimes caught in the crossfire.

1931: CHILD SLAIN, FOUR SHOT AS GANGSTERS FIRE ON BEER WAR RIVAL: "Five children were wounded, one of them mortally, early last night by gangsters who opened fire with shotguns and machineguns on a man lounging in front of the Helmar Social Club at 208 East 107th St. [NY]. The intended victim escaped injury by lying down, and, as the gangsters' car sped away, got up and disappeared. . . . The shooting, which occurred less than four blocks from the East 104th Street police station, was ascribed by police to the Harlem-Bronx beer war between the gangs of Joe Rao, an ally, temporarily, of Arthur (Dutch Schultz) Flegenheimer, and Vincent Coll. More than fifty detectives were sent out last night with orders to bring [the gangmembers] in for questioning." New York Times, July 29.

(Shootings like these prompted Police Commissioner Mulrooney to order New York police officers to shoot gangsters and other gunmen "above the waist.")

1931: "Last night, at the end of another day of gang warfare, the casualty list stood as follows: DEAD: Guido Ferreri, twenty-six years old, clothing manufacturer of 1616 Ocean Parkway, Brooklyn. Killed with a shotgun by two men in automobile in front of his home. WOUNDED: Adolph Joseph (Dogs) Gazzola, twenty-seven, liquor-runner and policy racketeer of 303 East 105th St.; wounded four times by an unidentified assailant and taken to Mount Sinai Hospital in critical condition." New York Times, August 1.

---

wire: a highly skilled pickpocket. See tool.

wise guy: a sucker; an easy mark.

yegg: a safeblower. Mostly obsolete after the 1920s.

NEW YORK CITY POLICE SLANG
OF THE 1940S

blow: to skip bail or skip town.

canary: a snitch or informer; one who "talks."

coffee sergeant: a station-house errand runner and coffee-maker.

collar: an arrest. To arrest.

contract: a favor, as "fixing" a parking or speeding ticket.

dip: a pickpocket.

heist: a theft.

lammister: a fugitive, from "on the lam."

lush worker: a criminal who mugs drunks.

NEW YORK CITY'S RISING HOMICIDE RATE
BEFORE & DURING PROHIBITION

Year	Homicides
1917	108
1918	156
1919	178
1920	184
1921	206
1922	237
1923	195
1924	265
1925	248
1926	213
1927	180
1928	214
1929	222
1930	316

There were two hundred homicides in the first seven months of 1931 alone, according to the *New York Times*.

persuader: a billy club or pistol.

pie wagon: a patrol wagon.

pokey: jail.

press the bricks: walk a beat.

rap: a criminal charge.

Roscoe: a gun, especially one that can be concealed under clothing. See also John Roscoe.

sap: to hit someone with a billy club or blackjack.

scratch: money. Also, mention of an officer in the news.

shill: an assistant of a confidence man.

signal thirty-two: radio alert that a man is armed.

singer: a snitch; a stool pigeon.

skylarker: a suspicious person.

skins: dollars.

sparrow cop: an officer assigned to Central Park.

tin: a badge.

well-heeled: armed.

Transportation

CARS

Thanks largely to Henry Ford and mass production, by 1920 one in every thirteen Americans owned an automobile. In 1924, one could buy a Ford for the astoundingly low price of $290. Ford did a number of things to help make it easier for Americans to buy cars. He paid his workers what was considered a huge wage at the time, $5 a day. Second, he let people buy on credit.

In 1919, the average nationwide speed limit was twenty miles per hour; fifteen in residential areas, and ten in cities. In some places, six miles per hour was the limit around sharp curves. In those early days, truckers took thirteen days to reach California from New York. As roads improved, however, so did the speed limits, which reached a national average of thirty-five to forty miles per hour in 1931. In 1921, 387,000 miles of paved roads crisscrossed America. By 1941, that figure would triple.

In 1919, about 90 percent of all cars were open to the air. In 1924, only about 60 percent were. By 1927, 82.9 percent of all cars were closed.

Allen: four-cylinder car built from 1914 to 1922. A total of twenty thousand cars were sold.

Auburn: built from 1900 to 1937. Rarely sold more than four thousand cars per year until 1925. With advanced designs, more than twenty-eight thousand were sold at its peak in 1931.

Buick: sold various models from 1903 on.

Cadillac: first manufactured in 1902, Cadillacs were always high-quality cars. However, they were originally designed for the middle class until the 1920s, when their reputation as a luxury car grew. From 1930 on they were considered one of the most prestigious automobiles on the road. A V-16 went for $5,350 to $15,000 in 1930.

car company failures: Between 1900 and 1938 more than one thousand car companies failed and went out of business. Some of these included:

Briscoe	1921
Brooks	1926
Cameron	1921
Case	1927
Chalmers	1924
Crawford	1924
Davis	1928
Detroit Electric	1938
Dorris	1926
Elcar	1930
Flint	1927
Kissel	1931
Locomobile	1929
Marmon	1933
Maxwell	1925
McFarlan	1927
Mercer	1925
Moon	1930
National	1924
Paige	1927
Peterson	1924
Peerless	1932
Pierce-Arrow	1938
Pilot	1924
Premier	1927
Pullman	1925
Star	1928
Stearns-Knight	1930

Stevens-Duryea	1927
Stutz	1935
Velie	1928
Willys-Knight	1932
Winton	1924

Chevrolet: built from 1911 on. 1932 models sold for as little as $495. Chevrolet actually outsold Fords throughout most of the 1930s.

Chevrolet Model AD: introduced in 1930, this was Chevy's answer to Ford's Model A. The six-cylinder, two-door sedan outsold its rival Ford year after year. It was nicknamed the "Cast Iron Wonder" or "Stovebolt Six," after its cast iron pistons. Its advertising slogan touted "six for the price of a four."

Chrysler: built from 1923 on.

Chrysler Airflow: introduced in 1934, an ugly car that was initially rejected by the public because of its rounded, aerodynamic or streamlined design. It had an eight-cylinder engine and could burn up the road at 95.7 miles per hour, a record that, for mass-production passenger cars, held for twenty-three years.

Cord: an advanced-design, sporty car that the youngsters of the day probably would have called "awesome" had that word been in use. Distinctively modern in appearance, the Cord boasted retractable headlights, a wraparound grille, and front-wheel drive. Built from 1929 to 1937, with pricetags ranging from $1,995 to $3,575.

DeSoto: originating in 1928, a clunky-looking, run-of-the-mill automobile costing under $1,000 throughout the 1930s. Ninety thousand were sold in its first year. The 1939 model had a sliding sunroof. A convertible coupe became available in 1940.
1939: "Are you bothered by the old-fashioned 'wobble-stick gearshift?'
  DeSoto's is on the steering post—out of knees way."
  DeSoto advertisement.

Doble: a sophisticated steam-powered car, second in fame only to the Stanley, that had the ability to get up to steam from a cold start in just one and a half minutes and boasted a range of fifteen hundred miles on only twenty-four gallons of water! The Doble was also a luxury car, priced at $8,000. Only forty-five Dobles were made between 1914 and 1931.

Dodge: built from 1914 on.

Duesenberg J: a distinctively elongated, luxurious, gas-guzzling American-made car, considered one of the great classics of the era. It was famous for its acceleration, its 265 horsepower motor catapulting it from zero to one hundred miles per hour in seventeen seconds; up to ninety miles per hour in second gear alone, with an overall top speed of 116 mph. Ironically, it was considered one of the quietest cars on the road, despite its massive power. Its engine was characteristically enameled a bright green. Its instrument panel was easily the busiest of its time. Some of its gauges included a stopwatch, an ammeter, an altimeter/barometer, a brake and oil pressure gauge, an rpm counter, an engine thermometer, and warning lights telling the driver when to change the oil and when to add water to the battery. The Duesenberg came with a long list of optional luxuries and was commonly equipped with radios, bars and vanity cases. The Duesenberg sold for well over $10,000 from 1928 to 1937, and only a few hundred were made. Still, it was the favorite car of numerous celebrities. William Randolph Hearst, Clark Gable, Gary Cooper, Mae West, Elizabeth Arden, Mayor Jimmy Walker of New York and the Kings of Spain and Italy were all proud Duesenberg owners.

Durant: built from 1921 to 1932, and selling 55,000 units in its peak year of 1922.

ethyl: dry gas, touted as superior to regular gas. Drivers told filling station attendants to "fill it with ethyl" from about 1930 on.

flivver: originally, a nickname for the Ford Model T. Later, any old, broken-down car.

Ford Model A: the very popular successor to Ford's Model T. It was introduced with massive consumer interest in December 1927. A four-cylinder, three-speed, it was available as a two-door phaeton or tourer, a roadster, a sedan and a pickup. Unlike the Model T, it came in an array of colors, including Niagara Blue and Arabian Sand. It was replaced by the Model B and the V-8 in 1932.

Ford Model T: Ford's classic four-cylinder automobile, manufactured from 1908 to 1927, with few yearly changes, including color, which was almost always black. Affectionately known as a Tin Lizzy or a flivver, the Model T was the butt of hundreds of affectionate jokes in its day, and for good reason. It wouldn't start in the cold. It needed a running start to mount hills. (It could, however, mount steep hills in reverse, because the gear ratio was lower in reverse than in forward; also, its gravity-fed fuel line tended to go dry when the car was tilted uphill in the forward position.) It rattled, and it frequently overheated. Worst of all was its crank start, which, when it kicked back, was responsible for innumerable broken arms and sprained wrists. Author Frederick Lewis Allen gives this account of its challenging starting method: "[The driver] climbs in by the right-hand door (for there is no left-hand door by the front seat), reaches over to the wheel, and sets the spark and throttle levers in a position like that of the hands of a clock at ten minutes to three. Then, unless he has paid extra for a self-starter, he gets out to crank. Seizing the crank in his right hand carefully, for a friend of his once broke his arm cranking, he slips his left forefinger through a loop of wire that controls the choke. He pulls the loop of wire, he revolves the crank mightily, and as the engine at last roars, he leaps to the trembling running board, leans in, and moves the spark and throttle to twenty-five minutes to two. . . . Finally he is at the wheel with the engine running as it should. . . ." *Only Yesterday, An Informed Survey of the 1920s.*

Driving the flivver was somewhat easier than other cars of the period. It had three floor pedals: the one on the left was first gear, the one in the middle was reverse, and the one on the right was the brake. The car was started off by first unblocking the handbrake lever and pressing down the left pedal. Releasing this pedal shifted the car into second.

With its twenty-horsepower motor, the T could reach a top speed of forty to forty-five miles per hour. Farmers especially loved the car because it could not only be used to truck things around, but its back wheels could be quickly replaced with adaptive tractor tires; the T was used by thousands of farmers to plow their fields!

In 1923, one out of every two cars sold was a Ford. And no wonder. The original 1908 price of $850 dropped precipitously to an incredible

$310 (including self-starter) by 1926, the lowest price of any car. It was finally replaced by the Model A in December 1927.

Some classic Model T jokes from the period:

"Can I sell you a speedometer?"

"I don't use one. When my Ford is running five miles an hour, the fender rattles; twelve miles an hour my teeth rattle; and fifteen miles an hour the transmission drops out."

"I hear they're going to magnetize the rear axle of the Ford."

"What's the idea?"

"So it will pick up the parts that drop off."

"He named his Ford after his wife."

"That's funny."

"Not at all! After he got it he found out that he couldn't control it."

"The Ford is the best family car. It has a tank for father, a hood for mother, and a rattle for baby."

1920: "BROKEN ARMS PREVENTED FROM FORD CRANKING. Non-Kick Device Makes Cranking Safe. . . . Any time the Ford Motor fires back or kicks, the 'Non-Kick' Device automatically disengages the clutch, allowing the motor to reverse without injury to yourself or the car. Thousands of satisfied users. Better than insurance because it prevents sprained wrists, broken arms, with their pain and suffering. . . . Newspapers and statistics show thousands hurt each month cranking Fords. About 5,000,000 Fords without starters. Only 30 percent of 1,250,000 cars Ford will make in 1921 will be sold with starters, so Ford People tell us, leaving 875,000 new cars sold without starters. . . .." *Advertisement for non-kick device.*

PRICES FOR 1919:

Touring	Runabout	Coupe	Sedan
$525	$500	$650	$775

PRICES FOR 1925:

Touring	Runabout	Coupe	Sedan	Four-Door Sedan
$290	$260	$520	$580	$660

1920s: "You didn't have a heater or a defroster in the T. My father carried a lantern on the floor and he had a little bag of salt. He'd rub the salt on the windshield every now and then, and in winter he'd have about an inch of eyespace to see through." *Errol McCutcheon.*

1920s: "We'd all pile into the T for a ride, five kids and Mumma, and Dad would crank. We all just sat there and held our breath, waiting and hoping, and Dad would crank and crank and crank. A lot of times I was worried Dad might drop dead from cranking. But then after awhile the motor would start up and everyone would holler and cheer." *Mary McCutcheon.*

Ford V-8: introduced to replace the Model A in March of 1932. The V-8 roadster or coupe could be bought for under $500 and drew wide consumer interest because of its reported top speed: seventy-eight miles per hour. John Dillinger loved the car and wrote to Henry Ford to tell him so: "Hello old pal: Arrived here at 10 A.M. today. Would like to drop in and see you. You have a wonderful car. Been driving it for three weeks. It's a real treat to drive one. Your slogan should be: Drive a Ford and watch the other cars fall behind you. It can make any other car take Ford's dust. Bye-bye." *John Dillinger.*

gas rationing: see Section 4: World War II, On the Homefront.

Hupmobile: a sporty, medium-priced American car, popular in the 1930s. Hupmobile went out of business in 1942.

Lincoln: originating in 1921, a high-quality V-8 luxury car, priced from $4,300-$6,600. It was easily the favorite car of gangsters and bootleggers for its capaciousness (lots of room for running booze down from Canada) and top speed of eighty miles per hour. (The classic V-12 originating in 1932 could go one hundred miles per hour). Police had no choice but to acquire Lincolns in the 1920s in order to keep up with the criminals. Notable feature: Greyhound radiator ornament.

Moon: an upscale car built from 1905 to 1930. Notable for its Rolls-Royce look-alike radiator. Its 1926 model was called the Diana, after the moon goddess. Its 1929 model was called the Prince of Windsor, named after the Prince of Wales.

Morris "bullnose": a cheap car as popular in England in the 1920s as the Model T and A were in America. It had four cylinders, a round or "bullnose" radiator, and it was available as a two-seater with rumble seat, or as a four-seater without rumble seat.

Nash: built from 1916 through the period, the Nash was known for its styling and special innovations. Notable innovations included its "twin ignition" system, which first appeared in 1928, its dashboard starter buttons and shatterproof glass (1930), its "Syncro-Safety Shift" mounted not on the floor but on the dashboard (1932) and its aircraft-like instruments (1934). Its "Weather-Eye" heating and ventilation system (1938) remained one of the best climate control systems available anywhere for twenty years. A 1939 Nash Ambassador Six could be bought for $1,200.

1946: "Wonderful things have developed since you last bought an automobile. . . . Overnight plane service to London . . . radar . . . television . . . and now—in the new, low-price Nash 600—the 'coming thing' in cars has come. . . . No doubt about it—not when you hear what a new Nash 600 does, and offers! You get economy of twenty-five to thirty miles on a gallon at moderate highway speeds—500 to 600 miles on a tankful! Instead of the usual interior dimensions you get a car so roomy that the front seat is divan size and the rear seat can be made into a soft, double bed at night, if you like. Instead of the usual heater, Nash offers the Weather-Eye Conditioned Air System—so that the whole car is draftless, dustless—and warm as your living room, in cold weather. . . ."

Nash Motors full-page magazine ad, August.

Oldsmobile: made from 1896 on.

Packard: a large, heavy, expensive car built from around the turn of the century through the end of the 1950s. A notable model was its powerful V-12 or "Twin-Six," made from 1915-1924. Its Boattail Speedster was popular during the 1920s and early 1930s, but cost $5,210 in 1929. Packard manufactured cheap cars during the Depression. Its 120 model sold for $795 in 1936. Air conditioning was offered as an option starting in 1940. In 1941, it began its popular Clipper line.

1937: "If Bill and I look like the cat that swallowed the canary, please excuse us. We just got something that's been our heart's desire—a Packard! The joke of it is that our new car has started our neighborhood gossiping. People say that Bill must have had a big raise, or come into some money, or something. They seem a little envious, too. And we're human enough to let it. You see, there *hasn't* been any raise. It's simply that we woke up to a few facts. Just about the time our well-worn small car began to limp, Bill and I walked by a Packard showroom. We stopped to admire the Packard 120 and Packard Six that were in the window. And I said to Bill, 'Of course we can't afford a Packard, but let's go in anyway. After all, a cat can look at a queen. So in we went—and got the surprise of our lives . . . for the Packard Six we picked, payments came to less than $35 a month (after down payment)!'" *Packard ad, July.*

rumble seat: a passenger seat that folded out at the trunk and was open to the air. Also known as a dickey seat.

1930s: "I couldn't take a rumble seat today because it was really rough, like riding in the back of a truck. But when you were young, you loved it out in the air and you got good tans and sunburns." *Mary and Errol McCutcheon.*

Peerless: top-end luxury car of the 1920s and earlier. A description of some of the luxuries of its "Salon-Sedan" appeared in a 1914 trade journal: "The interior colors of the car are dark mahogany, ivory, and green, blending from the darker to the lighter shades. Dark green linoleum covers the floorboards and is bound with German silver moulding. The carpet is high-piled English Axminster. At the floor and the sidewalls is a baseboard of mahogany about four inches wide. Above this is the wool frieze cloth and a chair rail of the same design as the baseboard, only smaller. Around the windows is a veneering of ivory enamel and the sashless panes are set in a veneer of three quarters of an inch wide mahogany. The shades are silk taffeta. The festooned draperies are silk broche lined with silk taffeta. The dome ceiling is lined with plain wool tapestry laid in a panel with flush lights in each of the four corners. Pillows are of Italian brocade with silk-tinseled velvet border. A toilet case is of mahogany with fittings of silver and mahogany-colored goat skins. All the interior metal parts are quadruple silver plated. At the rear corners are two disappearing Pullman electric lights for reading. Compartments are furnished for gloves, books, papers and slip covers." Peerless stopped manufacturing cars in 1934 and began making beer instead.

Pierce-Arrow: among the most luxurious cars ever built, a typical 1914 model was equipped with deep velour upholstery and carpets, Waltham clocks, umbrella compartments, smoking cases and special buttons to signal one's chauffeur. Options included gold-plated hardware. Pierce-Arrow offered electric starting and lighting as early as 1913. Its smooth ride was actually quieter than a Rolls-Royce. Distinctive feature: fender-mounted headlights. A top of the line model went for $7,200 in 1914. A cheap touring model, selling three or four thousand per year, was available for $2,875 in 1924. Pierce-Arrow went out of business after the 1938 model year.

Plymouth: manufactured from 1928 on.

Pontiac: manufactured from 1926 on.

REO: This car company was named after Ransom E. Olds, of Oldsmobile fame, and was in business from 1904 to 1936. Two of their better-known models were the Flying Cloud and the Wolverine.

Stanley Steamer: the classic steam-propelled car, manufactured from the turn of the century to 1925. Under the hood sat not an engine (that was under the car in front of the rear axle) but a drum-shaped boiler covered with asbestos and a network of pipes with a blowtorch-like burner, a pilot flame and several pumps. The pilot light could be left on overnight to maintain a low head of steam. If turned off, the steamer was "fired up" again by lighting the pilot with an acetylene torch. (The pilot light burned gasoline, the main burner, kerosene.) Speed was controlled by a simple hand throttle mounted on the steering column. The Stanley Steamer, after 1915, could run 300 miles on a single tank of water. As early as 1906, a Stanley reached the record speed of 127.66 miles per hour. Only about 1,000 Steamers were produced each year, at a cost of about $2,000.

struggle-buggy: students' nickname for a car, because making out in one was a struggle.

Studebaker: in the 1920s, a car-maker nearly as popular as Ford, building over 100,000 cars in 1922 alone. Its popularity didn't last, however. In 1932-33, its claim to fame was the six-cylinder Rockne, named after Notre Dame football coach Knute Rockne. It sold for just $600 but failed to catch the fancy of the buying public. Some suspected the name might be a problem. So the Rockne was promptly followed up with another car with a terrible name, the Dictator, built through 1937. Studebaker also made a huge, fast car called the President, which did enjoy respect and popularity and sold for a modest $1,625. Thanks to improved styling, production rebounded with 106,470 cars made in 1939.

Stutz: built from 1911 to 1935. Stutz's most famous model was its two-seater Bearcat speedster of 1914, later revived in various modes through the 1920s and 1930s. However, it also built excellent touring cars. These were so advanced and considered so safe to drive (they had hydraulic brakes and safety glass and were built low to the ground to help prevent rollovers) that the company offered a year's free insurance to anyone that bought one.

tin can: slang term for a car.

tin Lizzie: affectionate term for a car, especially a Ford, from 1917 and after. Later, any old, broken-down car.

war-time production: Production of civilian cars was halted by the government on February 9, 1942, so vehicles could be made for the military. Ford opened its Willow Run Michigan Bomber Plant three months later. Along with Willys, it also made jeeps. Nash-Kelvinator built aircraft engines. Chrysler built tanks. GM aided the war effort with heavy-duty trucks. Production of civilian cars resumed in 1945, but these models were only slightly facelifted versions of the 1942 line. Cars changed little, in fact, until the 1947 model year.

wisecracks: a faddish practice of high school and college boys of writing wisecracks, slogans and cute names—in paint or chalk—all over their jalopies, late 1920s, early 1930s. Some typical lines:

STANDING ROOM ONLY.

THE MAYFLOWER—MANY A PURITAN HAS COME ACROSS IN IT.

FOUR WHEELS, NO BRAKES.

ABANDON ALL HOPE YE WHO ENTER HERE.

USE CAN OPENER.

OPEN ALL NIGHT.

CHICKEN, HERE'S YOUR ROOST.

THIS SIDE UP.

HOT HANNA.

GALLOPING GERTRUDE.

(In front of the radiator): BEWARE–OLD FAITHFUL SPOUTS EVERY FIVE MINUTES!

1931: "A gang of youths in a collegiate Ford, its dilapidation camouflaged by many a chalked wisecrack, spied the immobile figure, and brakes howled to a stop. . . ." American Mercury, *February*.

AIR TRAVEL

Airplane travel was as exciting to the 1920s citizen as rocket travel was to his 1960s counterpart. Magazines and newspapers devoted an astonishing amount of space to anything that was remotely new in the way of flying: crashes, innovations, record speeds, acrobatics, record distances; they were all grist for the public's insatiable appetite for aviation news. When Charles Lindbergh flew solo across the Atlantic in 1927, he was met in France by an estimated one hundred thousand people. When he returned home, his ticker tape parade up Broadway was watched by four million awestruck fans. Lindbergh's celebrity status exceeded that of any president or movie star. But the sheer breadth of Lindbergh's fame would later ruin his life as he tried desperately to avoid the ever-probing eyes of the press and an adoring public.

AIRPLANE TRAVEL TIMES AND FARES, 1929:

Route	Miles	Hours	Stops	Fare
Boston-New York	220	1:45	2	$ 25
New York-Washington	201	2:15	1	$ 30
Chicago-San Francisco	1,943	22:30	10	$200
Chicago-Salt Lake City	1,319	14:30	6	$146
San Francisco-Los Angeles	379	5:00	3	$ 45
Miami-Havana	261	2:15	1	$ 55
El Paso-Dallas	575	7:00	5	$ 71
Seattle-Los Angeles	1,099	14:00	7	$125

Graf Zeppelin: many air enthusiasts in the 1920s believed that dirigibles would one day be as popular as airplanes as a means of travel. Their optimism sprung from the success of the Graf Zeppelin, a large, hydrogen-filled dirigible that carried its passengers with the luxury of a pullman car. It made its first commercial transoceanic flight in October of 1928 and its first around-the-world flight in August of 1929. On the world flight (which carried six hundred canaries, a gorilla and a chimpanzee, as well as human passengers), cruising speed averaged sixty miles per hour, with a total travel time, from Lakehurst, New Jersey, to Lakehurst, New Jersey, the long way, of twelve days and eleven minutes. Bankers were impressed enough by the flight to put up money for the construction of four new dirigibles, with which Germany established an airline offering weekly runs between Europe and the U.S. Officials at the Empire State Building were so impressed they immediately drew up plans to erect a mooring mast atop the famed building in anticipation of future landings and takeoffs.

As romantic as lighter-than-air travel was, however, the dirigibles' relatively slow air speed, expensive fares (dirigibles required large crews; the Graf Zeppelin, in addition to the commanding officer, had three watch officers, three navigators, three elevator men, three rudder men, three radio men, three sailmakers, one engineering officer, two keel engineers, fifteen mechanics, two electricians, two cooks and two stewards) and potentially explosive gasbags doomed them to failure and they would all but disappear from the skies after the Hindenburg disaster (See Section Eight: Radio and Radio Shows) in May of 1937.

CHRONOLOGY OF FLIGHT

1919: First daily passenger service begins February 5, in Berlin, Germany. Service is soon offered elsewhere in major cities around the world.

1919: U.S. seaplane crosses Atlantic, May 27.

1919: Florida airline opens passenger service to Havana, November.

1920: Oxygen-breathing device for high altitude tested.

1920: First retractable landing gear.

1923: First nonstop flight across the U.S., May 3.

1924: First successful automatic pilot system developed.

1924: First circumnavigation of world by air.

1925: First movies shown in flight, German airlines.

1927: Lindbergh flies to Paris, May 21. He is the ninety-second person to cross the Atlantic but the first to do it alone. See Chronologies: History, Events, Innovations and Fads.

1928: Amelia Earhart first woman to fly across Atlantic.

1929: Blind flying system developed.

1930: First female flight attendants, May 15, on United Airlines.

1930: First woman, Amy Johnson of England, flies around the world solo.

1930s: In the early part of the decade, United Airlines flies the Boeing twin-engine 247, which carries just ten passengers. TWA flies the twelve-seat DC-1, and the fourteen-seat DC-2, put in service in 1934. Soon after, American Airlines leads the way with the DC-3, carrying twenty-one passengers. Each of these planes can fly across the U.S. in under twenty hours.

1937: First pressurized plane.

1937: Automatic landing system developed.

1939: Fifty-two-passenger DC-4 put in service.

1943 on: Lockheed Constellation carries sixty-five to ninety passengers.

1928: "Coffee, tea, butter, sausages, marmalade formed a glutinous mess and overspread the unlucky ones sitting with their backs to the stern. I in my chair slid the length of the saloon, crashing into the unfortunate artist, Professor Dettmann, who in turn fell over

Robert Hartman's heavy movie camera, which fell full weight on Frederick Gilfillan. Breathless moments passed, leaving not a few blanched faces, and the thought—we were facing death.'' Lady Hay-Drummond-Hay, Hearst reporter and only woman passenger on Graf Zeppelin's first Atlantic crossing, describing a near-disaster as the dirigible's bow was tipped violently up by a strong headwind just south of the Azores. Passengers paid $3,000 each on that first transatlantic run. By the 1930s, the crossing would cost under $1,000.

1929: "Except for brief electrical storms, navigation was simple for Capt. Lehmann on the Graf's final leg to Friedrichshafen . . . [but passengers'] nerves were jumpy because one Frederick S. Hogg, retired Mount Vernon businessman, had smoked a cigar in the ship's lavatory. One spark might have blown her up. Some of the other passengers wanted passenger Hogg imprisoned. Capt. Lehmann only reprimanded him, took his cigars and pocket lighter ignominiously away." Time, *September 16.*

1929: "The directors of Empire State, Inc., believe that in a comparatively short time the Zeppelin airships will establish transatlantic, transcontinental, and transpacific lines, and possibly a route to South America from the port of New York. Building with any eye to the future, it has determined to erect this mooring tower." *Official announcement, December 11.*

Clothing and Fashions

f there was anything that shocked 1920s America as much as gang shootings and poisoned hooch, it was the startling trend in women's clothing to show more skin. Hemlines were going up, up, up. Necklines were coming down, down, down. To conservatives, the trend was nothing less than a sign of the devil. Some Philadelphia clergymen were so upset that they organized themselves into pseudo arbiters of fashion and put forth an "acceptable" dress they called the "moral gown" for "nice" women to wear. Predictably, women stayed away from it in droves. But the moral hysteria was hard to ignore.

- In 1920, a London surgeon wrote in *The Daily Mail* that insufficient clothing about the necks and throats of women was causing an increase in goiter. Calling the new fashion of low necklines "evil," he claimed to have counted no less than sixty-seven women who had "necks so puffy they were noticeable." The puffiness, he said, was "due to enlargement of the thyroid gland."
- In 1921, a noted criminologist attributed the "Crime wave" of the time to the "scandalous dress of our women." According to *Outlook Magazine*, nobody laughed at the assertion.
- Another credible "scientist" claimed that the fashion trend of wearing bras to flatten the chest was "causing rickets in newborns."
- In 1925, thirty-two women were denied admittance to an

audience with Pope Pius XI because they were improperly clothed. (The Catholic church was in an uproar over women's fashions; the Archbishop of the Ohio diocese actually issued a warning against "bare female shoulders;" Pope Benedict also made a pronouncement against "the present immodesty and extravagance in women's dress.")

"Dress reform is sorey needed . . ." one conservative wrote of the early 1920s. "Modesty has given way to daring, beauty to undisguised attempts to exhibit charms, and form has been supplanted by shape." It was, indeed, a common theme.

But what was to blame for these scandalous fashions? Disillusionment with the war? Women's newly won right to vote? The naughty love scenes at the movie houses? Prohibition? Flappers? The list of possible culprits was long.

It didn't matter. Women were simply sick of male-dictated fashions and were saying so.

The new fashions were rejected by conservative men because, admittedly, they "appealed to the male's baser instincts" and corrupted him. The women of the day countered that *that* was the man's problem, not the woman's. The new clothes were more comfortable and eminently more practical.

Much to the horror of the older generation, hemlines rose as high as knee level by the end of the decade. Fortunately for these squeamish people, hemlines dropped again in the 1930s and stayed below knee level through much of the 1940s. War conservation saw a slight shortening of women's dresses to knee level, an event that again brought out the Catholic church. In May of 1941, Pope Pius XII cautioned 4,000 Catholic Action girls against experimenting with "daring styles." "Certain dresses are more comfortable and hygienic," he said, "but if they prove dangerous for the soul they must be unfailingly rejected."

babushka: a kerchief worn over the hair and tied under the chin, first seen in the U.S. in 1938.

balmaccan: a casual, loose coat with raglan sleeves, popular on college campuses from the 1930s on.

beads: long strings of beads were worn widely by women throughout the 1920s.

Bermuda shorts: very popular among men for warm weather from the early 1940s.

blitzies: a woman's undergarment combining blouse and panties, worn from 1942 on. The shirttail of the blouse came between the legs and fastened to the front.

blucher: a man's half boot, originating in the 1930s.

bobbed hair: the short haircut of the flapper, the "in" style of the 1920s, and widely condemned as indecent by members of the clergy and other conservatives. The bob became nearly universal among young women in the 1920s, but many older women eventually adopted the style as well. The Marcel permanent wave—actually an arrangement of several soft waves—was a popular bobbed fashion, as was the straight Dutch bob with bangs and the "boyish" bob cut over the ears. Those who resisted the bob wore their long hair pulled back in a knot.
1922: "So far as I can see, conditions are no better than a year ago. Skirts are even shorter, waists as low as ever, more bobbed hair than ever, girls more shameless in their flirtations. . . ."
Literary Digest, *June 17.*
1922: "The revolution in morals and manners is still for the degradation of young people rather than for their betterment. I can see no place in society for bobbed hair, dresses that do not cover the knee-cap, and like contraptions."
G.W. Ingersoll, superintendent of schools, Constantine, MI, June.
1922: "The shameless dancing and the brief dressing of young girls have struck our Western country very hard. Bobbed hair and bobbed skirts are becoming almost unendurable in our small Western towns." *T.W. Conway, superintendent of schools, Tularosa, NM.*
1922: "Unfortunately, the bobbing of hair doesn't always have the same effect. When Samson was shorn, they made him go to work."
Hartford Times.

1926: "We don't believe mother is a Christian woman. She bobs her hair; and the Bible says in the eleventh chapter of first Corinthians that a woman should not cut her hair. She wears jewelry and bright colored clothes. A Christian woman shouldn't do those things."
Edith Benedict, aged ten, who testified against her mother in court proceedings concerning guardianship, quoted in Golden Book Magazine, *July.*

bobby sox: ankle-length sox, usually white, worn by teen girls from the mid-1940s on. A very popular fashion.

bras: these were made to flatten the breasts, not accentuate them, in the 1920s. This was only one of the ways women attained the fashionable "boyish" look. Bras designed to uplift and accentuate appeared in the 1930s.

conservation of fabric: the government ordered fabric to be conserved during wartime. As a result, men's and women's clothing lost cuffs, superfluous pockets and pocket flaps, and other frills, from spring 1942 on. Even men's boxer shorts suffered, when waistbands and buttons were replaced with side ties, from 1942 to 1945.

chemise: a straight, narrow, slip-like dress, the most popular dress of the 1920s. The chemise helped give the young, fashionable lady the popular "boyish" look, with a low or slight waistline.

Chesterfield: a man's formal overcoat, usually black or gray, with a velvet collar, popular in the 1920s, 1930s and 1940s.

cigarets: The World War I soldier who first took up cigarets was initially regarded as "effeminate" by his fellow pipe and cigar smokers. However, cigaret-smoking quickly caught on after the war, and both men and women took up the fashion. Women, of course, were looked-down upon for smoking initially, but by 1920 lady smokers were a common sight on the streets of any big city. One tobacconist in New York in 1920 claimed that half his customers were female.
1922: "The girls of the younger set are worse than the boys. They smoke and drink, that is, a great number of them, as tho it were nothing. . . ." Literary Digest, *June 17.*

1922: "There is no doubt but that the growth of the cigaret, especially among the young women of our country, is demoralizing."
M. Pusey, Editor of Gold and Blue, *Latter Day Saints University.*

1922: "The co-eds are taking up cigaret-smoking in increasing numbers." *C. Brooks, Dean, University of Alabama, June.*

1922: "As regards cigaret smoking, I know that 70-80 percent of the girls I am acquainted with indulge—girls of good families whose mothers may not feel inclined to accept this high percentage, but they are not with their daughters at dances, parties, etc., where smoking by the girls is most common."
Editor of the Punch Bowl, *University of Pennsylvania.*

cigaret case: very fashionable and carried by both men and women in the 1920s and 1930s.

cigaret holder: as long as twelve inches were stylish and considered debonair throughout the 1920s.

cloche: a closefitting, bell-shaped hat worn pulled over the forehead, the perfect hat for bobbed hair, widely worn by women in the 1920s and 1930s.

dinner jacket: a man's white formal jacket, popular in the 1930s and 1940s.

dirndl: a skirt with gathered waistline, first worn in the U.S. in 1937.

dress: the chemise was the most popular style of dress in the 1920s. Clingy, close-fitting dresses with flounces and drapery to create uneven hemlines were worn in the 1930s. One of the most popular dresses of the 1930s was the shirtwaist dress, with straight or flaring skirts. The barebacked evening dress—especially that which touched or swept the floor—came into vogue in the 1930s as well. See dirndl, hemlines, swing skirt.

fatigues: the World War II soldier's "nonfighting" work clothes, comprised of blue denim shirts and dungarees.

flapper fashions: the flapper, any young (under twenty), bold woman who wore bobbed hair, heavy makeup, short skirts, unfastened (flapping) galoshes, and stockings rolled below the knees and typically smoked and drank, was widely influential among young women and almost uniformly hated by the clergy and other conservatives during the early 1920s. She was largely responsible for the rising hemlines and dropping decolletes of the period which ultimately moved Pope Benedict to make a pronouncement against "the present immodesty and extravagance in women's dress," and clergymen from fifteen denominations in Philadelphia to design an acceptable dress, called the "moral gown" for "decent" women to wear. See moral gown.

1922: "If one judges by appearances, I suppose I am a flapper. I am within the age limit. I wear bobbed hair, the badge of flapperhood. (And, oh, what a comfort it is!) I powder my nose. I wear fringed skirts and bright-colored sweaters, and scarfs, and waists with Peter Pan collars, and low-heeled 'finale hopper' shoes. I adore to dance. . . . I attend hops and proms, and crew races and other affairs at men's colleges. But none the less some of the most thoroughbred superflappers might blush to claim sistership or even remote relationship with such as I. I don't use rouge, or lipstick, or pluck my eyebrows. I don't smoke, or drink, or tell 'peppy stories.' I don't pet . . . and I haven't a line! But then—there are many degrees of flapper. There is the semi-flapper; the flapper; the superflapper. . . . I might possibly be placed somewhere in the middle of the first class." *Ellen Page,* Outlook, *October.*

1925: "This Jane, being nineteen, is a flapper. . . . She is heavily made up . . . poisonously scarlet lips, richly ringed eyes. . . . [Her skirt] comes just an inch below the knees, overlapping by a faint fraction her rolled and twisted stockings. . . . She wears the newest thing in bobs, even closer than last year's shingle. It leaves her just about no hair in back. . . . The corset is dead . . . the petticoat defunct . . . the brassiere has been abandoned since 1924. . . . [This is] The Style, Summer of 1925. . . . These things and none other are being worn by all of Jane's sisters and her cousins and her aunts. They are being worn by ladies who are three times Jane's age. . . ." New Republic, *September 9.*

hair, men's: from the 1920s, short hair parted on the side, in the middle, or brushed back in a pompadour. The "slick" look was in vogue, so various hair oils, Vaseline and brilliantine were liberally used. Most men were clean-shaven; a few had very neatly trimmed mustaches. Hairstyles remained much the same throughout the 1930s, and beards were virtually nonexistent. The 1940s saw the same styles of short hair, with one notable new style, the Army "butch" or crew cut.

1936: "He was a tall young man with considerable brilliantine, and he smiled a great deal." Reader's Digest, May 1936.

hair, women's: See also bobbed hair. The most popular hairstyle by far in the 1920s was the short bob. Hair was worn slightly longer in the 1930s, but bobs still prevailed. A longer pageboy bob became popular among young women toward the end of the 1930s. The shoulder-length bob, softly waved or curled and parted, was the most popular style in the early 1940s. Bangs were widely worn throughout the war period. Tweezing and pencilling eyebrows became popular during this time.

hats, men's: from the 1920s on, the homburg, the fedora and the derby were widely worn, the fedora being the least formal and worn most often for general use. In 1945, *Good Housekeeping Magazine* estimated that 80 percent of all men wore snap-brim, felt fedoras. The fedora typically had a crease down the middle of the crown and a brim that was rolled up slightly in back. The homburg was worn for more formal occasions and was favored by lawyers, bankers and stockbrokers. A straw, banded sailor hat, known as the "hay-skimmer" or British boater, was popular in the 1920s and 1930s but was replaced by the Panama and coconut straw hat in the 1940s. Straw hats frequently replaced the felt fedora for summertime wear. Pork pie hats were big with college men, zoot-suiters and jitterbugs. Top hats were essential for formal occasions in the 1920s, 1930s and 1940s. Berets were donned for golfing. A billed tweed cap was also worn for sporting activities. The soft, folding military cap, the garrison cap, was also widely seen among soldiers throughout the war.

1932: "A correspondent takes me to task for describing the hat, which is known in America as a 'derby' and in France as a melon, as a 'bowler.' " Literary Digest, August 6.

1937: "While the season for Panama hats officially opens May 15 north of the Mason-Dixon line, retail sales don't reach their peak until July 1. This week leading hat stores reported a rush of . . . business, with volume running 25 percent above last year's. . . . The finest hats—those selling in this country at $50 to $500 apiece—are made in the village of Monte Cristi, on Ecuador's mountainous Pacific Coast. J.P. Morgan, Herbert Hoover, and the Duke of Windsor are among those owning $500 Panamas." Newsweek, *July.*

hats, women's: women liked wide-brim hats, toques, turbans, tams, berets and pillboxes, sometimes dressed with plumes, bows or flowers, throughout the 1920s and 1930s. The definitive woman's hat of the period, however, was the cloque. See cloche. The Empress Eugenie hat was popular beginning in 1931. This was a small, derby-like, black velvet hat with rolled brim, and trimmed with a black ostrich plume. It was commonly pulled down over the eyes. Hats were often worn this way or at a rakish angle off to the side. Nearly any object passed for a woman's hat in the 1930s, as attested by numerous jokes heard throughout the decade. See below.

1931: "Best's watched the Eugenie revival sweep Paris . . . and here they are. . . . Heads up! Hair back! Brims dipping into the right eye! Wear your new [Eugenie] hat with a 'manner', either madcap or marquise!" *Best Department store ad, New York.*

1935: "Waste baskets, salad bowls, pie plates, socks, shaving mugs–anything goes as a hat if a woman puts it on her head." Harper's Monthly, *March.*

1935: " . . . she thought the late-revered Eugenie hats attractive because they were merry. But most men thought Eugenie hats unbecoming because they seemed out of place against modern backgrounds." Harper's Monthly, *March 1935.*

hemlines: Women's hemlines typically hovered at nine to twelve inches off the ground in 1920, thirteen inches and higher in 1925, fifteen inches to knee height from 1927 to 1929. Members of the clergy and other conservatives were shocked by the ever-growing amount of leg visible in the 1920s, especially when hemlines reached knee height. Clothing manufacturers were also upset because less material was being used. But at the beginning of the 1930s, hemlines dropped back to a relatively safe ten to twelve inches. However, they gradually rose again to fifteen to seventeen inches by 1939. They stayed just below the knee through World War II.

hip flask: a whiskey flask carried in a voluminous hip pocket during Prohibition. It was widely seen as a trendy thing to do in the 1920s, but the practice disappeared with the repeal of Prohibition in 1933.

jeans: among the young of both sexes, they were as popular in the 1940s as they are today. Throughout the 1940s, jeans and sloppy Joe sweaters were the favorite combination of teen and college girls. From 1944 through much of the 1950s, jeans worn by kids and teens were typically folded up at the cuffs, sometimes as high as the knees.

1944: "After school the girl promptly changes into an old shirt and blue jeans, rolled to the knees."

Ladies Home Journal, *December, chronicling the life of a typical teenage girl.*

1946: "On the first warm, sunny day, at girls' colleges, they emerge from their winter wrappings, shedding layers of size forty sweaters, baggy slacks, enormous fleece-lined boots, and dad's raccoon coat (Yale '12), for the campus spring outfit of frayed and faded blue jeans rolled to the knee, men's shirts with flapping tails, and moccasins, run down at the heel. . . ." New York Times Magazine, *April 7.*

jewelry: very long, multiple strings of beads, pearl necklaces, large earrings and multiple bracelets were commonly worn by the fashionable woman of the 1920s.

Juliet: a woman's hairstyle in which the crown is kept smooth and the hair curled into a soft fluff below the ears, popular for two or three years following Norma Shearer's appearance in the movie, *Juliet,* in 1936.

knickerbockers: more casually known as knickers, short, knee length or slightly longer pants, worn by men on the golf course and by boys under age fourteen for everyday wear in the 1920s and early 1930s. Long stockings were worn with them. Knickers were largely abandoned by both boys and golfers in the 1930s.

Lindbergh jacket: a sport jacket of wool or leather with fitted wrist and waistbands, fashioned after the jacket of aviator Charles Lindbergh, 1920s.

makeup: much to the horror of the more conservative older generation, rouge, lipstick and heavy mascara became all the rage among young women from 1920 on. Lipstick was typically deep red and was often put on "bee sting" style, the lips made full and pouty in the middle and left bare at the ends.

military look: during and just after World War II, college girls made themselves fashionable by donning pea jackets, military pins, insignia and wings, pilot's helmets, and even complete uniforms.

1946: "In the last years college girls have added numerous military garments and appurtenances to their costume. This was one of the war's curious little reverberations. . . . When girls could filch them from the returning males, they took over their uniforms in toto. A general, visiting his daughter at one of the colleges, was unpleasantly startled when captains in pigtails and sailors in page-boy hairdos strolled negligently around campus. Soon notices were posted in the college dormitories reminding students of the penalty for impersonating service men." New York Times Magazine, *April 7.*

moral gown: A "morally acceptable" ankle-length dress with high neckline, designed by Philadelphia clergymen representing fifteen denominations in response to the shocking trend of rising hemlines and dropping decolletage of 1921. In more than a dozen states in 1921 bills were put before legislatures to standardize the length of women's skirts and the height of decolletage.

1921: "In Utah a statute providing fine and imprisonment for those who wear on the streets skirts higher than three inches above the ankle is pending. The Philadelphia 'moral gown,' with its seven and a half inches of 'see level,' as one visitor called it, would cease to be moral in Utah if this law goes through. . . . A bill is before the Virginia legislature which would raise the decolletage—front and back. It provides that no woman shall be permitted to wear a shirtwaist or evening gown displaying more than three inches of her throat. She must not have skirts higher than four inches above the ground or any garment of diaphanous material. . . . In Ohio a bill has been drafted prescribing that no decollete shall be more than two inches in depth and that no garment composed of any transparent material shall be sold, nor any 'garment which unduly displays and accentuates the lines of the female figure.' " New York American.

1921: "At noon the girl workers hurry along the stone-walled canyons, gay as a crocus bed in spring sunshine. . . . Not one in ten is wearing the modest and durable frock recently recommended by . . . clergy-men. . . .'' New Republic, *November 23.*

Norfolk jacket: popular man's, belted jacket, most often in tweed and plaid, through the 1930s and 1940s.

nylons: hugely popular in 1939, nylon was commandeered for use in the military and virtually disappeared from the civilian world during the war. Consequently nylon hose became one of the most popularly traded items on the black market, at home and abroad, until 1945. Until nylon became easily obtainable again, many women simply employed leg makeup to make their legs look pretty. Some even went so far as to draw seam lines on the back of their legs.

pajamas and sleepwear: women's lounging pajamas came into vogue not only for bed but for the beach and for evening wear in the 1930s. The legs of pajamas were so broad they were often mistaken for skirts. The evening pajamas were often barebacked and typically worn with a bolero. Two-piece pajama sets made of flannel or other material were commonly worn by men for sleepwear from the 1920s on. Floor-length nightgowns were popular among women throughout the period.
1931: "You can go to a not-too-white-tie dinner in this pink and green printed crepe pyjama. It is more formal if you take off the bolero." Vogue, *June.*

pants, men's: notably baggy and high-waisted throughout the period. From 1924-1926, the cuffs of the legs were sometimes as wide as twenty-four inches. Extra baggy pants were called "Oxford bags" and were a favorite of college students.

parka: a winter coat, originating in the 1930s.

platinum blonde: wildly popular hair color after Jean Harlow appeared with it in the movie *Hell's Angels* in 1930.

plus fours: knickers that, when unbuckled, hung four inches below the knee, popular for golf in the 1920s.

polo coat: a man's large, tan overcoat of camel's hair, worn for casual affairs and motoring in the 1920s.

raccoon coat: a long, heavy, shaggy coat made of raccoon pelts, a favorite among both male and female college students and widely seen at football games when the weather turned cold throughout the 1920s.

sack suit, man's: from the 1920s, baggy with wide, padded shoulders. Gangsters and other colorful characters frequently wore broad pinstripes and loud checks.

shoes, men's: from the 1920s on Oxfords in black or brown. Saddle shoes in black and white or brown and white were popular as sportswear. Loafers became popular at the beginning of the 1940s.

shoes, women's: various high-heels and pumps were worn, but these were slightly heavier and clunkier-looking than modern versions. Slingbacks, wedge sandals and platform soles all first appeared in the 1930s.

shoulder pads: wide, square shoulders were omnipresent on both men's and women's fashions throughout the war. It was easily the definitive look of the period.

slacks: exploded in popularity among women from the beginning of 1942 on. In Chicago, Marshall Field's, The Fair, and Goldblatt Bros. reported trouser sales skyrocketing, as much as five and ten times higher than in 1941. Nationwide, sales increased a whopping 500 percent. Brooklyn high school girls actually struck for the right to wear pants to school. A fad of college women wearing masculine fashions may have started the pants craze in 1940. Later, women working in war plants helped to expand the trend. Previously, women had worn pants only when camping.

1940: " . . . the amateur interpreters are having a field day trying to decide what deep meaning lies within the fact that so many college girls have outfitted themselves with strictly masculine fashions . . . shirts, jackets, sweaters and even slacks."
New York Times Magazine, *November 3.*

1942: "U.S. women by the millions have renounced skirts in favor of slacks. . . . Not since Mrs. Amelia Bloomer created an international uproar in 1849 by appearing in voluminous Turkish trousers has such a feminine trouser sensation swept the country." Time, *April 13.*

1942: "As men are being warned that two-pants suits, vests and trouser cuffs will soon be only a memory, women are breaking out in a rash of pants. . . ." *Life, April 20.*

slacks chemise: a one-piece undergarment functioning as bra and pantie, worn by women under slacks from 1942 on.

sloppy Joe: a long, baggy pullover sweater worn by schoolgirls, originating in 1940.

sneakers: especially popular among children from the late 1930s on.

soup-and-fish: slang term for a tuxedo. Used from 1920s on.
1922: "Getting into the soup-and-fish. . . ." *Sinclair Lewis,* Babbitt.

sportswear, men's: from the 1920s, voluminous knickers ending below the knee were essential for golfing or other sport. Berets, sleeveless pullovers or other sweaters, knee-high argyle socks and saddle shoes were de rigeur as well.

sportswear, women: shirtwaist dress or loose skirt and blouse, a pullover or other type sweater and long socks made for popular golf wear in the 1920s.

stockings, woman's: silk and rayon hose in beige, taupe and gray grew in popularity throughout the 1920s.

swimsuit, men's: European men often went topless in the 1920s, but American men were more conservative and at least wore a tank top with their trunks. Tops began to disappear in the 1930s, but as late as 1935, forty-two men on an Atlantic City beach were arrested for wearing bathing trunks with no tops. A city representative was quoted as saying, "We'll have no gorillas on our beaches."

swimsuit, women's: the long knit suits of the early 1920s were worn with stockings or tights to avoid showing any skin on the legs. Showing a bit of bare leg on the beach could bring an arrest. Backless, one-piece suits came into vogue in 1932. The skin-tight, backless maillot was a sensation in 1933. The first halter and pants suit appeared in 1934. Two-piece suits with bra or halter tops in bold prints came into vogue in the 1930s and 1940s.

swing skirt: a round-cut or flaring skirt worn by young women when dancing to swing music or "jitterbugging" in the 1940s. The swing skirt was most often worn with a sloppy Joe sweater and bobby socks.

trench coat: popular among men for wet weather in the 1930s and 1940s.

undershirt: Men stopped wearing undershirts almost overnight after Clark Gable appeared without one in the movie, *It Happened One Night*, in 1934.

1939: ". . . the fashion of going without undershirts began when Clark Gable undressed in the tourist camp in *It Happened One Night*. The sale of masculine underwear declined so sharply immediately afterwards that knitwear manufacturers and garment workers unions were reported to have sent delegations to the producers asking them to take out the scene." Current History, *November.*

zoot suit: sometimes referred to as the "drape shape," a man's suit characterized by tapering, tight-cuffed pants ("pegs") sometimes rising as high as the armpits and ballooning as much as thirty-two inches at the knees, and a long coat with wide, padded shoulders and wide lapels. Originated in 1937 in New York and popularly worn among the fashionable set through the 1940s. The suit was typically either black with vertical white stripes or wildly colorful with jacket and pants of oddly contrasting patterns. To round out the fashion, a knee-length key chain was worn and a handkerchief was allowed to protrude from the jacket pocket. A wide-brimmed hat and oversized bow tie were frequently a part of the attire as well. The zoot suit was not universally accepted among the general population because a certain brash or nervy personality was required to wear one without looking silly. However, "quieter" versions were made, and thousands of young men took their pants in tightly at the cuff to give themselves at least a touch of dangerous zoot chic. Zoot is thought to be a corruption of "suit." A Hollywood song, "A Zoot Suit," sang the suit's praises in 1941.

1942: ". . . for exotic detail the West coasters have made the Harlem boys look like a bunch of undertakers. Hollywood superzooters sport porkpie hats with monstrous brims, spaniel-eared suspenders, string ties, pearl buttons as big as silver dollars, and trouser cuffs so tight they have to be zippered.'' Newsweek, *September 7.*

1943: ''Last week practically everybody . . . was ferreting out the origins of the zoot suit. . . . Lew Eisenstein, proprietor of Lew's Pants Store, on 125th St., back in 1934, had a lot of about five hundred pairs of pants that he couldn't seem to move. While Lew was away on a business trip, his wife and one of the salesmen decided to see what would happen if they took in the bottoms of several pairs . . . the pants were no sooner in the window than they were snapped up by style-conscious colored boys. . . . By the time [Lew] got home, the style was sweeping along as irresistably as a tidal wave. . . . Overnight 'pegs' replaced the high-rise trousers, which had bell bottoms and in extreme cases rose as high as the wearer's armpits . . . another white haberdasher on Lenox Avenue claims credit for the first drape-shape coat and for the pork pie hat which most of the zoot suit boys affect.'' New Yorker.

COLLEGE FAVORITES

When asked by *Vogue* what they most liked to see women dressed in, college men answered, ''sports clothes,'' particularly sweaters and skirts; tweeds ''with a dash''; ankle socks and sports shoes.

MILITARY UNIFORMS OF WORLD WAR II

Army uniforms were olive drab; for the air force and marines, forest green; for the navy, navy blue and white. Fatigues, blue denim shirts and dungarees, were worn by all branches of the service for non-combat work. Rank was shown, among other ways, by shoulder insignia in the army, marines and air force, by sleeve cuff stripes in the navy.

Army, Air Force and Marines

Rank	Insignia
General of Army, Air Force	Four or five silver stars
Lieutenant General	Three silver stars
Major General	Two silver stars

WHAT THE GROOM WORE IN 1938

(Excerpted from *Esquire*, June 1938:)

"The groom wears a one-button oxford grey morning coat with grey striped trousers, plain black calf shoes, double breasted waistcoat, white pleated shirt with wing collar, blue-grey ascot, pearl stickpin, white pocket handkerchief and lilies of the valley boutonniere.

"An usher wears a one-button morning coat, striped trousers, double breasted white linen waistcoat, soft white shirt, white starched turn-over collar, grey Spitalfields tie (four-in-hand), white linen spats, plain black calf shoes, white handkerchief, white carnation boutonniere.

"A page boy wears a black Eton jacket, single breasted waistcoat, striped trousers, plain black shoes, white shirt, white Eton collar, narrow black tie, silk hat.

"The best man wears a morning coat, checked trousers, black shoes with button tops, fawn waistcoat, blue shirt and white cuffs and collar.

"A guest wears an oxford grey jacket (double-breasted) . . . trousers, pink broadcloth shirt, white starched turn-over collar, black satin tie, pearl stickpin, pink carnation, white pocket handkerchief, plain black shoes, black Homburg, white mocha gloves."

Brigadier General	One silver star
Colonel	Silver eagle
Lieutenant Colonel	Silver oak leaf
Major	Gold oak leaf
Captain	Two silver bars
First Lieutenant	One silver bar
Second Lieutenant	One gold bar
Chief Warrant Officer (W-4)	Silver bar with 3 enamel bands
Chief Warrant Officer (W-3)	Silver bar with 2 enamel bands
Chief Warrant Officer (W-2)	Gold bar with 3 enamel bands
Chief Warrant Officer (W-1)	Gold bar with 2 enamel bands

Navy

(Stripes were gold; the first number represents the number of two-inch-wide stripes; the second number, the half-inch stripes; the third number, the, quarter-inch stripes.)

Rank	Stripes
Fleet Admiral	1-4-0
Admiral	1-3-0
Vice Admiral	1-2-0
Rear Admiral	1-1-0
Commodore	1-0-0
Captain	0-4-0
Commander	0-3-0
Lieutenant Commander	0-2-1
Lieutenant	0-2-0
Lieutenant (junior grade)	0-1-1
Ensign	0-1-0
Chief Warrant Officer (W-4)	0-1-0 (1 break)
Chief Warrant Officer (W-3)	0-1-0 (2 breaks)
Chief Warrant Officer (W-2)	0-1-0 (3 breaks)
Chief Warrant Officer (W-1)	0-0-1 (3 breaks)

RADIO AND RADIO SHOWS

I n one of the most heralded memos of all time, David Sarnoff, future Chairman of the Board of RCA, wrote in 1916 to the general manager of the Marconi Co., his vision of a new home appliance:

I have in mind a plan of development which would make radio a "household utility" in the same sense as the piano or phonograph. The idea is to bring music into the house by wireless.

While this has been tried in the past by wires, it has been a failure because wires do not lend themselves to this scheme. . . .

The receiver can be designed in the form of a simple "Radio Music Box" and arranged for several different wave lengths, which should be changeable with the throwing of a single switch or pressing of a single button. . . .

The Radio Music Box can be supplied with amplifying tubes and a loudspeaking telephone, all of which can be neatly mounted in one box. The box can be placed on a table in the parlor or living room. . . .

Baseball scores can be transmitted in the air by the use of one set being installed at the Polo Grounds. . . .

This proposition would be especially interesting to farmers and others living in outlying districts removed from the cities. By the purchase of a Radio Music Box they could enjoy concerts, lectures, music, recitals, etc, which may be going on in the nearest city within their radius. . . .

The manufacture of the Radio Music Box . . . in large quan-
tities would make possible their sale at a moderate figure of
perhaps seventy-five dollars per outfit. . . .

The first such "Radio Music Boxes" for home use came off the
assembly line in 1922, at a cost of between fifty and one hundred dollars. Eleven million dollars worth of sets sold that first year. Sales doubled the next year and doubled again the year after that. All across the
country, stores sold out of these wonderful appliances almost as quickly
as they got them in. (The sets were a great improvement over the
home-made crystal sets built by radio enthusiasts out of Quaker Oats
boxes, wire and copper the year before.) Soon the most common news
story of the day was that of a new radio owner falling off his roof as he
installed his first antenna.

The radio broadcasting era itself began in earnest at 6:00 P.M. on
November 2, 1920, with the broadcast of the Harding-Cox election
returns from station KDKA in Pittsburgh. This famous first was quickly
followed by others, including the first play-by-play sporting event (Ray
vs. Dundee boxing match) on April 11, 1921, and the first live musical
program on November 27, 1921. By the end of 1921, more than thirty
new stations were vying for their own famous "firsts."

With radio's exploding popularity came numerous myths. Some
believed that radio waves could start a fire in the home during thunder-
storms. Others thought the waves were making them sick, and many
diseases were blamed on them. Some religious folks saw radio as "the
work of the devil."

Mostly, radio was adored and as programming improved, it grew
into a kind of family centerpiece, with Ma and Pa and the kids gathered
around the console after supper for staticky news, music and entertainment. TV, basically, without the picture.

NBC was formed in 1926 and branched off into "Red" and "Blue"
networks. CBS formed a year later. Mutual got its start in 1934. Eventually NBC sold its blue network in 1943, and soon after ABC was born.

Mayor Fiorella Laguardia reading the Sunday comics during a newspaper delivery strike. The Orson Welles science fiction broadcast that
terrified a nation. The eyewitness account of the Hindenburg disaster.

The Scopes Monkey Trial. The bulletin of the bombing of Pearl Harbor. Radio enjoys a rich history. Richest of all perhaps, was its Golden Age of programming, with its selection of fifteen-minute, half-hour and one-hour programs as diverse as that of TV today. Below is a small fraction of that programming from the early 1920s through the 1940s.

Air times are Eastern Standard Time unless otherwise noted. Because air times and days often varied for some shows, a complete schedule history is impractical. In general, the most common or long-running time slots are given whenever possible.

Music and news dominated broadcasting in the early days. Music was usually the norm after 10:00 P.M. Soap operas almost invariably ran in the mornings and afternoons, while comedies, mysteries, crime, variety and other programs were aired evenings.

RADIO SHOWS

The Abbott and Costello Program: starring Bud Abbott and Lou Costello. The comedy show that made the "Who's on First?" routine famous. First aired on NBC in 1942. Typical gag:
"You can be mastoid of ceremonies."
"A mastoid is a pain in the ear."
"See what I mean?"

The Adventures of Christopher Wells: starring Les Damon as Christopher and Vicki Vola as Stacy McGill, Wells's assistant. Wells was a newspaper reporter who got into trouble with various criminals. First aired on CBS in 1947.

The Adventures of Nero Wolfe: starring Sydney Greenstreet or Santos Ortega as Wolfe. A mystery show first airing on ABC in 1943.

The Adventures of Ozzie and Harriet: starring Ozzie, Harriet, David and Ricky Nelson. (David and Ricky were also played by other actors.) The show opened with the Billy May Orchestra and a running voice-over: "The solid silver with beauty that lives forever is International Sterling.

179

From Hollywood, International Silver Company, creators of International Sterling, presents *The Adventures of Ozzie and Harriet*, starring America's favorite young couple–Ozzie Nelson and Harriet Hilliard!" A hugely popular show first airing on CBS on October 8, 1944. Typical joke: "I was lit up once. I was so lit up the air-raid warden had to take me home under an umbrella." (Ozzie)

The Aldrich Family: starring various actors as Henry Aldrich, and Agnes Moorehead and Dickie Van Patten in supporting roles. The show opened with Henry's mother, Alice, shouting, "Henry! Henry Aldrich!" and Henry answering, "Coming Mother!" Although airing earlier as a sketch on *The Rudy Vallee Show*, the first full-length program was broadcast on NBC Blue in 1939. It was sponsored by Jell-O. Tuesday nights at 8:30.

Amanda of Honeymoon Hill: starring Joy Hathaway as Charity Amanda Dyke. A serial drama of Southern romance and marriage with a large supporting cast. First aired on the Blue network in 1940.

The American Album of Familiar Music: various singers warbled popular songs of the day in this long-running program featuring Frank Munn, Donald Dame, Evelyn MacGregor and others. The opening featured the orchestra and voice-over: "*The American Album of Familiar Music* . . . presenting America's widely discussed young singing star Donald Dame. . . ." First aired in 1931, sponsored by Bayer Aspirin.

The American School of the Air: an educational program airing weekday afternoons on CBS in 1930. The program dramatized current events and history and included a geography lesson given by the world-touring "Hamilton Family." The show was required listening in many American schools.

Amos 'n' Andy: starring Freeman Gosden in the roles of Amos Jones, Kingfish (George Stevens) and Lightnin', and Charles Correll as Andy. Possibly the most popular radio program of the era, debuting on March 19, 1928, over WMAQ in Chicago and airing initially at 11:00 P.M. and later at 7:00 P.M. The first NBC network broadcast was on August 19, 1929. The entire nation scheduled their agendas around the program's fifteen-minute, five-night-per-week, seven o'clock broadcast. Stores and movie theaters broadcast the show to keep patrons from rushing home at air time. Even President Calvin Coolidge demanded to be undisturbed when the show was on.

Amos and Andy lived in Harlem, ran the "Fresh-Air Taxi Company" and belonged to the "Mystic Knights of the Sea" Lodge. Lines made famous by the show: "Holy mackerel, Andy!" "Ow wah, ow wah, oh wah!" "I'se regusted!" and "Check and double-check." The show was partially based on racial stereotype, following the lives of naive black men, with material that would be considered widely offensive today. The show was sponsored by Pepsodent from 1929-1937 and by Campbell's Soup from 1937-1943. It later ran once per week as a thirty-minute show sponsored by Rinso.

The Andrews Sisters Eight-to-the-Bar Ranch: a weekly musical variety show starring Patti, Maxine and LaVerne Andrews, with Gabby Hayes. First aired by ABC in 1945.

Archie Andrews: a comedy based on the comic strip characters, Archie, Jughead, Betty, Veronica and Reggie, created by Bob Montana. First aired by Mutual in 1943. Typical line: "I got a way of looking into a dame's eyes that makes her completely forget what I look like."

Arthur Godfrey Time: a very popular morning variety show, with live orchestra music, talk and humor, hosted by one of the decade's favorite stars, Arthur Godfrey. Over CBS throughout the 1940s. Nine o'clock mornings.

Aunt Jemima: starring Harriette Widmer as "Aunt Jemima," a five-minute, once-a-week music program for Aunt Jemima Pancake flour, on CBS from 1942-1943. Vocalists included the Old Plantation Sextet and Mary Ann Mercer.

Baby Rose Marie: starring new child star Rose Marie, who sang and acted. First aired on NBC Blue in 1932.

The Baby Snooks Show: starring Fanny Brice as Baby Snooks. A comedy show with a theme song of "Rock-a-Bye Baby." Its running opening and voice-over: "Sanka is the coffee that lets you sleep . . . but now . . . [CRASH from orchestra] Wake up! It's time for . . . [CRASH] Baby Snooks! [Audience applause and theme song] Yes, it's *The Baby Snooks*

Show starring Fanny Brice as Baby Snooks, with Hanley Stafford as Daddy, Carmen Dragon and his orchestra, Bob Graham, vocalist, and yours truly Harlow Wilcox . . . the coffee that is one-hundred per-cent flavor-rich . . . so you'll always enjoy it. And ninety-seven percent caffeine free . . . so it will never interfere with sleep. . . ."

Bachelor's Children: an award-winning, fifteen-minute, five-days-per-week soap opera depicting American family life, starring Hugh Studebaker as Dr. Bob Graham, with a large supporting cast. Aired on CBS at 8:45 A.M. and again at 2:30 for West Coast listeners, and sponsored by Old Dutch Cleanser, from 1935 to 1946.

Backstage Wife: a five-day-per-week network soap opera aired at 4:15 P.M. beginning in 1935. The show revolved around the life of Mary Noble, the wife of matinee idol, Larry Noble, and was supported by a huge cast. Opening announcer: "*Backstage Wife*, the story of Mary Noble and what it means to be the wife of a famous Broadway star—dream sweetheart of a million other women." Various times and stations later.

Beat the Band: a musical quiz show hosted by "The Incomparable Hildegarde." Listeners sent in clues to songs and the members of the band had to guess the titles. When the band was stumped, the participating listener won fifty dollars and two cartons of Raleigh cigarettes. On NBC beginning in 1940.

Believe It Or Not: astonishing facts, hosted by Robert Ripley, with vocalist Harriet (Ozzie and Harriet) Hilliard. On NBC beginning in 1930.

Ben Bernie: a CBS music program hosted by Ben Bernie, with vocalists Little Jackie Heller, Buddy Clark, Mary Small, Jane Pickens and many others. His orchestra was heard on various broadcasts and on his own show at nine o'clock Tuesday nights throughout the 1930s. He closed the show with the same voice-over during the theme song: "And now the time has come to lend an ear to—Au revoir. Pleasant dreams. Think of us . . . when requesting your themes. Until the next time when possibly you may all tune in again. Keep the Old Maestro always in your schemes. Yowsah, yowsah, yowsah. Au Revoir. . . . This is Ben Bernie, ladies and gentlemen, and all the lads wishing you a bit of pleasant dreams. May good luck and happiness, success, good health, attend your schemes. And don't forget, should you ever send in your request-a, Why, we' sho try to do our best-a, Yowsah. Au revoir, a fond cheerio, a bit of a tweet-tweet, God bless you . . . and pleasant dreams.''

Big Bands, Live: the big bands of the era frequently did live remote radio broadcasts from ballrooms and nightclubs throughout the U.S. Sometimes as many as half a dozen big bands could be tuned in on any given Saturday night. The shows were typically hosted by a local announcer, with the orchestra leader introducing the songs and musicians. Popular big bands of the era included the Dorsey Brothers, Glen Miller, Harry James, Charlie Barnet, Gene Krupa, Cab Calloway, Benny Goodman, Xavier Cugat, Duke Ellington, and Guy Lombardo.

The Black Castle: a fifteen-minute mystery thriller with various actors, first airing over Mutual in 1943. Its creepy opening: ''Now up these steps to the iron-studded oaken door which yawns wide on rusted hinges, bidding us enter. [over organ music] Music? Do you hear it? Wait . . . it is well to stop. For here is the Wizard of the Black Castle.'' [animal howls and sinister laughing] *The Wizard*: ''There you are. Back again, I see. Well, welcome. Come in, come in. [animal howls] You'll be overjoyed at the tale I have for you tonight!''

Blondie: comedy based on the comic strip characters, Blondie and Dagwood Bumstead, created by Chic Young. Penny Singleton, Anne Rutheford, Alice White and Patricia Van Cleve all played Blondie at one time or another, with Arthur Lake as Dagwood. The familiar opening: ''Uh-uh-uh . . . don't touch that dial! Listen to . . .'' [voice of Dagwood] ''Blooooooonnnnndie!'' On CBS starting in 1939. Wednesday nights at 7:30.

The Bob Hope Show: comedy show featuring sketches and gags and frequent appearances by Judy Garland and other guest stars. A very popular show on NBC Blue starting in 1934, and sponsored by Pepsodent. Typical joke: ''Have the prices gone up! I went to the market and asked the butcher for a ten-pound turkey. He said, 'OK, how do you want that financed?' ''

Brenda Curtis: a soap opera starring Vicki Vola as Brenda, Hugh Marlowe as Jim, and Agnes Moorehead as the mother-in-law. On CBS starting in 1939.

The Brighter Day: a soap opera starring Margaret Draper as Liz Dennis. The opening: "*The Brighter Day*. Our years are as falling leaves, we live, we love, we dream . . . and then we go. But somehow we keep hoping, don't we, that our dreams come true on that brighter day." On NBC from 1948.

Buck Rogers in the 25th Century: a science fiction adventure program, running from 1931 to 1939, with Matt Crowley and various other actors in the role of Buck. The show featured such futuristic concepts as atomic disintegrators, psychic restriction rays and molecular expansor beams, all invented by "Dr. Huer." Breathless listeners could sign on to become "Solar Scouts" and receive "planetary maps" by sending in a strip from a can of Cocomalt. The opening: [big drum roll followed by echoing announcement] "Buck Rogers in the Twenty-fifth Century!" Six o'clock on various weeknights.

Burns and Allen: a comedy show, usually with a musical number by the orchestra in the middle, starring George Burns and Gracie Allen. Gracie, in her naive, child-like voice, had most of the funny lines, while George played the straight man. A running character on the show was Mel Blanc as a weepy, meek postman who was henpecked by his wife but told everyone to "keep smiling." Advertisements for the sponsor's "Swan" soap were cleverly interwoven into the program by the announcer. On CBS on Monday nights from 1941 to 1945. Typical dialogue:

"Gracie, what's this check stub, one pullover, twenty-five dollars? I don't want to sound like a cheapskate, but isn't that a lot of money for a pullover?"

"The man on the motorcycle said it was the regular price."

"You got it from a man on a motorcycle?"

"Yes, I went through a red light and he drove up and said, 'Pull over!' "

The Buster Brown Gang: hosted by singer, Ed McConnell, a children's program featuring songs, comedy sketches and storytelling, performed before a live studio audience of children. On NBC from 11:30 A.M. to noon Saturdays in 1943. Sponsored by Buster Brown Shoes.

Captain Midnight: an adventure serial with Ed Prentiss, Bill Bouchey or Paul Barnes as Captain Midnight. Opening: [sound of clock gonging midnight and diving airplane] *Announcer*: "Caaptaainn Midniightt!" First aired over Mutual in 1940. Various weeknights at 5:45.

Captain Tim Healy's Stamp Club: a children's fifteen-minute stamp collecting news show sponsored by Ivory Soap. Beginning on NBC in 1938, it aired regularly at 5:15 P.M. on Tuesday, Thursday and Saturday.

Charlie Chan: a mystery series with the well-known Chinese detective created by E.D. Biggers, originating on the Blue network in 1932.

The Chase and Sanborn Hour: beginning as a music program in 1928 and eventually evolving into a comedy-variety show. It was hosted first by Maurice Chevalier, followed by Eddie Cantor, then Edgar Bergen and occasionally was also known by the name of its host. With Eddie Cantor, it was the highest rated show of 1933 and 1934. Sunday nights at eight o'clock.

Cheerio: a talk show featuring a host known only as "Cheerio." The program aired six days a week at 8:30 A.M. on NBC, from 1927 through the early 1930s.

The Chicago Theatre of the Air: a hugely popular variety program featuring musical comedy performed in front of a live audience in Chicago on Saturday nights and airing over Mutual beginning in 1940.

The Cisco Kid: a Western adventure series starring Jackson Beck as The Cisco Kid and Louis Sorin and sometimes Mel Blanc as Pancho. The opening: *Cisco Kid*: "Of all the senoritas I have known, you are the most beautiful." *Woman*: "Oh, Cisco!" [followed by theme song] Airing over Mutual beginning in 1943.

Clara, Lu and Em: a soap opera featuring three women, Clara, Lu, and Em, who liked to gossip. First airing over the Blue network in 1931.

Clicquot Club Eskimos: a musical program featuring a banjo-playing orchestra leader, first airing over NBC in 1926.

The Colgate Sports Newsreel Starring Bill Stern: a very popular program, from 1939 to 1951, featuring sports news and profiles of famous athletes by Bill Stern, who was widely known for his coverage of a wide variety of sporting events. Its opening: "Bill Stern the Colgate shave-cream man is on the air, Bill Stern the Colgate shave-cream man with stories rare. Take his advice and you'll look nice, Your face will feel as cool as ice, With Colgate Rapid shaving cream . . . Good evening, ladies and gentlemen. This is Bill Stern bringing you the 187th edition of the Colgate shave cream Sports Newsreel. . . ."

The Collier Hour: a variety program sponsored by *Collier's Magazine.* One of its feature segments was a serialization of *Fu Manchu.* First airing over the Blue network in 1927.

The Cuckoo Hour: one of the earliest radio comedy programs, originating on January 1, 1930, and running until 1938. Opening announcement: "Good evening, friends—and what of it? The next fifteen minutes are to be devoted to a broadcast of *The Cuckoo Hour,* radio's oldest network comedy program, and if you don't think that's something—well, maybe you're right. The Cuckoos feature Raymond Knight, the radio humorist, as station KUKU's Master of Ceremonies, and Ambrose J. Weems, and a lot of other disreputable characters. We now turn you over to station KUKU." *Voice of Knight*: "Good evening, fellow pixies, this is Raymond Knight, the Voice of the Diaphragm enunciating. . . . " Airing on Wednesday nights at 9:30.

Death Valley Days: the classic western, with Tim Frawley as the Old Ranger and Harvey Hays as the Old Prospector, airing on the Blue network from 1930 until its name was changed to *Death Valley Sheriff* in 1944. Friday nights at 8:30.

Dick Tracy: a crime-adventure serial based on the comic strip by Chester Gould, running from 1935 to 1945. Opening: "And now . . . Dick Tracy!" followed by radio code sound effects and the voice of Dick Tracy: "This is Dick Tracy on the case of . . . Stand by for action! [siren sound effect] Let's go, men!" And final voice-over, "Yes, it's Dick Tracy, Protector of Law and Order!"

Doc Barclay's Daughters: soap opera airing over CBS in 1938.

Dr. Christian: drama first airing over CBS in 1937, with scripts written and sent in by listeners.

Dr. Dolittle: the stories of Hugh Lofting, presented with a fifteen-minute format at 5:15 twice a week on the Blue network in 1936.

Dr. I.Q., the Mental Banker: a quiz show with live audience participation, hosted by Lew Valentine as Dr. I.Q. Announcers roamed the studio audience and hand-picked members to answer questions put forth by Dr. I.Q. Those with correct answers won silver dollars, while those with incorrect answers won a box of Mars candy bars. First aired over NBC on Monday nights in 1939. Opening: "Presenting, Dr. I.Q.! . . . Mars Incorporated, makers of America's most enjoyable candy bars, bring you another half-hour of fun with your genial master of wit and information—Dr. I.Q., the Mental Banker! And now here is that wise man with the friendly smile and the cash for your correct answers . . . Dr. I.Q.!" [audience applause] *Dr. I.Q.*: "Thank you, thank you, Mr. Anthony. And good evening, ladies and gentlemen. My assistants are stationed throughout the audience with portable microphones which enable members of the theater audience to remain in their seats while answering questions which I ask from the stage. . . ."

Easy Aces: domestic comedy starring Goodman and Jane Ace as themselves. Wife Jane was famous for her malapropisms, such as "Up at the crank of dawn," or "When I get the urge I'm completely uninhabited!" A fifteen-minute format airing from 1930 to 1945. Seven o'clock weeknights over NBC.

The Ed Sullivan Show: a variety show hosted by New York newspaper columnist Ed Sullivan, over CBS beginning in 1931. Jack Benny made his radio debut on this show in 1931.

The Eddie Cantor Show: a comedy-variety show starring Eddie Cantor and a large cast including vocalists Dir. .h Shore and Deanna Durbin. Also known as *The Chase and Sanborn Hour.* Airing from 1931 through the decade.

The Edgar Bergen and Charlie McCarthy Show: a comedy-variety show starring ventriloquist Edgar Bergen and his dummies, Charlie McCarthy, Mortimer Snerd and Effie Klinker, with Don Ameche as MC (Ameche also played the husband in a running feature with Frances Langford, called the Bickersons, about a bickering husband and wife.)

Also known as *The Chase and Sanborn Hour,* until Bergen joined the show in 1936. A running gag was the monocled Charlie ribbing Bergen about moving his lips all the time when he made Charlie talk. A long-favorite Sunday night program. Typical line:

"How long was your last cook with you?"

"She was never with us. She was against us."

Eight o'clock Sunday nights over CBS.

Ellery Queen: a detective-mystery show starring Hugh Marlowe as Ellery Queen, originating on CBS in 1939.

The Eveready Hour: radio's first big production variety show, featuring jazz, opera, drama, poetry, lectures, comedy and one-act plays based on actual events. Sponsored by Eveready batteries, beginning in December of 1923.

Father Coughlin: a Roman Catholic priest who provided commentary on religion and current events and was, at one time, considered one of the most influential personalities in the country after the President. His program was frequently controversial, and attempts were made on his life twice. He was first heard in Detroit in 1926, then on CBS at four o'clock on Sundays through the mid-1930s. When CBS cancelled the show, he formed his own network, and he continued to broadcast until the early 1940s.

Fibber McGee and Molly: a comedy show starring Jim Jordan as Fibber, Marian Jordan as Molly (and six other parts), Hal Peary as Throckmorton P. Gildersleeve and Marlin Hurt as Beulah, the maid, with various other cast members. Famous running lines from the show: "Tain't funny, McGee." "Heavenly days!" "Somebody bawl for Beulah?" "Dad-rat the dad-ratted. . . ." Most famous running gag: Fibber opening a hall closet door with a horrible crash of junk falling out, with comment: "Gotta straighten out that closet one of these days."

Originally known as *The Johnson Wax Program With Fibber McGee and Molly* in 1935, the show played on Tuesday nights at 9:30 over CBS until 1952.

Typical humor:

"We're not going anyplace if I don't get this blasted suitcase open pretty quick."

"Bang it on the floor. That's the way they come open for the red-caps."

The Fire Chief: a humor-variety show starring vaudeville comedian Ed Wynn over NBC Red Tuesday nights at 9:30. It debuted on April 28, 1932, and ran until May of 1935.

Fireside Chats: commentary by Franklin Delano Roosevelt while in office in the 1930s.

The Fitch Bandwagon: a variety show starring Phil and Alice Faye Harris and others. Theme song: "Laugh a while, let a song be your style, use Fitch Shampoo. Don't despair, use your head, save your hair, use Fitch Shampoo." The show featured famous bands of the day and aired at 7:30 Sundays, just before Edgar Bergen, beginning in 1937 over NBC.

Flash Gordon: a science fiction adventure series starring Gale Gordon or James Meighan as Flash, first airing over Mutual in 1935.

The Frank Sinatra Show: a variety program starring Frank Sinatra, over CBS beginning in 1943.

The Fred Allen Show: a comedy-variety show starring Fred Allen, with a large supporting cast and numerous guest stars. The show began in 1932 as *The Linit Show*, then *The Linit Bath Club*, *The Salad Bowl Revue*, *The Sal Hepatica Revue* and *The Texaco Star Theater*. It changed to a half-hour from a previous hour format in 1942. The show continued to run over ABC on Sunday nights at nine o'clock.

The Fred Waring Show: a musical program starring Fred Waring and his Pennsylvanians. Musicians appearing on the show included Honey and the Bees, The Lane Sisters, Stella and the Fellas, guitarist Les Paul, and many others. The show first aired in the early 1920s and continued through the 1930s on CBS.

Fu Manchu: a mystery program starring John Daly as Chinese villain Fu Manchu. Over CBS in 1932.

Gangbusters: the 1930s equivalent of today's *America's Most Wanted* TV program. The show featured narrated, true crime stories, with a closing description of the wanted criminals. Listeners frequently tipped off the police to numerous suspects, reportedly resulting in actual arrests. The opening: [very loud sound effects of marching feet, machine-gun fire and a siren] "Calling the police! Calling the G-men! Calling all Americans to war on the underworld! . . . Gangbusters! With the cooperation of leading law-enforcement officials of the United States, Gangbusters presents facts in the relentless war of the police on the underworld . . . authentic case histories that show the never-ending activity of the police in their work of protecting our citizens." The show, sponsored by Palmolive Brushless Shaving Cream, aired over CBS at ten o'clock on Wednesday nights.

Gene Autry's Melody Ranch: a variety show featuring western music and adventure, starring Gene Autry, with The Cass Country Boys and the King Sisters, sponsored by Wrigley's Gum. On Sunday afternoons on CBS starting in 1940, later moving to eight o'clock Saturday nights.

Girl Alone: a soap opera starring Betty Winkler as Patricia Rogers, the girl alone, with a large supporting cast. First airing over NBC in 1935.

The Goldbergs: originally titled, *The Rise of the Goldbergs*, a kind of humorous soap opera revolving around a poor, New York Jewish family, who spoke with thick dialects. Each show started with Gertrude Berg's line, "Yoo hoo! Is anybody?" Some typical dialect: "God forbid I should laugh from you, Molly! It vould be a fine day if I should laugh from you! If it vasn't for you, vould dere be a Molly Cloik und Soot Company? . . . Ah, Molly, a man ain't a voman. A man don't talk much, but de moe he's got in de heart de less his tongue vaggles. . . ." First airing on November 20, 1929, and running until 1945 on NBC. Weekdays at 5:15.

Grand Central Station: a drama starring Hume Cronyn and Nancy Coleman. Its opening: [sound effects of chugging train] "As a bullet seeks its target, shining rails in every part of our great country are aimed at Grand Central Station, heart of the nation's greatest city. Drawn by the magnetic force of the fantastic metropolis, day and night great trains rush toward the Hudson River, sweep down its eastern bank for 140 miles, flash briefly by the long red row of tenement houses south of 125th street, dive with a roar into the two-and-one-half mile tunnel which burrows beneath the glitter and swank of Park Avenue and then

... Grand Central Station! Crossroads of a million private lives ... gigantic stage on which are played a thousand dramas daily!" Friday nights at eight o'clock over NBC Blue starting in 1937.

The Grand Old Opry: a variety program featuring country and western music and humor, featuring Cousin Minnie Pearl, Roy Acuff (who during World War II was voted the most popular singer, beating out Frank Sinatra and Bing Crosby), Ernest Tubb, Gene Autry, Hank Williams, The Cumberland Valley Boys and many others. Its most famous line was probably the lively, "Howdy!" exclaimed by Cousin Minnie Pearl. The show originated as *The WSM Barn Dance* in 1925, but its name was soon changed to *The Grand Old Opry* in February 1926. Performed in front of a live audience, the show gradually grew from a one-hour program to five hours, aired on Saturday nights by WSM Nashville. NBC picked up thirty minutes of the show for network broadcasting beginning in 1939.

The Great Gildersleeve: a sit-com starring Hal Peary as Throckmorton P. Gildersleeve, bachelor and uncle of two troublemaking children. Gildersleeve was a spin-off character from the Fibber McGee and Molly program. Airing over NBC beginning on August 31, 1941. Sunday nights at 6:30.

The Green Hornet: a mystery-adventure program starring Al Hodge (and three other actors) as Britt Reid, the Green Hornet, and Raymond Hayashi (and others) as Kato. Its opening: "The Green Hornet! [Sound effect of hornet buzzing] He hunts the biggest of all game! Public enemies who try to destroy our America! [Theme song, 'Flight of the Bumblebee,' starts] With his faithful valet, Kato, Britt Reid, daring young publisher, matches wits with the underworld, risking his life that criminals and racketeers, within the law, may feel its weight by the sting of the Green Hornet!" Airing over Mutual in 1938 and continuing through the forties. Saturday nights at eight o'clock.

The Guiding Light: a soap opera, starring Ed Prentiss as Ned Holden, and Sarajane Wells or Mercedes McCambridge as Mary Ruthledge, with a large supporting cast. First airing in 1938 over NBC.

The Happiness Boys: the comedy duo of Billy Jones and Ernie Hare, who sang, cracked jokes and performed brief skits. They began over local WEAF in New York in 1923 and then were broadcast nationally over NBC in 1927 at eight o'clock Friday nights. The immensely popular show, one of the first-ever comedy-oriented programs, aired through the late 1930s. Its opening song:

"How do you do, everybody, how do you do?
How do you do, everybody, how are you?
We are here we must confess just to bring you happiness
Hope we please you more or less, how do you do?
How do you do, oh, how do you do?
How do you doodle-doodle-doodle-doodle-do?
Billy Jones and Ernie Hare wish to say to you out there
How do you doodle-doodle-doodle-doodle-do?"

The Helen Hayes Theater: a drama series, featuring various adapations of famous stories, and hosted by Helen Hayes. First airing over NBC Blue in 1935.

Hilltop House: a soap opera starring Bess Johnson as Bess Johnson, a superintendent of a boarding school, with a large supporting cast. Aired by both Mutual and CBS in 1937. The title was changed to *The Story of Bess Johnson* in 1941.

Hollywood Hotel: a drama series featuring Hollywood movie stars in the leading roles, hosted by Dick Powell, Fred MacMurray and others. First airing over CBS in 1934.

Houseboat Hannah: a soap opera starring Henrietta Tedro as Hannah O'Leary, debuting over Mutual in 1937.

I Love a Mystery: a mystery program revolving around three detectives, Jack Packard (the brainy one), Doc Long (the lock-picker), and Reggie Yorke (the strong one), at the A-1 Detective Agency. Their motto was, "No job too tough, no mystery too baffling." Beginning as a five-nights-per-week program on NBC at 7:15 in 1939, evolving into a half-hour weekly series in 1940.

Information, Please! a quiz show featuring a panel of experts who tried to answer tough questions submitted by listeners. Listeners who stumped the panel won a set of the *Encyclopedia Britannica.* Airing over NBC Blue from May 17, 1938, through the 1940s.

Inner Sanctum: a hugely popular, albeit bloody and violent, mystery-horror program with various guest stars (including Boris Karloff), and hosted by Raymond Johnson. A typical opening: "Lipton Tea and Lipton Soup present, Inner Sanctum Mysteries, starring Boris Karloff. . . ." [Sound of organ music and creaking door] "Good evening, friends of the Inner Sanctum. This is your host to welcome you through the squeaking door into the land of ghosts, vampires, and other gay, hilarious people. Friends, are you looking for an apartment? Well, we have just the place for you. It's sturdily built. Completely of marble. With cold running water—every time it rains. You don't have to worry about the landlord putting you out. The lease is forever. All you have to do to get this little love nest is call your undertaker and get yourself a little bit dead. [Laughs]" [*Woman*] "Mr. Host, I assure you no one is the least bit interested in your offer." [*Host*] "But Mary, just think, once you're dead you can appear on Inner Sanctum. . . ." The host and co-host typically interspersed the show's introduction with plugs for Lipton products.

The introduction above was taken from a show broadcast on November 12, 1945. The program debuted on January 7, 1941 over the Blue Network. Sunday nights at 8:30.

Jack Armstrong, the All-American Boy: an adventure serial starring Jim Ameche or Charles Flynn (and sometimes others) as Jack Armstrong, sponsored by Wheaties. The sponsor gave out such premiums as Jack Armstrong pedometers, Jack Armstrong whistling rings, Jack Armstrong secret decoders and other trinkets. The show's theme song, sung by The Norsemen:

"Wave the flag for Hudson High, boys,
Show them how we stand!
Ever shall our team be champion,
Known throughout the land!
Rah Rah Boola Boola Boola Boola
Boola Boola Boola Rah Rah Rah
Have you tried Wheaties?

They're whole wheat with all of the bran.
Won't you try Wheaties?
For wheat is the best food of man!
They're crispy and crunchy the whole year through.
Jack Armstrong never tires of them
And neither will you.
So just buy Wheaties
The best breakfast food in the land!''

First airing over CBS in 1933 and continuing until 1951. Weekdays at 5:30.

The Jack Benny Program: a comedy-variety show starring Jack Benny, Mary Livingstone, Dennis Day, Phil Harris, Mel Blanc, and Eddie Anderson (as Rochester, Jack's valet). The show's most famous line was Jack Benny's, "Now cut that out!" Ongoing humor featured Jack's sub-par violin-playing, his money-hoarding (the longest live audience laughter in radio history occurred when a robber told Benny, "Your money or your life!" and Jack had to think it over), and the polar bear that lived in his cellar and ate the gas man. Sunday nights at seven over CBS from 1932 on.

John's Other Wife: a soap opera revolving around the life of store-owner, John Perry and his secretary, "the other wife." Over NBC in 1936.

Joyce Jordan, Girl Interne: a medical serial starring Rita Johnson and others as Joyce Jordan. The show first aired over CBS in 1938. The name was changed to *Joyce Jordan, M.D.* in 1942.

Jumbo: a variety-drama revolving around the circus and two feuding circus owners, Mr. Considine and Matt Mulligan. Jimmy Durante played a press agent in the show, which was performed in front of a live audience of 4,500 at the Hippodrome Theater in New York. Tuesday nights at 9:30 on NBC starting in 1935. Sponsored by Texaco.

The Kate Smith Show: a variety program featuring singing, comedy and drama. Smith, known as "The Songbird of the South," was best-known for her singing of "God Bless America" and the first eight bars of "When the Moon Comes Over the Mountain." Airing on CBS starting in 1936.

Kay Kyser's Kollege of Musical Knowledge: a musical program that featured light quizzes in between numbers, hosted by Kay Kyser, and Mervyn Bogue as Ish Kabibble, on Wednesday nights on NBC beginning in 1938.

Kraft Music Hall: a variety show hosted by Bing Crosby from 1936 to 1946, and by Al Jolson until 1948. The show featured such regular guests as Peggy Lee, Mary Martin, Victor Borge and others.

Land of the Lost: a children's adventure show. The show revolved around Isabel and Billy, children who were led into plots by a glowing red fish called The Red Lantern. Over ABC in 1944.

Let's Pretend: a children's drama originally titled *The Adventures of Helen and Mary*, sponsored by Cream of Wheat. Opening:

"Cream of Wheat is so good to eat
That we have it every day.
We sing this song, it will make us strong
And it makes us shout hooray.
It's good for growing babies
And grownups too to eat.
For all the family's breakfast
You can't beat Cream of Wheat. . . ."

Voice-over: "Cream of Wheat—the great American family cereal, presents, *Let's Pretend!*" From 1934 through the 1940s on CBS.

Life Can Be Beautiful: a soap opera sponsored by Spic and Span, beginning in 1938 over CBS. One o'clock weekdays.

Li'l Abner: a hillbilly comedy based on the comic strip by Al Capp. John Hodiak played Li'l Abner. The announcer was Durward Kirby. First airing over NBC in 1939.

Little Orphan Annie: an adventure program starring Shirley Bell as Little Orphan Annie and Henry Saxe as Daddy Warbucks, based on the comic strip characters by Harold Gray. Annie's most famous line from the show: "Leapin' lizards!" The show first aired over the Blue network in 1931 and was sponsored by Ovaltine. Weekdays at 5:45.

The Lone Ranger: a western adventure program starring George Seaton (and others) as The Lone Ranger and John Todd as Tonto. Memorable lines included Tonto always referring to the Lone Ranger as "Kemo Sabe," and bystanders who watched the Lone Ranger pass and asked, "Who was that masked man?" The show first aired on January 30, 1933, and continued throughout the forties. Its famous opening was the theme song of the William Tell Overture in the background: [sound of hoofbeats and the voice of the Lone Ranger] "Hi-yo Silver!" *Announcer*: "A fiery horse with the speed of light, a cloud of dust and a hearty hi-yo Silver! The Lone Ranger! . . . With his faithful Indian companion, Tonto, the daring and resourceful masked rider of the plains led the fight for law and order in the early western United States. Nowhere in the pages of history can one find a greater champion of justice. Return with us now to those thrilling days of yesteryear. . . . [Sound of hoofbeats] From out of the past come the thundering hoofbeats of the great horse Silver. The Lone Ranger rides again!" *Lone Ranger*: "Come on, Silver! Let's go, big fellow! Hi-yo Silver! Away!" Over the Mutual Network. Friday and other nights at 7:30 or 8:00.

Lum and Abner: a popular, long-running comedy starring Chester Lauck as Lum Edwards and Norris Goff as Abner Peabody. The action took place in a store in Pine Ridge, Arkansas. The show began over NBC on April 26, 1931, and continued over each of the networks over the next twenty-four years. Monday nights at 6:30.

Lux Radio Theater: a Hollywood production that took popular movies and adapted them to radio plays, with parts played by leading film actors. Barbara Stanwyck and Don Ameche frequently turned up as performers. Hosted by Cecil B. deMille. On Monday nights over the Blue network from June 1, 1936, to June 6, 1955.

Ma Perkins: a serial drama starring Virginia Payne as Ma Perkins, a lumberyard operator in the town of Rushville Center, with a huge supporting cast. The popular soap opera, sponsored by Oxydol, debuted on December 4, 1933, and enjoyed a twenty-seven-year run. Weekdays at 3:30 over CBS.

Major Bowes and His Original Amateur Hour: an amateur talent show hosted by Major Edward Bowes or Jay Flippen. Its theme song was

WAR OF THE WORLDS BROADCAST

It happened on the evening of October 30, 1938, and it threw thousands of Americans into a panic. Telephone lines were clogged with calls, women and children weeped, men secured ammunition and guns. The Red Cross and the National Guard would have to be mobilized.

What was happening?

The radio broadcast of H.G. Wells's "The War of the Worlds," a science fiction drama about Martians invading the earth. It was a classic American event.

The radio play was clearly presented as just that, *a play*: "The Columbia Broadcasting System and its affiliated stations present Orson Welles and the Mercury Theater on the Air in "The War of the Worlds" by H.G. Wells. . . . Ladies and gentlemen, the director of the Mercury Theater and the star of these broadcasts, Orson Welles. . . ."

But according to research headed by Hadley Cantril of Princeton University, of the six million people who heard the show, over a million believed the program to be an *actual news report* and were frightened out of their wits. Many listeners apparently either tuned in late or somehow missed the other disclaimers made throughout the show. The impact of the broadcast had on the nation is reflected in these newspaper headlines of the following day:

FAKE RADIO WAR STIRS TERROR THROUGHOUT THE U.S.

MANY FLEE HOMES TO ESCAPE "GAS RAIDS FROM MARS"

PHONE CALLS SWAMP POLICE AT BROADCAST OF WELLS FANTASY

When the broadcast announced that Martians were actually attacking people all over the U.S., thousands of people prepared themselves for the onslaught.

PITTSBURGH—A man returned home in the midst of the broadcast and found his wife, a bottle of poison in her hand, screaming: "I'd rather die this way than like that."

SAN FRANCISCO—An offer to volunteer in stopping an invasion from Mars came among hundreds of telephone inquiries to police and newspapers during the radio dramatization of H.G. Wells's story. One excited man called Oakland police and shouted: "My God! Where can I volunteer my services? We've got to stop this awful thing!"

INDIANAPOLIS—A woman ran into a church screaming: "New York destroyed; it's the end of the world. You might as well go home to die. I just heard it on the radio." Services were dismissed immediately.

BREVARD, N.C.—Five Brevard College students fainted and panic gripped the campus for a half hour with many students fighting for telephones to inform their parents to come and get them.

PROVIDENCE, R.I.—Weeping and hysterical women swamped the switchboard of the Providence Journal for details of the "massacre." The electric company received scores of calls urging it to turn off all lights so that the city would be safe from the "enemy."

After learning that the broadcast was only a sort of Halloween prank, the public demanded punishment for the show's producer, Orson Welles. He was hounded by reporters for days. Outraged (and embarrassed) citizens threatened him. Lawsuits were filed against him and the Mercury Theater. Welles claimed over and over: "I had no idea this would happen. I had no idea. . . ."

"Tonight the Columbia Broadcasting System and its affiliated stations coast-to-coast has brought you 'The War of the Worlds' by H.G. Wells, the seventeenth in its weekly series of dramatic broadcasts featuring Orson Welles and the Mercury Theater on the Air. Next week we present. . . ."

"There's No Business Like Show Business." On various networks from 1934 to the end of the forties. Eight o'clock Sunday nights.

Mandrake the Magician: an adventure program based on the comic strip by Falk and Davis, starring Raymond Johnson as Mandrake. First airing over Mutual in 1940.

Manhattan Merry-Go-Round: a program that presented live music from "imagined" nightclubs around New York. Its opening announcement: "Here's the Manhattan Merry-Go-Round that brings you the bright side of life, that whirls you in music to all the big night spots of New York town to hear the top songs of the week sung so clearly you can understand every word and sing them yourself." Airing Sunday nights at nine o'clock on NBC starting in the early 1930s. Sponsored by Dr. Lyon's Tooth Powder.

Mercury Theater on the Air: hosted by Orson Welles, a high-quality weekly drama program. Its greatest claim to fame was its production of H.G. Wells's, *The War of the Worlds*, which panicked thousands of listeners who believed the broadcast was a real news bulletin. Debuting over CBS in 1938. Late evenings.

The Milton Berle Show: a comedy starring Milton Berle, first airing on NBC in 1939.

Mr. District Attorney: a law-and-order drama starring Dwight West or Raymond Johnson as the District Attorney, sponsored by Bristol Meyers. Its opening: *Announcer*: "Mr. District Attorney, champion of the people, defender of truth, guardian of our fundamental rights to life, liberty, and the pursuit of happiness." *The District Attorney*: "And it shall be my duty as District Attorney not only to prosecute to the limit of the law all persons accused of crimes perpetrated within this county but to defend with equal vigor the rights and privileges of all its citizens." Wednesday nights on NBC from 1939 through the 1940s.

Myrt and Marge: a fifteen-minute, five-days-a-week soap opera starring Myrtle Vail as Myrt and Donna Fick as Marge, with a large supporting cast. The story revolved around the backstage life of the two women, who were actresses. Over CBS beginning in 1931 and continuing throughout the decade.

The National Barn Dance: a country and western music program broadcast in front of a live audience. The show had a large cast of regulars, including Little Georgie Gobel, and various musical groups. Beginning on September 30, 1933, and airing regularly at 10:30 Saturday nights on NBC.

Nick Carter, Master Detective: a detective show starring Lon Clark as Nick Carter. First aired over Mutual in 1943.

Old Fashioned Revival Hour: a religious program hosted by Reverend Charles Fuller, heard throughout the 1940s over Mutual.

One Man's Family: the longest-running soap opera on radio, beginning on NBC on April 29, 1932, and ending May 8, 1959. The serial followed the lives of San Franciscans Henry and Fanny Barbour and their five children, Paul, Hazel, Claudia, Cliff and Jack, and their children. Its opening announcement: "*One Man's Family* is dedicated to the mothers and fathers of the younger generation and to their bewildering offspring." The once-a-week, 30-minute show aired over NBC on Friday nights from 9:30 to 10:00 Pacific Standard Time. (The show aired from San Francisco.)

The O'Neills: a soap opera starring Kate McComb as Mrs. O'Neill. Airing over CBS in 1934. Weekdays at 5:30.

Our Gal Sunday: a soap opera starring Dorothy Lowell as Sunday, with a large supporting cast. Its theme song was "Red River Valley." Its opening announcement: "Our Gal Sunday . . . the story of an orphan girl named Sunday, from the little mining town of Silver Creek, Colorado, who in young womanhood married England's richest, most handsome lord, Lord Henry Brinthrope. The story asks the question, Can this girl from a mining town in the West find happiness as the wife of a wealthy and titled Englishman?" Starting on March 29, 1937, over CBS at 12:45.

The Palmolive Beauty Box Theater: a musical-variety show starring Jessica Dragonette and Benny Fields. Over NBC beginning in 1934.

Peewee and Windy: a comedy show revolving around the lives of two sailors on shore leave. Airing throughout the early 1930s on NBC.

Pepper Young's Family: a soap opera starring Curtis Arnall (and others) as Larry (Pepper) Young, with a large supporting cast. Its opening announcement: "Pepper Young's Family . . . the story of your friends, the Youngs, is brought to you by Camay, the mild beauty soap for a smoother, softer complexion." Over NBC starting in 1936. Mornings at 11:15.

Perry Mason: a law-and-order drama based on the stories of Erle Stanley Gardner. It starred Bartlett Robinson (and others) as Perry Mason, and Gertrude Warner (and others) as Della Street. Over CBS in 1943.

The Phil Baker Show: a comedy show starring comic and accordion-player, Phil Baker, from 1933 to 1940.

Popeye the Sailor: a children's program based on the famous comic strip. Det Poppen played Popeye and Olive La Moy played Olive Oyl. Sponsored by Wheatena. Starting in 1935 over NBC.

Portia Faces Life: a soap opera revolving around the life of Portia Blake Manning, a successful woman lawyer. Weekdays at 5:15. First airing over CBS in 1940.

Pretty Kitty Kelly: a soap opera starring Arline Blackburn as Kitty. The show aired Monday through Friday at 5:45, beginning March 15, 1937.

The Quiz Kids: very popular quiz program in which extremely difficult questions were posed to an exceptionally bright panel of youngsters. Listeners marveled at the intelligence of the panel, but it was learned years later that the children were secretly coached with some questions. The MC was Joe Kelly. On Wednesday evenings, then moving to Sunday afternoons over NBC, with its debut on June 28, 1940.

The Red Skelton Show: a comedy-variety show starring Red Skelton, who played such characters as Clem Kadiddlehopper, J. Newton Numskull, and Junior, the Mean Widdle Kid. Ozzie Nelson and Harriet Hilliard were vocalists on the show. Tuesday nights at 10:30 over NBC, starting in 1941.

The Right to Happiness: a serial drama starring Claudia Morgan as Carolyn Kramer Nelson, with a large supporting cast. Its opening announcement: "And now, Ivory soap's own story—The Right to Happiness. . . . Happiness is the sum total of many things—of health, security, friends, and loved ones. But most important is a desire to be happy and the will to help others find their right to happiness as well. . . . The Right to Happiness . . . A very human story. . . ." Over NBC beginning in 1939. Weekdays at 1:30.

Rin-Tin-Tin: an adventure program starring Rin-Tin-Tin, the Wonder Dog. Over NBC Blue in 1930.

The Road of Life: a medical soap opera starring Ken Griffin (and others) as Dr. Jim Brent, with a huge supporting cast. First airing over CBS in 1937.

The Robert Burns Panatela Program: a comedy-variety show starring George Burns and Gracie Allen, with Guy Lombardo and his Royal Canadian Orchestra. First airing over CBS in 1932.

Robinson Crusoe Jr.: a children's program starring Lester Jay as Robinson Brown. The show revolved around the adventures of an upper-class boy and his comrades who were marooned on an island. First airing over CBS in 1934.

The Romance of Helen Trent: a soap opera in search of romance for an over-thirty-five fashion designer, starring Virginia Clark (and others) as Helen Trent, with a large supporting cast. Its theme song was a hummed version of "Juanita." Its opening announcement: "The Romance of Helen Trent . . . who sets out to prove for herself what so many women long to prove, that because a woman is thirty-five . . . or more . . . romance in life need not be over . . . that romance can live in life at thirty-five and after." First airing over CBS in 1933 and continuing into the 1940s.

Roy Rogers: a western adventure program starring Roy Rogers, Dale Evans and Gabby Hayes, with the musical groups, Sons of the Pioneers and Riders of the Purple Sage. Airing from 1944 through the 1950s.

The Rudy Vallee Show: a high-quality variety program, also known as *The Fleischmann Yeast Hour*, hosted and produced by Rudy Vallee. Vallee, who was famous for singing through a megaphone with his nasal voice, introduced a number of budding stars on his radio show, among them, Edgar Bergen and Charlie McCarthy, Alice Faye, Bob Hope, Milton Berle, Eddy Cantor and Carmen Miranda. *The Aldrich Family* was a spinoff from Vallee's show. Rudy's catchphrase was "Heigh-ho, everybody!" From 1929 to 1939.

Second Husband: a soap opera starring Helen Menken as Brenda Cummings and Joe Curtin as Grant Cummings, the second husband. First airing over CBS in the evenings in 1937, then moving to 11:15 A.M., Monday through Friday in 1942.

Seth Parker: a hugely popular serial program of hymn singing and drama, starring Phillips Lord as Seth Parker. The show took place in Jonesport, Maine, and revolved loosely around Parker and his neighbors, who gathered at Parker's house to sing hymns. Many radio listeners liked to sing along with the hymns. First airing over NBC Sunday nights at 10:30 in 1933.

The Shadow: a crime program starring Robert Hardy Andrews or Orson Welles as Lamont Cranston (The Shadow) with Agnes Moorehead (and others) as Margot Lane. Its chilling theme song was "Omphale's Spinning Wheel," which played in the background with this opening announcement, *The Shadow*: "Who knows what evil lurks in the hearts of men? The Shadow knows! [laughs]" *Announcer*: "Again, Blue Coal dealers present radio's strangest adventurer, the Shadow, mystery man who strikes terror into the very hearts of lawbreakers and criminals. . . . Today, Blue Coal brings you the Shadow's greatest adventure, 'The Silent Avenger.' . . . The Shadow's exciting adventure begins in just a moment, but first, I'd like to remind you homeowners that right now, when Winter is changing into Spring, is the most treacherous time of all the year. But you can protect your family's health and save valuable dollars by burning Blue Coal. It's Pennsylvania's finest anthracite. Order a trial ton from your nearest Blue Coal dealer tomorrow." The Shadow was, in reality, Lamont Cranston, a wealthy, young man-about-town who hated criminals. Once visiting the Orient, Cranston learned a strange and mysterious secret—the hypnotic power to cloud men's minds so they couldn't see him. Cranston's friend and companion, the lovely Margot Lane, was the only person who knew to whom the voice of the invisible Shadow belonged. The show's closing was equally memorable. *Announcer*: "You've just heard a dramatized version of one of the many copyrighted stories which appears in *The Shadow* magazine. All the characters and all the places named are fictitious. Any similarity to persons living or dead is purely coincidental." [creepy music, voice and creepy laugh of the shadow] "As you sow evil, so shall you reap evil. Crime does not pay. The Shadow knows. [laughs]" This opening and closing of the show aired in 1938. Later shows varied slightly. Over Mutual beginning in 1936.

Sherlock Holmes: a detective program starring Richard Gordon, Louis Hector, Basil Rathbone (and others) as Sherlock Holmes, and Leigh Lovel (and others) as Dr. Watson. Holmes most repeated line was, "Elementary, my dear Watson." Based on the stories by Sir Arthur Conan Doyle. Airing over NBC beginning in 1930.

Smith Brothers: a humor program featuring the duo of Scrappy Lambert and Billy Hillpot, who sang and told jokes. Sponsored by Smith Brothers cough drops. From 1926 to 1934 over NBC Red on Wednesday nights.

The Smith Family: one of radio's first sit-coms, starring vaudevillians Jim and Marian Jordan, who went on to become Fibber McGee and Molly. Airing over WENR in Chicago in 1925.

Stage Door Canteen: a variety program, with MC Bert Lytell. Debuting over CBS in 1942.

Stella Dallas: a soap opera starring Anne Elstner as Stella Dallas, with a large supporting cast. Airing over NBC from October 25, 1937, throughout the 1940s and into the 1950s. Its opening announcement: "We give you now, Stella Dallas—a continuation on the air of the true-to-life story of mother love and sacrifice, in which Stella Dallas saw her own beloved daughter Laurel marry into wealth and society and, realizing the differences in their tastes and worlds, went out of Laurel's life. These episodes in the later life of Stella Dallas are based on the famous novel of that name by Olive Higgins Prouty, and are written by Frank and Anne Hummert." Weekdays at 4:15.

The Story of Mary Marlin: a soap opera starring Joan Blaine (and others) as Mary Marlin, a United States senator, with a huge supporting cast. Over NBC beginning on January 1, 1935, at five o'clock.

Superman: the classic superhero series starring Clayton Collyer or Michael Fitzmaurice as Clark Kent and Superman, with a cast of characters that not only included Lois Lane, Perry White and Jimmy Olson, but Batman and Robin as well. The actors typically deepened their voices mid-line as Clark Kent was transformed into Superman. Its opening: "Kellogg's Pep, the super-delicious cereal, presents: The Adventures of Superman! Faster than a speeding bullet! [sound of bullet ricochet] More powerful than a locomotive! [steaming train] Able to leap tall buildings at a single bound! [wind burst effect] Look! Up in the sky! [Trio of voices] "It's a bird!" "It's a plane!" "It's Superman!" First airing over Mutual in 1940.

Take It or Leave It: a quiz show. Phil Baker, Bob Hawk, Gary Moore or Jack Paar held the MC position in various years. Contestants tried to correctly answer questions until they reached the sixty-four dollar question. The show later became known as *The Sixty-Four Dollar Question.* First airing over CBS in 1940.

Terry and the Pirates: an adventure program based on the comic strip by Milton Caniff. It starred Jackie Kelk (and others) as Terry Lee. Over NBC in 1937.

The Thin Man: a detective show based on the character created by Dashiell Hammett. Over NBC in 1941.

Today's Children: a soap opera starring Helen Kane as Kathryn Carter, with a large supporting cast. Originating over NBC in 1933 and airing throughout the 1940s.

Tom Mix: a western adventure program, with various actors playing the part of Tom Mix. Mix resided at the T-M Bar Ranch in Dobie Township. His horse was Tony, the Wonder Horse. His friends were known as the "Straight Shooters." Sponsored by Ralston. First airing over NBC in 1933.

Tommy Riggs and Betty Lou: a comedy show featuring ventriloquist Tommy Riggs and his disembodied voice as Betty Lou, his niece. First airing over NBC in 1938.

Town Hall Tonight: comedy program featuring one of the most highly regarded comedians of the day, Fred Allen. Wednesday nights from 1935 to 1940.

The True Story Hour with Mary and Bob: a one-hour drama series starring Nora Stirling as Mary and William Brenton as Bob. Airing over CBS from 1928 to 1932.

Truth or Consequences: a humorous quiz show in which contestants failing to answer questions were given the consequences of carrying out stunts or tasks. The MC was Ralph Edwards. Wrong answers were always signaled by "Beulah the Buzzer." Its opening: [over audience laughter]: "Hello, there. We've been waiting for you. It's time to play Truth—[organ]—or Consequences!" [sound of Beulah the Buzzer]. Over NBC beginning in 1940. Saturday nights at 8:30.

Twenty Thousand Years in Sing Sing: a crime series starring Warden Lewis E. Lawes. First heard over NBC in 1933.

Uncle Don: a children's variety program featuring songs, stories, games, advice, birthday greetings, reading of the Sunday comics, and more. Hosted by Don Carney, the show was heard in eighteen states over WOR in New York, from 6:00 to 6:30 P.M., from September 1928 to 1949. Its theme song was, "Hello, Little Friends, Hello."

> "Hello nephews, nieces, mine.
> I'm glad to see you look so fine.
> How's Mama? How's Papa?
> But tell me first just how you are.
> I've many, many things to tell you, on the radio.
> This is Uncle Don, your Uncle Don,
> Hello, little friend, hello."

Valiant Lady: a soap opera starring Joan Blaine (and others) as Joan Hargrove-Scott, the Valiant Lady, with a large supporting cast. First heard over NBC in 1938.

Vic and Sade: a comedy show starring Art Van Harvey as Vic Gook, Bernadine Flynn as Sade Gook, Billy Idelson as the Gook's son, Rush, and Clarence Hartzell as Uncle Fletcher. The Gooks were a middle-class family who lived "in the little house halfway up in the next block," in Crooper, Illinois, near Peoria. Vic worked for "Plant No. 14 of the Consolidated Kitchenware Company." Sade went to a lot of washrag sales. Uncle Fletcher, who answered everything with, "Fine!" and was hard of hearing, had a penchant for reminiscing about friends and acquaintances who had died. He also rode the garbage route with Mr. Gumpox on his garbage wagon. Colorful characters referred to on the show included, Ishigan Fishigan of Sishigan, Michigan, Blue Tooth Johnson, Smelly Clark, Gus Plink and Godfrey Dimlock. Its theme songs were "Oh, You Beautiful Doll," and "Shine On, Harvest Moon." Its opening announcement: "And now, folks, get ready to smile again with radio's home folks, Vic and Sade, written by Paul Rhymer." This fifteen-minute show was so popular it had several air times, including 3:15 weekday afternoons and 10:30 evenings, five times per week. It sometimes aired mornings as well. It premiered over NBC Blue on June 29, 1932, and continued for fourteen years. It was voted most outstanding radio program of 1936.

Walter Winchell: Winchell, "your New York correspondent," delivered news and commentary in a breathless, rapid-fire style while a code signal (which he worked himself) beeped in the background. One of the highest rated reporters on the air. His famous opening: "Good evening, Mr. and Mrs. North and South America and all the ships at sea . . . let's go to press!" Over NBC at various times, including Sunday nights at 9:30.

What's the Name of That Song?: a musical quiz show in which contestants (chosen prior to the show for their ability to sing) were awarded five dollars if they could correctly identify one of three songs from excerpts that were played. The contestants were awarded more money if they could sing the first line and more money still if they could complete the entire song. Hosted by Dud Williamson, beginning over Mutual in 1944.

When a Girl Marries: a soap opera starring Mary Jane Higby as Joan Field Davis and John Raby as Harry Davis, with a large supporting cast. Its opening announcement: "When a Girl Marries . . . this tender, human story of young, married love is dedicated to everyone who has ever been in love. . . ." First heard over CBS in May of 1939.

The Whistler: a mystery program starring Bill Forman (and others) as The Whistler. The Whistler was only an observer and commentator on the unfolding dramas and played no role in the stories themselves. The theme song was whistled during the opening: "I am the Whistler. And I know many things, for I walk by night. I know many strange tales hidden in the hearts of men and women who have stepped into the shadows. Yes, I know the nameless terrors of which they dare not speak." Over CBS on Sunday nights from 1945 to 1954.

Wilderness Road: a serial drama revolving around the lives of an 18th-century pioneer family, the Westons, Sam, Anne, Peter, David, John, Mary and Simon. It also starred Ray Collins as Daniel Boone. Over CBS beginning in 1936.

Will Rogers: possibly the most popular humorist of the 1920s and 1930s, Rogers is widely credited with boosting national morale during the Depression. With his down-home, colloquial style, Rogers's witty observations on politics and current events became a radio mainstay from as early as 1922. He liked to poke fun at politicians and was the first to mimic a president (Coolidge) over the air, much to the mixed horror and delight of listeners. He could be heard on various broadcasts over the years, but on one program, *The Gulf Show* (Sunday nights at nine o'clock) he had a regular fifteen-minute monologue. Typical observations: "But with Congress, every time they make a joke, it's a law. . . . And every time they make a law it's a joke." Or this on the Hoover Dam: "I see by the papers this morning that they are going to change the name of Hoover Dam. That is the silliest thing I ever heard of in politics. They are going to take the name of Hoover away from that dam. Lord, if they feel that way about it, I don't see why they don't just transfer the two names."

The Witch's Tale: eerie tales starring Adelaide Fitz-Allan as Old Nancy, the Witch of Salem. Hosted by Alonzo Deen Cole. Its opening: [tolling of clock] "The Witch's Tale! [howling wind] "The fascination for the eerie . . . weird, blood-chilling tales told by Old Nancy, the Witch of Salem, and Satan, the wise black cat. They're waiting, waiting for you now. . . ." Over Mutual in 1934 at nine o'clock Tuesdays.

Woman in White: a serial drama starring Luise Barclay (and others) as Karen Adams Harding, the Woman in White. Harding was a nurse who was romantically involved with a surgeon. Over NBC from 1937 through the 1940s.

Yesterday's Children: an education program in which notable people talked about the most memorable or most influential books they ever read. Even Franklin Roosevelt appeared on this show. Hosted by Dorothy Gordon. Over NBC Blue in 1940.

Young Dr. Malone: a soap opera starring Alan Bunce (and others) as Dr. Jerry Malone, with a huge supporting cast, many of whom worked at the "Three Oaks Medical Center." Over NBC Blue beginning in 1939. Weekdays at 2:00.

Young Widder Brown: a soap opera starring Florence Freeman as Ellen Brown, who had a romance with Dr. Anthony Loring. Over NBC in 1938. Weekdays at 4:45.

Your Hit Parade: a widely listened to Saturday night music program featuring orchestras that played the most popular songs of the week, as determined by various surveys. The number one song of the week was always played at the end of the show. Vocalists on the show included Frank Sinatra, Doris Day, Dinah Shore, Bonnie Baker, Buddy Clark and many others. One of the most popular songs, up until 1945, was "I Hear a Rhapsody," which was first played on January 4, 1941, and went on to number one ten times. "I'll be Seeing You" and "White Christmas," in 1944 and 1942, respectively, also claimed ten number one spots.

The top ten songs of September 21, 1935:

1. I'm in the Mood for Love
2. You're All I Need
3. Cheek to Cheek
4. East of the Sun
5. Without a Word of Warning
6. Accent on Youth
7. I Couldn't Believe My Eyes
8. Page Miss Glory
9. Rhythm and Romance
10. I'm on a Seesaw

The top ten songs of May 23, 1942:

1. Don't Sit Under the Apple Tree
2. Somebody Else Is Taking My Place
3. Tangerine
4. Sleepy Lagoon
5. Skylark

6. Moonlight Cocktail
7. Johnny Doughboy
8. Jersey Bounce
9. Miss You
10. She'll Always Remember

First airing over NBC in 1935 and continuing into the 1950s.

SCOPES EVOLUTION TRIAL

The entire Scopes evolution trial (or Scopes monkey trial), with witness testimony, cross-examinations and the brilliant arguments of attorneys Clarence Darrow and William Jennings Bryan, was broadcast in its entirety by WGN, from Dayton, Tennessee, from July 10-21, in 1925, at a cost of $1,000 a day.

Radio Terms

As a growing new medium, radio quickly developed its own peculiar slang. A few of the more common terms from the 1930s and 1940s:

abie: a radio personality or entertainer who is a sure money-maker. 1938: "You settle for a conventional music program with a comedian, and everybody starts looking for an abie. Cantor, Benny, Crosby, Baker, Bergen, and most of the other names are all tied up." Fortune, *May.*

adenoid: a vocalist with a "tight" voice.

canary: a vocalist, especially a soprano. 1938: "Joe Blow gets off another gag, and everybody laughs again. The canary sings. The orchestra plays a tune. . . ." Fortune, *May.*

cat: any swing musician.

cliff-hangover: the original word for "cliffhanger," a serial thriller.

crawk: an animal imitator. (Keep in mind how vital sound effects were.)

fairy godfather: an undemanding sponsor.

THE HINDENBURG DISASTER

The most unforgettable live radio news of the century was the coverage of the Hindenburg explosion on May 6, 1937, by Herb Morrison of WLS, Chicago. As the dirigible approached its mooring in Lakehurst, New Jersey, Morrison calmly described the scene. He quickly broke into pitiful sobs, however, as the dirigible burst into flames and plunged to earth.

"The ship is gliding majestically toward us, like some great feather. We're standing here beside the American Airline flagships, waiting to rush them to all points in the United States when they get the ship moored. It's practically standing still—now they have dropped ropes out of the nose of the ship. The rain has slacked up a bit. The back motors of the ship are just holding it . . . just enough to keep it from . . . [sound of explosion] . . . *it's burst into flame!* Get this, Charlie! Get this, Charlie! It's crashing! Terrible! Oh my! Get out of the way please! It's burning—bursting into flame and it's falling on the mooring mast and . . . the folks . . . oh, this is terrible! This is one of the worst catastrophes in the world . . . oh, it's burning! [sound of explosion] Oh, four or five hundred feet into the sky it's a terrific catastrophe ladies and gentlemen [Morrison begins to cry], it's smoke and flames now and the plane is crashing to the ground, not quite to the mooring mast . . . oh, the humanity. . . ." Morrison's broadcast was heard coast to coast.

fish bowl: the studio observation booth, used by advertising clients and radio executives.

1938: "You're pretty excited by this time, but you stay away from the studios while they're servicing the script. . . . You take your wife and some of the company men down and sit in the fish bowl, chewing a cigar and looking important." Fortune, *May.*

flesh peddler: a talent agent.

gaffoon: a sound effects man.

1941: "When the script calls for the sound of marching feet . . . a gaffoon, or sound effects man, works [a] machine in which nine blocks of wood . . . strike a plywood base in measured marching cadence." Popular Science, *June.*

Franklin Roosevelt's "day that will live in infamy" address to Congress on the bombing of Pearl Harbor was heard over the radio at noon on December 8, 1941. A record sixty million Americans tuned in. Also scheduled on the radio that day, from a listing of New York network affiliate stations:

3:00 WEAF—Against the Storm
    WOR—Variety Musicale
    WJZ—Orphans of Divorce
    WABC—The Helping Hand
3:15 WEAF—Ma Perkins
    WJZ—Honeymoon Hill
    WABC—News for Women
3:30 WEAF—Guiding Light
    WOR—Dance Orchestra
    WJZ—John's Other Wife
3:45 WEAF—Vic and Sade
    WJZ—Just Plain Bill
3:55 WABC—News
    WQXR—News
4:00 WEAF—Backstage Wife
4:15 WEAF—Stella Dallas
4:30 WEAF—Lorenzo Jones
    WOR—Happy Jim Parsons
4:45 WEAF—Young Widder Brown
5:00 WEAF—When a Girl Marries
    WOR—Little Ophan Annie
5:15 WEAF—Portia Faces Life
    WOR—Mandrake
    WJZ—Secret City
    WABC—The Goldbergs
5:30 WEAF—We, the Abbotts
    WOR—Jack Armstrong
    WJZ—Flying Patrol
    WABC—The O'Neils

5:45 WEAF—Vagabonds Quartet
    WOR—Captain Midnight
    WJZ—Tom Mix Straight Shooters
    WABC—Scattergood Baines
6:00 WEAF—String Orchestra
    WOR—Uncle Don
6:15 WJZ—Sports—Bill Stern
    WABC—Hollywood—Hedda Hopper
6:30 WJZ—Lum and Abner
6:45 WEAF—Three Suns Music
    WJZ—Lowell Thomas
7:00 WEAF—Fred Waring Orchestra
    WOR—Sports-Stan Lomax
    WABC—Amos 'n' Andy
7:15 WOR—Lone Ranger
7:30 WABC—Blondie
    WQXR—Treasury of Music
8:00 WEAF—James Melton, Tenor
    WJZ—I Love a Mystery
8:30 WEAF—Richard Crooks, Tenor
    WJZ—True or False
8:45 WOR—Hoff Orchestra
9:00 WEAF—Dr. I.Q.
    WOR—Gabriel Heatter, Comments

9:30 WEAF—That Brester Boy
   WOR—Duchin Orchestra
   WMCA—Variety Musicale
   WQXR—Eddy Brown
     Orhcestra
10:00 WEAF—Percy Faith
     Orchestra

WOR—Raymond Gram
   Swing
WABC—Orson Welles,
   Variety-Drama
(Most programs after ten
were comprised of news
and recorded music.)

hog-calling contest: "A strenuous commercial audition for announcers." *Variety Radio Directory,* 1937-1938.

Madame Cadenza: a ditzy female singer.

on the beach: unemployed; laid off.

scoutmaster: an advertising agency executive.

spieler: a radio announcer or commentator.
1938: "You're all set except for a spieler, and after a hog-calling contest you get one for $250." Fortune, *May.*

town crier: a loud singer.

woodchopper: a xylophone player.

woodshed: a rehearsal for a show. From 1935 on.

SECTION NINE

MUSIC AND DANCE

I f it was done by our grandparents and great-grandparents, then
dancing in the 1920s must have been about as exciting as watching paint dry, right? Listen to what the critics of the period had
to say:

College dances "are mere animal exhibitions of agility and
feeling. There is nothing of grace in them, and [they] serve as
an excuse for actions that would be severely censored anywhere but
on the modern dance floor." *University of Maryland Review.*

"To glide gracefully over a floor, keeping time to the rhythm and
harmony of music, is a pleasant recreation and is pleasing to witness,
but to jig and hop around like a chicken on a red-hot stove, at the
same time shaking the body until it quivers like a disturbed glass of
jello, is not only tremendously suggestive but is an offense against common decency. . . ." *New Mexico College of Agriculture Round Up.*

"The outstanding objection to the modern dance is that it is im-
modest and lacking in grace. It is not based on the natural and harm-
less instinct for rhythm, but on a craving for abnormal excitement.
And what is it leading to? The dance in its process of degradation has
passed from slight impropriety to indecency, and now threatens to
become brazenly shameless." *Hobart College Herald.*

Hey, that sounds like *fun!* The provocative movements described
included those produced by the "shimmy" and the "Charleston," two
dances that were arguably every bit as wild as those we see today. Of
course, more timid souls had the one-step and others to show that they
were more "civilized" during the 1920s.

215

And the music? It was hot, too. Jazz. Swing. The crooners. Big bands. Swing bands. The morale-building war songs, the miss-you-when-you're-gone songs, the ballads. In the 1920s, Rudy Vallee and Paul Whiteman and his orchestra dominated the music scene. In the 1930s, it was Benny Goodman, Glen Miller, Tommy Dorsey, Duke Ellington, Ella Fitzgerald and, of course, Bing Crosby. Frank Sinatra also appeared on the scene in the 1930s but really made a name for himself in the 1940s.

Live music was easy to find. Bands and orchestras were playing everywhere. Tune into any major radio station on a Saturday night and you were likely to hear any number of orchestras, playing live-remotes from scores of ballrooms, dance halls and hotels across the country. "From high atop the Plaza Hotel in New York, we bring you the master of swing and sway, Sammy Kaye."

Big Apple: originating in and named after a black nightclub in Columbia, South Carolina, this dance swept the nation in 1937. It combined elements of square dancing and swing dancing with moves from the Charleston and religious revival meetings and often employed group dancing in a circle with a spirited caller. Steps included the "peck and pose," with partners pecking sweetly at their partner's right then left shoulders; the "cut that apple," with dancers doing a double Charleston, a pirouette to face out, a repeat and face in; an Indian rain dance-type step; a "praise Allah" move with dancers leaning back and raising their arms heavenward; a "London Bridge," the traditional square dance move; and to round things off, a fundamental hop similar to the Lindy Hop. Others steps included "the shag," "the Suzy Q," and the "truck."

1937: "Anybody can dance The Big Apple—anybody, that is, with the energy of a steam engine, the legs of Glen Cunningham, and the wind of an underwater swimming champion."

Arthur Murray in Literary Digest, *October 2.*

Charleston: hugely popular dance originating around 1903 but not widely publicized until the Broadway Negro revue, "Running Wild," of 1923. The dance has been described as a sort of "fast foxtrot" with some four hundred different steps. It was so wild and "orgiastic," that many colleges actually banned it.

However, Charleston dance contests were held nationwide throughout the mid-1920s, and even children could be seen mimicking the wild movements on sidewalks. In 1923, the floor of Boston's Pickwick Club buckled under the weight of one thousand clomping Charleston dancers, killing forty-four.

1925: "... the chorus assumed the most awkward postures—knock-knees, legs 'akimbo,' toes turned in until they met, squattings, comic little leaps sidewise. . . . Certain steps—where the dancer crosses his hands on his knocked-knees, weaves them back and forth, teetering at the same time on the ball of one foot (a step, I may say, extremely lovely to watch, when it is done by women . . .) are not in our present style of dancing at all. . . . The Charleston gives you liberty." *Source unknown.*

1926: "In the fervent crowd you must realize that the Charleston has taken the place of the blues and the shimmy. . . . The African tribes do nothing but the Charleston." Living Age.

dance halls: hugely popular throughout the period. Thousands of public dance halls were spread throughout America, some of them—called dance "palaces"—accommodating as many as five hundred to three thousand dancers. According to one set of statistics, in New York, which boasted more than six hundred dance halls, 14 percent of males between the ages of seventeen and forty and 10 percent of the females of the same age attended public dance halls at least once per week. Twenty-five percent of San Francisco youths regularly attended their local halls, according to *American Mercury* magazine. Admission ranged from fifty cents to a dollar and a half. The dancing was frequently overseen by women chaperones or dance-hall inspectors, who set various rules of acceptable moral conduct.

1924: "Male dancers are not permitted to hold their partners tightly. . . . Both partners should assume a light, graceful position. . . . Vulgar, noisy jazz music is prohibited. Such music almost forces dancers to use jerky half-steps and invites immoral variations. . . . Partners are not permitted to dance with cheeks close or touching. When dancers put their cheeks together it is simply a case of public lovemaking. . . . So-called neck-holds are prohibited. The gentleman's arm should encircle his partner's waist, his hand resting

lightly at her spine, just above the waistline; the lady's left arm should not encircle the gentleman's shoulders or neck."
Ordinances at one of the stuffier Cleveland dance halls.

foxtrot: one of the favorite dances of the 1920s. Couples typically danced the foxtrot very close together, often cheek to cheek, much to the horror of conservatives. *The Catholic Telegraph* huffed, ". . . the embracing of partners—the female only half dressed—is absolutely indecent; and the motions—they are such as may not be described, with any respect for propriety, in a family newspaper. Suffice it to say that there are certain houses appropriate for such dances; but those houses have been closed by law."

Lambeth Walk: the most popular dance of 1938, originating in Britain as the Cockney Strut. The dance was performed by couples who, according to one description, "strutted forward, linked arms, reversed position, faced each other, clapped and then, as a final step, jerked their thumbs over their shoulders, saying, "Oi" for no apparent reason." Actually, the "oi!" was an imitation of the coster's or apple-sellers salute on the street. The dance mixed elements of square dancing with swing and was said to be a milder version of the Big Apple. See the Big Apple. The dance was first seen in America at the St. Regis Roof in New York in August of 1938.

1938: "The [Lambeth] Walk has been officially recognized in Germany, for last week the government established the song composer's Aryan ancestry and permitted German dancers who had been doing the Lambeth Walk surrepticiously to strut, slap knees, and shout Cockney 'oi's' with the Fuhrer's blessing."
Newsweek, *September 12.*

Lindy Hop: in the 1940s, *Life* called the Lindy Hop America's "true national folk dance," but don't get the wrong idea. The Lindy, sometimes referred to as the jitterbug, was anything but mild. Men swung their partners around their backs, over their heads, through their legs; couples pranced, shuffled, twisted and jumped; they performed hip rotations, and they bopped across the floor like popping popcorn. Individual moves included the "boogie," "round-the-back," "jig-walk," "shorty George," "truckin'," "Suzy-Q," and the "twist." The

218

dance originated among blacks in the 1920s and was named after Lindbergh's flight across the Atlantic. The dance slowly evolved and incorporated new steps into the 1930s, when it broke out of its restricted social strata and gained national prominence. The dance was wildly popular in the early 1940s and made a natural fit with swing music.

1943: ". . . as recently as three years ago a jitterbug was anyone who bounced, wiggled and jumped in time to hot music without any particular knowledge of what he was doing. But the accomplished jitterbug of the present does the Lindy Hop . . . [a dance that] encompasses hundreds of individual steps, breaks and mutations. . . ." Life, *August 23.*

1943: "Under such a spell your true jitterbug is likely to do almost anything in the way of a dance step; he will go in for a bit of Lindy Hop . . . he will unwind his partner brusquely to arm's length and snatch her back again, swiveling his hips and turning his toes in and out the while, his face rapt and immobile. When he really gets going he may improvise all sorts of fantastic figures. . . ." New York Times Magazine., *November 7.*

swing: big band swing music was the most popular dance music, especially among young couples, from 1935 to 1942. Benny Goodman and his orchestra are widely credited with starting the swing craze.

Chronologies

HISTORY EVENTS, INNOVATIONS AND FADS

(Entries within individual years are not necessarily in chronological order.)

1919: Flu epidemic carries over from the fall of 1918. People panic and wear gauze masks in the streets. Ultimately, more than 400,000 Americans succumb to the disease.

First nonstop flight across Atlantic made by British flyers, Captain John Alcock and Lieutenant Arthur Brown in a Vickers-Vimy biplane, from St. Johns New Foundland to Ireland, in fifteen hours, fifty-seven minutes, June 15.

Signing of the Treaty of Versailles officially ends World War I on June 28.

Prohibition begins with the passing of the National Prohibition Act or Volstead Act by Congress on October 28. Sale of any beverage containing more than one-half of 1 percent of alcohol is deemed illegal.

A police strike in Boston in September produces widespread looting. New police are quickly hired.

First tabloid picture newspaper, the *New York Daily News*, begins publishing.

Jack Dempsey, the "Manassa Mauler," wins heavyweight boxing championship against Jess Willard on July 4.

Cincinnati Reds win World Series over Chicago White Sox.

1920: The first presidential election in which women nationwide are allowed to vote.

Warren G. Harding elected president.

Election results broadcast over radio for the first time, on November 2, over station KDKA in Pittsburgh.

First airmail service from New York to California.

Traffic lights introduced.

Several people die in Hatfield-McCoy feud in Kentucky.

Average life expectancy is fifty-four.

The divorce rate is just 13.4 percent.

Baby Ruth candy bar introduced. In 1923, they will be drop-parachuted by the thousands from airplanes flying over cities nationwide.

Babe Ruth joins Yankees, after working as a pitcher for the Red Sox. In his first year with the Yanks, he hits fifty-four home runs, thirty-five more than either league's second best hitter.

Eight members of the Chicago White Sox indicted for accepting bribes to throw the previous year's World Series against the Cincinnati Reds. All eight players are acquitted but banned from baseball. The national disgrace becomes known as the Black Sox scandal.

Cleveland Indians beat Brooklyn Dodgers in World Series.

1921:   Will Rogers rises to fame in this decade and into the next.

Jack Dempsey knocks out Georges Carpentier to defend world heavyweight boxing championship on July 2.

First Miss America Pageant, September 8.

Psychoanalysis popularized.

Babe Ruth hits fifty-nine home runs in his second year with the Yankees.

New York Giants beat the New York Yankees in World Series.

Wheaties, the Breakfast of Champions, is introduced.

Reader's Digest begins publishing.

Unknown soldier buried at Arlington Cemetery on Armistice Day, November 11.

Mae West imprisoned for ten days for appearing in a nasty play called *Sex*. She complains that prison underwear is too fuzzy.

1922:   Period of prosperity begins and will continue until the stock
        market crash of 1929.

Jazz music rises to prominence, led by Louis "Satchmo" Armstrong and other black musicians.

Warren Harding becomes the first president ever heard over
the radio with the dedication of the Frances Scott Key me-
morial in Baltimore on June 14.

First play-by-play broadcast of World Series begins from Polo
Grounds in New York City, on October 4. New York Giants
win over New York Yankees.

First radio commercial (by a real estate company) over WEAF
in New York on November 28.

Fatty Arbuckle, 320-pound comedian, acquitted for accidently
killing twenty-three-year-old actress Virginia Rappe while
having sex with her in September 1921.

"Day by day in every way I'm getting better and better" a
faddish self-help line chanted over and over again by fol-
lowers of pop psychologist/pharmacist Emile Coue. Coue
is hugely popular as "the power of positive thinking guru"
of the decade.

1923:   President Warren G. Harding dies in office on August 2. Vice
        President Calvin Coolidge is sworn in.

Auto sales boom. One out of every two cars sold in America
is a Ford.

U.S. Steel agrees to reduce the workday from twelve hours to
eight, paving the way for the standard forty-hour work week
throughout the U.S.

Mah Jong becomes a national craze. "The wave of the Mah
Jong craze has admittedly passed its crest. Yet there are
more people playing Mah Jong today than there were a
year ago, when the rage was the hottest. . . . It is no longer
the 'thing to do.' Instead, it is now the thing one does, if
one wants to do it." *New York Times*, August 10, 1924.

A massive earthquake rocks Tokyo and Yokohama, Japan, killing more than 100,000 and leveling 575,000 buildings. The
event is called the "greatest disaster the world has ever
known."

Time magazine begins publishing.

First baseball game played in newly built Yankee Stadium.

The Charleston, a fast fox-trot, originating among southern blacks, becomes all the rage across America. Several colleges ban the dance.

Free-spirited, nonconforming young women called "flappers" disturb parents and prudish conservatives nationwide.

New York Yankees beat the New York Giants in the World Series.

Electric shaver patented by Colonel Jacob Schick.

1924:   Calvin Coolidge reelected as president.

A bottom-of-the-line Ford without a self-starter can be purchased for $299, the lowest car price in history.

Gangster Dion O'Bannion gunned down and murdered in his Chicago flower shop by associates of arch rival, Al Capone.

Florida real estate boom. Many lose their shirts on shady get-rich-quick land deals involving swamps.

Washington Senators beat New York Giants in World Series.

1925:   First woman, Nellie Ross, is elected governor in Wyoming.

Resurgence of Ku Klux Klan is illustrated by a massive 40,000-member demonstration in Washington, D.C., on August 8.

New Yorker magazine begins publishing. First issue costs fifteen cents.

A rare total eclipse is seen in New York.

John Scopes, a twenty-four-year-old teacher, arrested for intentionally violating a Tennessee law forbidding the teaching of evolutionary theories. Scopes Evolution Trial or Scopes Monkey Trial held from July 10-21. Scopes is represented by Clarence Darrow. William Jennings Bryan is the prosecutor. The dramatic arguments are broadcast daily over the radio. One hundred reporters cover the story in person. Even though Darrow utterly humiliates Bryan on the witness stand, Scopes is convicted and fined. All the jury members but one read the Bible, but none have read a book on evolution. No scientists were allowed to testify. Bryan dies soon after the trial concludes.

Pittsburgh Pirates beat Washington Senators in World Series.

1926:   Movie star Rudolph Valentino, idol to millions of adoring women, dies suddenly at the age of thirty-one. Some distraught women commit suicide.

Henry Ford introduces forty-hour work week.

Gene Tunney defeats Jack Dempsey for heavyweight boxing title on September 23.

Nineteen-year-old Gertrude Ederle swims the English Channel, the first woman to do so, on August 6. Her time is almost two hours faster than the record held by the fastest man. New York City honors her with a ticker tape parade.

First motion picture with sound (music only), *Don Juan.*

St. Louis Cardinals beat the New York Yankees in World Series.

Scheduled airline flights begin.

Harry Houdini dies, from complications arising from being punched in the stomach, on October 31, at the age of forty-three.

1927:   On May 20, twenty-five-year-old aviator Charles "Lucky" Lindbergh takes off in the monoplane Spirit of St. Louis from Roosevelt Field, Long Island, and arrives in Paris, France, thirty-three and a half hours later. It is the first solo, nonstop, transatlantic flight. Lindbergh is welcomed by cheering crowds in Paris and is later honored with the largest ticker tape parade in history in New York. He will be considered the nation's greatest hero for years to come.

Mount Rushmore monument is dedicated.

Holland Tunnel, joining Manhattan and New Jersey, opens.

First Ford Model A introduced, with unprecedented consumer interest. Curious auto enthusiasts by the thousands line up to catch a first glimpse at exhibitions.

Gangster Al Capone's earnings estimated at $105 million.

Babe Ruth hits sixty home runs, a record that will hold for decades.

New York Yankees beat the Pittsburgh Pirates in World Series. These 1927 Yankees are considered by many sportswriters to be the greatest baseball team of all time.

Al Jolson stars in *The Jazz Singer*, popularly known as the first
motion picture with sound, or the first "talkie."
First Academy Award presented. *Wings* wins best picture
award.
First nationally broadcast radio program, the Rose Bowl football game, followed by a concert by the New York Symphony Orchestra, January 1.

1928: Herbert Hoover elected president.
Animated character by the name of Mickey Mouse introduced
in the cartoon "Plane Crazy" by Walt Disney.
Amelia Earhart becomes the first woman aviator to fly across
the Atlantic on May 25.
Jean Lussier goes over Niagara Falls in a specially made rubber
ball and survives, July 4.
New York Yankees beat the St. Louis Cardinals in World Se-
ries.
"I Faw Down an' Go Boom" a hit song.

1929: On February 14, five gangmembers, two dressed as police,
walk into a garage that doubles as a bootlegging depot in
Chicago's North Side and shoot and kill with submachine
guns, seven of rival George "Bugs" Moran's gang. The
shooters are suspected to work for Al Capone. It comes to
be known as the St. Valentine's Day Massacre.
The stock market crashes in October after reaching a record
high on September 3. The crash heralds the beginning of
a severe economic downturn. The Great Depression begins
nine months later.
Richard Byrd completes the first flight over the South Pole,
November 2.
Flagpole sitting, sometimes for days at a time, and dance mar-
athons are national crazes, from the second half of the
1920s into the 1930s. ". . . Baltimore was dotted with boys
and girls ranging from eight to thirteen who were determined to upset Avon Foreman's [juvenile] record as a flagpole sitter. Some of them came down as soon as father
got home, but since the ceremonies attending the Avon
Foreman descent from the flagpole, there has been an

average of some fifteen children roosting in various con-
trivances atop "flagpoles" ranging from ten to twenty feet
high. Two of them have broken legs and one an arm, but
others mount poles to replace the casualties and the sitting
goes on. . . . The corner druggist pays a dollar or two for
the right to advertise his business on the sacred totem. . . ."
New Republic, August 28, 1929.

The Graf Zeppelin flies around the world. Many believe zep-
pelins will be the great transport of the future.

Less than 10 percent of farms are equipped with rural electric
lines.

Leg of lamb is thirty-nine cents a pound. Bread is ten cents a
loaf. Milk is sixteen cents a quart.

The Philadelphia Athletics beat the Chicago Cubs in World
Series.

1930: Over 1,000 banks close nationwide, with many depositers losing their life savings.

Cigaret smoking rising steadily in popularity since the First
World War.

One in every five Americans owns a car.

New York Supreme Court Justice Joseph Crater vanishes and
is never heard from again, May 1.

The planet Pluto discovered.

"The Lone Ranger" radio show heard for first time over
WXYZ in Detroit.

A new song, "Life Is Just a Bowl of Cherries," introduced by
Rudy Vallee, September.

Wonder Bread introduced.

Bib-Label Lithiated Lemon-Lime Soda, containing lithium,
introduced with the slogan, "Take the ouch out of the
grouch." The soft drink's name was later changed to 7-Up
and its lithium content removed.

Philadelphia Athletics beat St. Louis Cardinals in World Series.

1931: Over eight hundred banks close nationwide.

Spurred by a "Ripley's Believe It or Not" cartoon, the Star
Spangled Banner officially becomes the national anthem.

Empire State Building opened.

In June, Wiley Post and Harold Gatty fly around the world in their plane, Winnie May, in eight days, fifteen hours and fifty-one minutes.

In October, Hugh Herndon and Clyde Pangborn complete the first nonstop flight across the Pacific, from Japan to the U.S., in a little over forty-one hours.

Al Capone convicted of tax evasion and sentenced to eleven years in prison.

St. Louis Cardinals beat the Philadelphia Athletics in World Series.

1932: Depression peaks. Fifty-six percent of blacks and 40 percent of whites, or thirteen million Americans are unemployed. Business failures skyrocket. Wages plummet to 60 percent less than that earned in 1929. Herbert Hoover cuts his own salary by 20 percent.

"Brother, Can You Spare a Dime" is a popular song reflecting the times.

On March 1, Charles Lindbergh's twenty-month-old baby is kidnapped from the second story of their home in New Jersey and ransomed for $50,000. The nation is outraged. Even Al Capone offers a $10,000 reward. The infant's body is found near Lindbergh's home on May 12. The kidnapper will not be found for two years.

Franklin D. Roosevelt elected president.

Government employees go on a five-day work week.

Amelia Earhart flies solo across the Atlantic, May 20.

The Bonus Army, a group of some seventeen thousand World War I veterans, camp out in Washington, D.C., and demand their service bonuses—not scheduled to be paid out for several years—early, to help them survive the Depression. The Senate refuses and a core group of two thousand disgruntled servicemen are finally driven out of Washington by troops led by Douglas MacArthur.

The nation grumbles over Prohibition; calls for its repeal intensify.

New York Yankees beat Chicago Cubs in World Series.

1933:   Roosevelt's "New Deal" initiated to help create new jobs, change the national monetary system, and launch a hodge-podge of new government agencies.

Assassination attempt on President-elect Roosevelt, February 15. The assassin, shouting "Too many people are starving to death!" misses Roosevelt but hits the mayor of Chicago, Anton Cermak, and kills him.

Hitler assumes power in Germany. After only one week in power he boycotts Jewish businesses. He also forbids all criticism of himself.

Of the floundering economy, Roosevelt asserts at his inauguration on March 4 that "the only thing we have to fear is fear itself."

Roosevelt gives the first of his nationally broadcast "fireside chats," Sunday night, March 12.

FBI launched by Roosevelt, headed by John Edgar Hoover. The bureau's creation is partially spurred by increasing gangster activity.

The unpopular and impossible to enforce law of Prohibition is repealed, December 5.

Average life expectancy fifty-nine years.

Banks reopen. Confidence growing with Roosevelt in charge.

Drought turns depleted soil to dust throughout the midwest. On November 11, a windstorm, called a "black blizzard," blows the first of forty million acres of soil away and produces a massive, choking dust storm stretching from Texas to Canada. The sand drifts as high as six feet in places, burying roads, fences and small trees. Farmers devastated.

First drive-in movie theater opens in June in Camden, New Jersey.

Sally Rand performs her fan dance at the Century of Progress Exposition at Chicago.

New York Giants beat Washington Senators in World Series.

1934:   Midwest drought continues.

Depression eases with lower unemployment and fewer business and bank failures.

Bank robber John Dillinger, "Public Enemy Number One,"

shot and killed by FBI leaving a movie theater in Chicago.

Half of all college men and a quarter of college women have engaged in premarital sex at least once, according to one national survey. Another survey reveals that seven out of ten men and women in their twenties have engaged in premarital sex.

Pitchers Dizzy and Daffy Dean help the St. Louis Cardinals beat the Detroit Tigers in World Series.

Walter Nilsson rides his unicycle from New York to San Francisco in one hundred and seventeen days.

Seventeen-year-old June Hovick wins a dance marathon in West Palm Beach by dancing for five months.

First Laundromat, Fort Worth, Texas.

1935:   Senator Huey Long assassinated, September 8.

Polio prevalent.

Hitler orders German radio stations not to play jazz music by blacks or Jews.

Ohio State star athlete Jesse Owens rises to prominence by setting six world records in track and field.

First major league night game held at Crosley Field in Cincinnati.

Babe Ruth's last year in baseball.

Detroit Tigers beat Chicago Cubs in World Series.

Board game, *Monopoly*, introduced by Parker Brothers.

1936:   Franklin Roosevelt reelected.

Drought and soil depletion deepens dust bowl in midwest. Farmers migrate en masse to more fertile ground in the west.

Eight hundred-foot-long dirigible Hindenburg makes first of regularly scheduled transatlantic flights as it arrives in Lakehurst, New Jersey.

To Hitler's dismay, black athlete Jesse Owens wins four gold medals in Olympics held in Berlin.

Hoover Dam completed.

Last public hanging held in Owensboro, Kentucky, June 10. Twenty thousand gather to witness the hanging of black murderer Rainey Bethea.

Humphrey Bogart stars in five movies.

New York Yankees beat New York Giants in World Series.

1937: Hindenburg explodes as it nears its mooring mast in Lakehurst, New Jersey. The event is broadcast live on radio by Herbert Morrison, May 6. See Section Eight: Radio and Radio Shows.

Japan wars with China.

The Golden Gate Bridge in San Francisco is dedicated.

Joe Louis knocks out James Braddock for World Heavyweight Boxing title. Louis will keep the title until 1950.

Amelia Earhart vanishes during an around-the-world flight attempt in her plane, the Flying Laboratory, July 3. She is never heard from again.

Blues singer Bessie Smith, injured in car crash in Mississippi, is refused admittance to Clarksdale hospital because she is black, and dies, September 26.

Humphrey Bogart appears in seven movies.

Miniature golf becomes a huge new popular pastime.

A survey by *Fortune* magazine reveals the best-loved comics of the day, in order:

1. Little Orphan Annie
2. Popeye
3. Dick Tracy
4. Bringing Up Father
5. The Gumps
6. Blondie
7. Moon Mullins
8. Joe Palooka
9. Li'l Abner
10. Tillie the Toiler

New York Yankees beat the New York Giants in World Series.

1938: Germany annexes Austria.

War of the Worlds Martian invasion play, based on a story by H.G. Wells, is broadcast nationally by Orson Welles and the Mercury Theater. Tens of thousands of listeners panic, believing the play—delivered as a series of bulletins—to be actual news. See Section Eight: Radio and Radio Shows.

Depression eases further. The number of out-of-work Americans on relief drops by one-third from the previous year.

Severe hurricane strikes the northeast unexpectedly. A one hundred-foot wave crashes over Providence, Rhode Island, and floods the streets. One hundred and fifty-three houses in Westhampton, Long Island, are washed or blown away. The storm ultimately kills seven hundred people and leaves sixty thousand homeless.

First Superman comic is published by *Action Comics* in June. It's a huge hit.

To the nation's amusement, a man named Douglas Corrigan flies in his plane to Ireland, which he mistakes for California. He is dubbed "Wrong Way Corrigan."

Minimum wage is twenty-five cents an hour. Hamburger costs nineteen cents a pound. A porterhouse steak costs forty-five cents a pound.

Time magazine's Man of the Year is Adolf Hitler.

New York Yankees beat the Chicago Cubs in World Series.

1939: Germany invades Poland, September 1.

On September 3 France and Great Britain declare war on Germany.

German submarine sinks British passenger ship, Athenia, killing thirty Americans on board, September 3.

Economy surges forward due to war in Europe.

Pan Am begins first regularly scheduled transatlantic air service with its airliner, the "Dixie Clipper."

Scientists split the atom.

New York World's Fair held in Flushing, Long Island, visited by thirty-two million people from April through October.

Americans are seeing an average of one movie per week. Admission ranges from twenty-two to fifty-five cents.

Gone With the Wind and *The Wizard of Oz* are playing at movie theaters.

Coffee is twenty-five cents per pound.

Helicopter invented.

Swallowing live goldfish becomes a national fad among

college students nationwide. One student swallows forty-three.

New York Yankees beat Cincinnati Reds in World Series.

1940: Franklin D. Roosevelt reelected president.

Germany occupies Denmark and Norway, April 9.

Germany invades Luxembourg, Belgium and the Netherlands, May 10.

Italy joins Germany and declares war on Britain and France, June 10.

France is defeated and surrenders to Germany, June 21.

Germany attacks Great Britain (The Battle of Britain) by air in August to soften them for a later invasion. British RAF planes, aided by airborne radar, defeat the German planes two to one.

Unemployment falls due to increasing factory orders spurred by the war.

Forty-hour work week officially adopted nationwide.

Olympic Games cancelled due to war in Europe.

First peacetime draft conducted in U.S. Many men believe they will be deferred from service if married and speed up their engagements.

Germany, Italy and Japan form economic and military alliance and become known as the Axis powers.

Movie star Tom Mix dies in car crash.

Cincinnati Reds beat Detroit Tigers in World Series.

M&Ms candy developed.

Richard and Maurice McDonald open their first drive-in restaurant near Pasadena, California. It will evolve into a chain of McDonalds across the country.

1941: Germany invades Soviet Union and soon makes massive inroads, June 22.

German submarine sinks U.S. destroyer, Reuben James, October 30.

Japanese launch surprise attack on Pearl Harbor in Hawaii, December 7. The battleships Arizona, California, Oklahoma and Utah are sunk and others heavily damaged. Three thousand Americans are killed. Japan also attacks the Philippines, Wake Island and Guam. The U.S. declares war on Japan the next day.

Germany and Italy declare war on U.S., December 11.

Blackouts and air raid tests staged in cities throughout U.S.

Rubber rationing goes into effect, December 27.

Lou Gehrig, first baseman for New York Yankees, dies at the age of thirty-seven, June 2.

Glen Miller's "Chattanooga Choo Choo" record a million-seller.

New York Yankees beat Brooklyn Dodgers in World Series.

1942:   U.S. forces demoralized with numerous early defeats in the Pacific, especially at the Bataan Peninsula in the Philippines and Corregidor in Manila Bay. Americans turn the tables, however, in May defeating the Japanese in the Battle of the Coral Sea, and in June, in the Battle of Midway. At Midway the Japanese lose 17 ships, 275 planes and 4,800 men.

April 18, Major General James Doolittle and his squadron of sixteen B-25s infiltrate Japan and bomb Tokyo and other cities. The attack provides a huge boost to U.S. morale.

Sugar rationing begins, May 5.

Gas rationing begins for eastern states of U.S., May 15.

Marines land on Guadalcanal in the Solomon Islands, August 7, the spearhead of an extended test of resolve, with ever-growing Japanese and American forces battling for supremacy until February 1943, when the Americans ultimately force a Japanese evacuation.

U.S. forces land in North Africa, November 7.

Coconut Grove nightclub fire kills 491 people in Boston, November 28.

National gas rationing begins, December 1.

Audie Murphy joins the army at the age of sixteen. He will go on to become the most decorated soldier in the war.

St. Louis Cardinals beat the New York Giants in World Series.

1943:   Shoe rationing begins, February 7. Americans limited to three pair per year.

Canned goods rationed, March 1.

Americans sink twenty-two Japanese ships and down fifty Japanese planes in the Battle of the Bismarck Sea, March 2-4.

Meat, cheese and fat rationed, March 29.

War Manpower Commission prohibits any vital worker from quitting his job, April 17. The action affects twenty-seven million employees.

Polio epidemic spreads across U.S.

U.S. captures Tunisia. British forces capture Tunis, May 7.

Two hundred and fifty thousand Axis troops taken prisoner in surrender of North Africa in May.

Zoot Suit Riots in Los Angelas on June 4; sailors and marines start fistfights with any Mexicans and blacks wearing zoot suits. Race riots in Detroit, June 20. Thirty-five people are killed and 500 injured in two day melee. Riots also break out in Harlem, August 1.

John F. Kennedy's PT boat rammed and cut in two by Japanese destroyer in the Solomon Islands. Kennedy and ten crew members swim to safety and are marooned for days on an island.

Lindy hop most popular dance.

Allied forces invade Sicily, July 10.

Allied planes bomb Rome, July 19.

Axis forces lose 167,000 men in fight for Sicily. Allies triumph, August 17.

Italy invaded by Allies, September 3.

Italy surrenders to Allies, September 8.

Italy declares war on Germany, October 13.

Dwight Eisenhower appointed Supreme Commander of Allied forces for the invasion of Europe, December 24.

New York Yankees beat St. Louis Cardinals in World Series.

1944:   Allied forces land at Anzio, Italy, January 22.

Eight hundred U.S. flying fortresses bomb Berlin, March 6.

Allied forces invade Normandy, France, June 6, D-Day. Known as Operation Overlord, it is the most massive military operation in history, ultimately involving over five thousand ships, three thousand planes and upwards of four million troops.

Germans begin use of V-1 rocket bomb, June 13. Use of the bigger V-2 commences in the fall.

Assassination attempt on Hitler, July 20, fails.

One hundred sixty-seven people killed and nearly five hundred injured as Ringling Brothers and Barnum and Bailey circus tent in Hartford, Connecticut, catches fire during a performance, July 6.

Twenty-five thousand Japanese soldiers killed in battle for Saipan. U.S. forces victorious.

Lieutenant George Bush on a bombing run on the island of Chi Chi Jima is shot down by the Japanese but quickly rescued by an Allied submarine, September 24.

Seventeen thousand Japanese soldiers killed as U.S. takes Guam, August 9.

Paris liberated, August 25.

U.S. forces infiltrate Germany for first time, September 12.

Out of desperation, Japanese adopt suicide bomber strategy. Kamikaze pilots and their suicide dives seen for first time at massive naval battle at Leyte, Philippine Islands, October 23-26.

Franklin D. Roosevelt reelected for record fourth term. Harry Truman elected Vice President.

Battle of the Bulge begins, December 16.

Band leader Glen Miller killed in air crash, December 24.

Twenty thousand cases of polio reported in U.S.

St. Louis Cardinals beat St. Louis Browns in World Series.

1945: National dimout ordered to help conserve dwindling fuel supplies. The dimout runs from January 15 to May 8.

Allied planes bomb Dresden. February 13-14. An estimated seventy thousand refugees die in the resulting firestorm.

The Japanese lose over twenty thousand men in the battle for Iwo Jima. U.S. Marines prevail March 16.

Two hundred seventy-nine U.S. B-29s napalm-bomb Tokyo, killing one hundred thousand, March 9-10.

U.S. invades Okinawa, April 1.

Franklin D. Roosevelt dies of a cerebral hemorrhage at sixty-three, April 12. Harry Truman assumes presidency.

Benito Mussolini and his mistress killed by a firing squad, April 28.

Adolf Hitler and wife Eva Braun commit suicide in Berlin, April 30.

British forces occupy Hamburg, May 3.

V-E, Victory in Europe, day. War in Europe ends, May 8.

One hundred thousand Japanese soldiers die at Okinawa before Japanese surrender on June 21.

Philippine Islands liberated, July 5.

First atomic bomb test-detonated near Alamogordo, New Mexico, July 16.

In blinding fog, a B-25 bomber crashes into the 78th and 79th floors of the Empire State Building, killing thirteen people, July 28.

Atomic bomb dropped on Hiroshima, Japan, by Colonel Paul Tibbets in the Enola Gay, on August 6. Eighty thousand perish.

Soviet Union declares war on Japan, August 8.

Atomic bomb dropped on Nagasaki, Japan, August 9. Forty thousand perish.

V-J, Victory in Japan, day, August 15. War in Pacific ends.

Official Japanese surrender document signed on the U.S.S. Missouri in Tokyo Bay, September 2.

Shoe rationing ends, October 30.

Nuremberg war crimes trials begin. Twenty-one war criminals put on trial for various atrocities.

Meat and butter rationing ends, November 23.

Tire rationing ends, December 20.

Bess Myerson wins Miss America title in Atlantic City.

Detroit Tigers beat the Chicago Cubs in World Series.

HIT SONGS

1919: The World Is Waiting for the Sunrise
How Ya Gonna Keep 'em Down on the Farm ("after they've seen Paree")

The Vamp
A Pretty Girl Is Like a Melody
1920: When My Baby Smiles at Me
Left All Alone Again Blues
Wild Rose
Mah Lindy Lou
The Japanese Sandman
1921: Second-hand Rose
April Showers
Ain't We Got Fun
Baby Face
Ma, He's Makin' Eyes at Me
I'm Just Wild About Harry
1922: Carolina in the Morning
Chicago
Toot, Toot, Tootsie, Goodbye
I Wish I Could Shimmy Like My Sister Kate
1923: Barney Google
Charleston
That Old Gang of Mine
Yes! We Have No Bananas
I Love Life
1924: California Here I Come
Hard Hearted Hannah
I Wonder What's Become of Sally
Indian Love Call
The Man I Love
Oh, Lady Be Good
Rose-Marie
Tea for Two
1925: A Cup of Coffee, a Sandwich and You
Sweet Georgia Brown
Don't Bring Lulu
1926: The Birth of the Blues
Bye Bye Blackbird
Do-Do-Do
Someone to Watch Over Me

1927: Ain't She Sweet
    Me and My Shadow
    Hallelujah!
    I'm Looking Over a Four Leaf Clover
    My Heart Stood Still
    Strike Up the Band
    'S Wonderful
    Thou Swell
1928: I Wanna Be Loved by You
    Let's Do It (Let's Fall in Love)
    Lover, Come Back to Me
    Nagasaki
    You Took Advantage of Me
1929: Am I Blue
    Stardust
    Can't We Be Friends?
    Happy Days Are Here Again
    I May Be Wrong
    Tip Toe Thru the Tulips With Me
    With a Song in My Heart
    You Do Something to Me
1930: Body and Soul
    But Not for Me
    Can This Be Love?
    Dancing on the Ceiling
    Embraceable You
    I Got Rhythm
    Love For Sale
    Bidin' My Time
1931: I Found a Million Dollar Baby (In a Five and Ten Cent Store)
    Of Thee I Sing
    When Your Lover Has Gone
    You're My Everything
    Where the Blue of the Night Meets the Gold of the Day
1932: April in Paris
    Brother, Can You Spare a Dime?
    Forty Second Street

I Guess I'll Have to Change My Plan
Louisiana Hayride
Night and Day
You're Getting to Be a Habit With Me
1933: It's Only a Paper Moon
Shadow Waltz
The Gold Digger's Song (We're in the Money)
1934: Anything Goes
Autumn in New York
I Get a Kick Out of You
You and the Night and the Music
You're the Top
You're a Builder Upper

From 1935 to 1945, the number one and two hits as surveyed by the radio program, "Your Hit Parade."

1935: Alone
Chasing Shadows
Cheek to Cheek
Don't Give Up the Ship
Double Trouble
East of the Sun
Eenie Meenie Miney Mo
Red Sails in the Sunset
You Are My Lucky Star
In a Little Gypsy Tea Room
Life Is a Song
A Little Bit Independent
Lullaby of Broadway
What's the Reason
I'll Never Say Never Again
I'm in the Mood for Love
In the Middle of a Kiss
Moon Over Miami
On Treasure Island
Paris in the Spring
Soon
1936: Did I Remember

The Way You Look Tonight
Is It True What They Say About Dixie
Goody Goody
Lost
Pennies From Heaven
In the Chapel in the Moonlight
The Music Goes Round and Round
Lights Out
Take My Heart
When Did You Leave Heaven
I'll Sing You a Thousand Love Songs
The Glory of Love
It's De-Lovely
A Melody From the Sky
You
Robins and Roses
Until the Real Thing Comes Along
I'm Gonna Sit Right Down and Write Myself a Letter

1937: Once in a While
Boo Hoo
It Looks Like Rain in Cherry Blossom Lane
Ebb Tide
September in the Rain
Goodnight My Love
That Old Feeling
Whispers in the Dark
A Sailboat in the Moonlight
This Year's Kisses
Carelessly
Harbor Lights
Rosalie
Remember Me
So Rare
With Plenty of Money and You
You Can't Stop Me From Dreaming
Sweet Leilani
Where Or When

1938: My Reverie
A-Tisket, A-Tasket
Ti Pi Tin
Jeepers Creepers
I've Got a Pocketful of Dreams
Love Walked In
Music Maestro Please
Say My Heart
Thanks for the Memory
You Must Have Been a Beautiful Baby
Bie Mir Bist Du Schoen
Change Partners
I Can Dream, Can't I
You're a Sweetheart
Cry Baby Cry
I Double Dare You
I Let a Song Go Out of My Heart
Please Be Kind
Vieni Vieni
Heart and Soul
Whistle While You Work

1939: Deep Purple
Over the Rainbow
Scatterbrain
South of the Border
And the Angels Sing
Moon Love
Stairway to the Stars
Wishing
Heaven Can Wait
Our Love
Blue Orchids
Day In Day Out
Indian Summer
My Prayer
Beer Barrel Polka
Three Little Fishes

1940:   I'll Never Smile Again
        The Woodpecker Song
        Careless
        When You Wish Upon a Star
        There I Go
        Frenesi
        Imagination
        Maybe
        Only Forever
        Make Believe Island
        Practice Makes Perfect
        Darn That Dream
        Ferryboat Serenade
        Fools Rush In
        Sierra Sue
        Trade Winds
        We Three
        It's a Blue World
        When the Swallows Come Back to Capistrano
        Blueberry Hill
1941:   I Hear a Rhapsody
        Amapola
        Daddy
        There'll Be Bluebirds Over the White Cliffs of Dover
        You and I
        I Don't Want to Set the World on Fire
        Tonight We Love
        The Hut Sut Song
        Chattanooga Choo Choo
        Intermezzo
        Marie Elena
        My Sister and I
        Wise Old Owl
        There'll Be Some Changes Made
        Till Reveille
1942:   White Christmas
        There Are Such Things

Deep in the Heart of Texas
Don't Sit Under the Apple Tree
Jingle Jangle Jingle
He Wears a Pair of Silver Wings
My Devotion
Sleepy Lagoon
Somebody Else Is Taking My Place
Blues in the Night
One Dozen Roses
I Don't Want to Walk Without You
Tangerine
I Left My Heart At The Stage Door Canteen
Mister Five By Five
When The Lights Go On Again

1943: My Heart Tells Me
You'll Never Know
Sunday, Monday, or Always
As Time Goes By
I've Heard That Song Before
Brazil
Comin' In On a Wing and a Prayer
Don't Get Around Much Anymore
Elmer's Tune
Paper Doll
People Will Say We're In Love
It's Magic
Moonlight Becomes You
Shoo Shoo Baby
All or Nothing at All
Let's Get Lost
That Old Black Magic
You'd Be So Nice to Come Home To
Oh What a Beautiful Morning

1944: I'll Be Seeing You
Don't Fence Me In
I'll Walk Alone
Long Ago and Far Away

The Trolley Song
Besame Mucho
I Love You
It's Love, Love, Love
Amor
Dance With a Dolly
I Couldn't Sleep a Wink Last Night
Mairzy Doats
Swinging on a Star
Is You Is or Is You Ain't My Baby
Time Waits for No One
1945: Symphony
Till the End of Time
Dream
It's Been a Long, Long Time
Sentimental Journey
Accentuate the Positive
Candy
If I Loved You
It Might as Well be Spring
My Dreams are Getting Better
I'll Buy That Dream
I'm Beginning to See the Light
I Can't Begin to Tell You
A Little On the Lonely Side
The More I See You
On the Atchison, Topeka and the Santa Fe
Laura
There, I've Said It Again

BOOKS

(A mix of bestsellers and notable books of the period.)

1919: *Winesburg, Ohio,* Sherwood Anderson
Ten Days That Shook the World, John Reed
The American Language, H.L. Mencken
1920: *The Man of the Forest,* Zane Grey

Main Street, Sinclair Lewis
This Side of Paradise, F. Scott Fitzgerald
The Age of Innocence, Edith Wharton
1921: *Mysterious Rider,* Zane Grey
The Sheik, Edith Hull
Three Soldiers, John Dos Passos
1922: *If Winter Comes,* A.S.M. Hutchinson
The Enormous Room, e.e. cummings
Tales of the Jazz Age, F. Scott Fitzgerald
Babbit, Sinclair Lewis
Julia, Booth Tarkington
1923: *Life of Christ,* Giovanni Papini
Etiquette, Emily Post
Lost Lady, Willa Cather
Through the Wheat, Thomas Boyd
1924: *In Our Time,* Ernest Hemingway
The Call of the Canyon, Zane Grey
Billy Budd, Herman Melville
The Autobiography of Mark Twain
So Big, Edna Ferber
1925: *The Man Nobody Knows,* Bruce Barton, (A bestseller in 1925
and 1926)
An American Tragedy, Theodore Dreiser
Manhattan Transfer, John Dos Passos
The Great Gatsby, F. Scott Fitzgerald
Arrowsmith, Sinclair Lewis
1926: *The Private Life of Helen Troy,* John Erskine
Abraham Lincoln, the Prairie Years, Carl Sandburg
The Sun Also Rises, Ernest Hemingway
Topper, Thorne Smith
1927: *Elmer Gantry,* Sinclair Lewis
Death Comes for the Archbishop, Willa Cather
1928: *The Bridge of San Luis Rey,* Thornton Wilder
Bad Girl, Vina Delmar
Scarlet Sister Mary, Julia Perterkin
The Man Who Knew Coolidge, Sinclair Lewis
1929: *All Quiet on the Western Front,* Erich Maria Remarque

A Farewell to Arms, Ernest Hemingway
Laughing Boy, Oliver Lafarge
Dodsworth, Sinclair Lewis
Look Homeward, Angel, Thomas Wolfe
1930:   *The Bridge*, Hart Crane
As I Lay Dying, William Faulkner
Cimarron, Edna Ferber
The Maltese Falcon, Dashiell Hammet
1931:   *The Good Earth*, Pearl Buck
Sanctuary, William Faulkner
The Glass Key, Dashiell Hammett
1932:   *Tobacco Road*, Erskine Caldwell
Light in August, William Faulkner
Beyond Desire, Sherwood Anderson
The Case of the Velvet Claws, Erle Stanley Gardner
Brave New World, Aldous Huxley
1933:   *Winner Take Nothing*, Ernest Hemingway
Rabble in Arms, Kenneth Roberts
Anthony Adverse, Hervey Allen
1934:   *Tender Is the Night*, F. Scott Fitzgerald
The Thin Man, Dashiell Hammett
Goodbye, Mr. Chips, James Hilton
1935:   *Tortilla Flat*, John Steinbeck
Judgement Day, James T. Farrel
Of Time and the River, Thomas Wolfe
1936   *Gone With the Wind*, Margaret Mitchell
The Big Money, John Dos Passos
1937   *Of Mice and Men*, John Steinbeck
1938:   *Our Town*, Thornton Wilder
The Unvanquished, William Faulkner
1939:   *The Grapes of Wrath*, John Steinbeck
Captain Horatio Hornblower, C.S. Forester
Abraham Lincoln, the War Years, Carl Sandburg
1940:   *For Whom the Bell Tolls*, Ernest Hemingway
You Can't Go Home Again, Thomas Wolfe
Native Son, Richard Wright
1941:   (Sales of the Bible increased 25 percent throughout the war)

The White Cliffs of Dover, Alice Miller
My Friend Flicka, Mary O'Hara
Berlin Diary, William Shirer
1942:   *The Moon Is Down*, John Steinbeck
The Robe, Lloyd Douglas
See Here, Private Hargrove, Marion Hargrove
1943:   *A Tree Grows in Brooklyn*, Betty Smith
Thirty Seconds Over Tokyo, Captain Ted Lawson
Here Is Your War, Ernie Pyle
Guadalcanal Diary, Richard Tregaskis
The Human Comedy, William Saroyan
1944:   *Brave Men*, Ernie Pyle
Forever Amber, Kathleen Winsor
1945:   *Cass Timberlain*, Sinclair Lewis
Black Boy, Richard Wright

MOVIES

In pre-television days, most people routinely went to the movies once per week. Children, if they lived nearby and could go on their own, went even more often. In 1929, an astonishing one hundred thousand Americans visited their local movie houses on a weekly basis.

1922: "Of 3,000 Chicago children who answered a [Parent Teacher Association] questionnaire, 87 percent said they attended from one to seven or more shows every week. With several hundred, attendance at the movies had become a fixed habit. Indeed, it is said, Friday, Saturday and Sunday now mean attendance at the movie as definately as Sunday used to mean attendance at Sunday-school."
Literary Digest, *June 17.*

(*Notable and popular movies.*)

1919:   *The Masked Rider* (a serial with fifteen episodes)
Trail of the Octopus (a serial with fifteen episodes)
Broken Blossoms (Lillian Gish)
True Heart Susie (Lillian Gish)
1920:   *Son of Tarzan* (a serial with fifteen episodes)
The Lost City (a serial with fifteen episodes)
Way Down East (Lillian Gish)

1921: *The Sheik* (Rudolph Valentino)
Under the Lash (Gloria Swanson)
Tarzan of the Jungle (a serial with fifteen episodes)
The Adventures of Tarzan (a serial with fifteen episodes)
Nanook of the North (documentary)
Orphans of the Storm (Lillian Gish)

1922: *A Dangerous Adventure* (a serial with fifteen episodes)
Blood and Sand (Rudolph Valentino)
Nosferatu (Max Shreck)
Robin Hood (Douglas Fairbanks, Sr.)

1923: *The Santa Fe Trail* (a serial with fifteen episodes)
The Hunchback of Notre Dame (Lon Chaney)
Down to the Sea in Ships (Clara Bow)

1924: *Battling Brewster* (a serial with fifteen episodes)
The Navigator (Buster Keaton)
Sherlock, Jr. (Buster Keaton)
The Thief of Bagdad (Douglas Fairbanks, Sr.)

1925: *Are Parents People?* (Betty Bronson)
The Big Parade (John Gilbert)
Go West (Buster Keaton)
The Gold Rush (Charlie Chaplin)
The Phantom of the Opera (Lon Chaney)
The Battleship Potemkin (Alexander Antonov)

1926: *Behind the Front* (Wallace Beery)
Dancing Mothers (Clara Bow)
Metropolis (Brigitte Helm)
The Scarlet Letter (Lillian Gish)
The Strong Man (Harry Langdon)
Tramp, Tramp, Tramp (Harry Langdon)

1927: *The Beloved Rogue* (John Barrymore)
The Cat and the Canary (Laura LaPlante)
College (Buster Keaton)
Flesh and the Devil (Greta Garbo)
The Jazz Singer (Al Jolson. Although this is popularly referred to as the first "talkie," it did not have sound all the way through.)
Orchids and Ermine (Colleen Moore)

1928: *Lights of New York* (The first "talkie" with sound all the way through.)
The Man Who Laughs

1929: *Applause* (Helen Morgan)
Cocoanuts (Marx Brothers)
The Mysterious Island (part silent, part sound; Lionel Barrymore)
On With the Show (first talkie in color)
Thunderbolt (George Bancroft, Fay Wray)
The Virginian (Gary Cooper)

1930: *All Quiet on the Western Front* (Lew Ayres)
Animal Crackers (Marx Brothers)
The Big House (Wallace Beery)
Morocco (Marlene Dietrich)
Murder (Hitchcock)

1931: *Charlie Chan Carries On* (Warner Oland)
Dracula (Bela Lugosi)
Frankenstein (Boris Karloff)
Monkey Business (Marx Brothers)
Svengali (John Barrymore)

1932: *The Big Broadcast* (Bing Crosby)
Dr. Jekyll and Mr. Hyde (Fredric March)
Dr. X (Fay Wray)
Grand Hotel (Greta Garbo)
Horsefeathers (Marx Brothers)
The Mummy (Boris Karloff)
Scarface (Paul Muni)
Tarzan, the Ape Man (Johnny Weismuller)

1933: *Alice in Wonderland* (Charlotte Henry)
Bombshell (Jean Harlow)
Dinner at Eight (Jean Harlow)
Duck Soup (Marx Brothers)
The Fatal Glass of Beer (W.C. Fields)
42nd Street (Ruby Keeler)
I'm No Angel (Mae West, Cary Grant)
The Invisible Man (Claude Rains)
Three on a Match (Bette Davis, Joan Blondell)

1934:   *Babes in Toyland* (Laurel and Hardy)
        The Black Cat (Bela Lugosi and Boris Karloff)
        Cleopatra (Claudette Colbert)
        Chained (Clark Gable, Joan Crawford)
        It Happened One Night (Clark Gable, Claudette Colbert)
        The Thin Man (William Powell, Myrna Loy)
1935:   *March of Time* (Current events newsreels featuring one na-
        tional, one foreign and one light story, lasting about twenty
        minutes; shown before the feature movie. They began in
        1935 and continued for years.)
        Anna Karenina (Greta Garbo, Fredric March)
        Barbary Coast (Miriam Hopkins, Edward G. Robinson)
        Bride of Frankenstein (Boris Karloff)
        Captain Blood (Errol Flynn)
        Dangerous (Bette Davis)
        Mutiny on the Bounty (Charles Laughton, Clark Gable)
        The Scarlet Pimpernel (Merle Oberon, Raymond Massey)
1936:   *Camille* (Greta Garbo)
        Desire (Marlene Dietrich)
        Follow the Fleet (Ginger Rogers, Fred Astaire)
        The Great Ziegfeld (William Powell, Myrna Loy)
        Pennies from Heaven (Bing Crosby)
        Showboat (Irene Dunne, Allan Jones)
        Things to Come (Raymond Massey)
1937:   *The Awful Truth* (Irene Dunne, Cary Grant)
        Captains Courageous (Spencer Tracy)
        Charlie Chan on Broadway (Warner Oland)
        A Day at the Races (Marx Brothers)
        The Good Earth (Luise Rainer)
        Lost Horizon (Ronald Colman)
        Stella Dallas (Barbara Stanwyck)
        Topper (Cary Grant)
1938:   *The Adventures of Robin Hood* (Errol Flynn, Olivia de Havilland)
        The Adventures of Tom Sawyer (Tommy Kelly, Jackie Moran)
        Blondie (Penny Singleton, Arthur Lake)
        Boys' Town (Spencer Tracy)
        Bringing Up Baby (Katherine Hepburn, Cary Grant)

Holiday (Katherine Hepburn)
Jezebel (Bette Davis)
The Lady Vanishes (Hitchcock)
Pygmalion (Wendy Hiller, Leslie Howard)
1939: *Andy Hardy Gets Spring Fever* (Mickey Rooney)
Beau Geste (Gary Cooper, Ray Milland)
Blondie Brings up Baby (Penny Singleton, Arthur Lake)
Drums Along the Mohawk (Henry Fonda)
Gone With the Wind (Clark Gable, Vivien Leigh)
Goodbye, Mr. Chips (Robert Donat, Greer Garson)
Gunga Din (Cary Grant, Douglas Fairbanks, Jr.)
Mr. Smith Goes to Washington (Jimmy Stewart)
Stagecoach (John Wayne)
The Wizard of Oz (Judy Garland)
1940: *All This and Heaven Too* (Bette Davis)
The Bank Dick (W.C. Fields)
A Chump at Oxford (Laurel and Hardy)
Fantasia (Disney)
The Grapes of Wrath (Henry Fonda)
Of Mice and Men (Burgess Meredith, Lon Chaney, Jr.)
Road to Singapore (Bob Hope, Bing Crosby)
Strike Up the Band (Judy Garland, Mickey Rooney)
1941: *Ball of Fire* (Gary Cooper)
The Black Cat (Basil Rathbone)
Buck Privates (Abbott and Costello)
Citizen Kane (Orson Welles)
High Sierra (Humphrey Bogart)
How Green Was My Valley (Roddy McDowall, Walter Pigeon)
The Maltese Falcon (Humphrey Bogart)
Never Give a Sucker an Even Break (W.C. Fields)
1942: *Andy Hardy's Double Life* (Mickey Rooney)
Blondie for Victory (Penny Singleton, Arthur Lake)
Casablanca (Humphrey Bogart, Ingrid Bergman, Paul Henreid)
For Me and My Gal (Gene Kelly, Judy Garland)
Jungle Book (Sabu)
The Magnificent Ambersons (Orson Welles)

> *Mrs. Miniver* (Greer Garson, Walter Pigeon)
> *Yankee Doodle Dandy* (James Cagney)

1943: *For Whom the Bell Tolls* (Ingrid Bergman, Gary Cooper)
> *Heaven Can Wait* (Don Ameche)
> *The Human Comedy* (Mickey Rooney)
> *The Oxbow Incident* (Henry Fonda)
> *Stage Door Canteen* (Cheryl Walker, William Terry)

1944: *Andy Hardy's Blonde Trouble* (Mickey Rooney)
> *Arsenic and Old Lace* (Cary Grant)
> *Double Indemnity* (Barbara Stanwyck, Fred MacMurray)
> *Gaslight* (Ingrid Bergman)
> *Lifeboat* (Hitchcock)
> *National Velvet* (Elizabeth Taylor)
> *The White Cliffs of Dover* (Irene Dunne)
> *Ziegfeld Follies* (Fred Astaire, Gene Kelly, Judy Garland)

1945 *A Bell for Adano* (John Hodiak, Gene Tierney)
> *Anchors Aweigh* (Frank Sinatra)
> *The Bells of St. Mary's* (Bing Crosby, Ingrid Bergman)
> *The Body Snatcher* (Boris Karloff)
> *The Corn Is Green* (Bette Davis)
> *The Seventh Veil* (Ann Todd, James Mason)
> *Spellbound* (Ingrid Bergman, Cary Grant)

Movie Serials

Serials were twenty-minute adventures run in theaters after the cartoons and before the main feature on Saturday mornings. (They were often repeated after the main feature as well). Each serial had anywhere from ten to fifteen weekly chapters, with twelve being average. Known more for their action than their scintillating dialogue, they usually ended on a "cliffhanging" moment in order to draw the hooked crowd, mostly children and teens, the following week. (For silent serials of the 1920s, a different breed altogether, see main movie listings.)

1929: *Tarzan the Tiger*
> *The Ace of Scotland Yard*

1930: *The Indians Are Coming*
> *The Lightning Express*

ADVERTISING

One of the first singing jingles heard over radio was this classic for
Pepsi, written in 1939, and performed by a vocal trio.

"Pepsi-Cola hits the spot
Twelve full ounces, that's a lot.
Twice as much for a nickel, too.
Pepsi-Cola is the drink for you.
Nickel, nickel, nickel, nickel.
Trickle, trickle, trickle, trickle. . . ."

When cigarets were "good" for you:

1930: "For years this has been no secret to those who keep fit and
trim. They know that Luckies steady the nerves and do not hurt
their physical condition. They know that Lucky Strikes are the
favorite cigarette of many prominent athletes who must keep
in good shape. They respect the opinions of 20,679 physicians
who maintain that Luckies are less irritating to the throat than
other cigarettes."

Here's another radio jingle. This one from 1944.

"I'm Chiquita Banana
And I've come to say
Bananas have to ripen in a certain way
When they are flecked with brown and have a golden hue
Bananas taste the best and are the best for you
You can put them in a salad
You can put them in a pie-aye.
Any way you want to eat them
It's impossible to beat them.
But bananas love the climate of the very, very tropical equa-
tor
So you should never put bananas in the refrigerator."

The Lone Defender With Rin-Tin-Tin
1931: *Battling With Buffalo Bill*
Danger Island

	King of the Wild
	The Lightning Warrior (Rin-Tin-Tin)
1932:	*The Hurricane Express*
	The Devil Horse
	The Airmail Mystery
1933:	*Fighting With Kit Carson*
	The Phantom of the Air
	Tarzan the Fearless (Buster Crabbe)
1934:	*The Law of the Wild* (Rin-Tin-Tin)
	Mystery Mountain (Clyde Beatty, Mickey Rooney)
	Perils of Pauline
	The Return of Chandu the Magician (Bela Lugosi)
1935:	*The Adventures of Rex And Rinty* (Rin-Tin-Tin)
	The Lost City
	The Miracle Rider (Tom Mix)
	The New Adventures of Tarzan
1936:	*Darkest Africa* (Clyde Beatty)
	Flash Gordon (Buster Crabbe)
	Undersea Kingdom
1937:	*Dick Tracy*
	Radio Patrol
	Secret Agent X-9
	Zorro Rides Again
1938:	*Dick Tracy Returns*
	Flash Gordon's Trip to Mars (Buster Crabbe)
	The Lone Ranger
	The Secret of Treasure Island
1939:	*Buck Rogers* (Buster Crabbe)
	Dick Tracy's G-Men
	Mandrake the Magician
	The Lone Ranger Rides Again
	Scouts to the Rescue (Jackie Cooper)
	Zorro's Fighting Legion
1940:	*Adventures of Red Ryder*
	Flash Gordon Conquers the Universe (Buster Crabbe)
	The Green Hornet
	Junior G-Men

The Shadow
Terry and the Pirates
1941: *Adventures of Captain Marvel*
Dick Tracy vs. Crime, Inc.
Jungle Girl
Riders of Death Valley
The Spider Returns
1942: *Captain Midnight*
Junior G-Men of the Air
Gangbusters
King of the Mounties
1943: *Batman*
G-Men vs. the Black Dragon
The Phantom
The Masked Marvel
1944: *Captain America*
Haunted Harbor
Zorro's Black Whip
The Tiger Woman
1945: *Brenda Starr, Reporter* (Joan Woodbury)
Jungle Queen
Jungle Raiders
The Monster and the Ape
The Royal Mounted Rides Again
Secret Agent X-9

BIBLIOGRAPHY

Magazines and Newspapers

American Mercury; *Colliers*; *Cosmopolitan*; *Current History*; *Esquire*; *Fortune*; *The Golden Book*; *Harper's Monthly*; *Ladies Home Journal*; *Life*; *Literary Digest*; *The Living Age*; *The Nation*; *New Republic*; *New York Times*; *New York Times Magazine*; *Outlook*; *Popular Science*; *Reader's Digest*; *Saturday Evening Post*; *Scribners*; *Vogue*; *Yank, The Army Weekly*.

Books

Allen, Frederick Lewis. *Only Yesterday, An Informal History of the 1920s.* Blue Ribbon Books, 1931.

Allen, Frederick Lewis. *Since Yesterday, the 1930s in America.* Harper and Row, 1939, 1940.

Allsop, Kenneth. *The Bootleggers.* Arlington House, 1961.

Appel, Benjamin. *The People Talk, American Voices From the Great Depression.* Touchstone, 1982.

Battle: True Stories of Combat in World War II. Saturday Evening Post. Curtis Books, 1965.

Bendiner, Robert. *Just Around the Corner, a Highly Selective History of the Thirties.* Dutton, 1968.

The Best From Yank, The Army Weekly. E.P. Dutton, 1945.

The Best Songs of the 20s and 30s. Harmony Books, 1973.

Boardman, Barrington. *Flappers, Bootleggers, Typhoid Mary and the Bomb, An Anecdotal History of the United States from 1923-1945.* Harper and Row, 1989.

Buxton, Frank, and Bill Owen. *The Big Broadcast, 1920-1950.* Viking Press, 1972.

Casey, R. *I Can't Forget.* Bobbs-Merill Company, 1941.

Chronicle of Aviation. International Publishing, 1992.

Cohen, Stan. *V for Victory, America's Homefront During World War II.* Pictorial Histories Pub., 1991.

Editors of *Consumers Guide. Cars of the 30s.* Beekman House, 1980.

Corbett, Ruth. *Daddy Danced the Charleston.* A.S. Barnes and Company, 1970.

Dick, Harold, and Douglas Robinson. *Graf Zeppelin and Hindenburg, The Golden Age of the Great Passenger Airships.* Smithsonian Institution, 1985.

Flexner, Stuart, and H. Wentworth. *Dictionary of American Slang.* Thomas Crowell Company, 1960.

Fussel, Paul. *Wartime.* Oxford University Press, 1989.

Garruth, Gorton. *What Happened When.* Harper and Row, 1989.

Georgano, G.N. *Encyclopedia of American Automobiles.* E.P. Dutton, 1968.

Goldin, Hyman. *Dictionary of American Underworld Lingo.* Twayne Publishers, 1950.

Goldston, Robert. *The Great Depression, The United States in the Thirties.* Fawcett, 1968.

Goodgold, Ed, and Ken Weiss. *To Be Continued.* Crown Publishers, 1972.

Green, William. *Famous Bombers of the Second World War.* Doubleday and Company, 1959.

Hargrove, Marion. *See Here, Private Hargrove.* Henry Holt and Company, 1942.

Hill, Edwin. *The American Scene.* Witmark Educational Publications, 1933.

Hunt and Norling. *Behind Japanese Lines.* University Press of Kentucky, 1986.

Ingersoll, Ralph. *The Battle Is the Pay-off.* Harcourt Brace and Company, 1943.

Kael, Pauline. *5001 Nights at the Movies.* Holt, Rhinehart and Winston, 1982.

Keegan, John. *The Rand McNally Encyclopedia of World War II.* Rand McNally, 1977.

Kinnard, Roy. *Fifty Years of Serial Thrills.* Scarecrow Press, 1983.

Lingeman, Richard. *Don't You Know There's a War On?* G.P. Putnams, 1970.

Morgan, William. *The O.S.S. and I.* W.W. Norton, 1957.

Morris, Joe Alex. *What a Year! (1929).* Harper and Brothers, 1956.

Mowry, George. *The Twenties: Fords, Flappers and Fanatics.* Prentice-Hall, 1963.

Nichols, David. *Ernie's War.* Touchstone, 1987.

O'Donnol, Shirley Miles. *American Costume, 1915-1970.* Indiana University Press, 1982.

O'Hara, John. *Butterfield 8.* Random House anthology, 1934.

O'Hara, John. *Hope of Heaven.* Random House anthology, 1934.

Phillips, Cabell. *The 1940s, Decade of Triumph and Trouble.* MacMillan, 1975.

Poindexter, Ray. *Golden Throats and Silver Tongues, the Radio Announcers.* River Road Press, 1978.

Polenberg, Richard. *America at War; the Homefront.* Prentice-Hall, 1968.

Post Stories of 1941. Saturday Evening Post. Little Brown, 1942.

Rogus, Agnes. *I Remember Distinctly, A Family Album of the American People, 1918-1941.* Harper and Brothers, 1947.

Rotha, Paul. *Movie Parade.* The Studio Publications, 1936.

Runyan, Damon. *Romance in the Roaring Forties.* Beechtree, 1986.

Sann, Paul. *The Lawless Decade, A History of the Twenties.* Crown, 1957.

Sarlat, Noah. *Combat!* Lion Library Editions, 1956.

Sklar, Robert. *The Plastic Age (1917-1930).* George Braziller, 1970.

Smith, S.E. *The United States Marine Corps in World War II, Vol. II.* Random House, 1969.

Spaeth, Sigmund. *A History of Popular Music in America.* Random House, 1948.

Stein, Ralph. *The American Automobile.* Random House.

Stern, Philip Van Doren. *A Pictorial History of the Automobile, 1903-1953.* Viking Press, 1953.

Thorp, Margaret. *America at the Movies.* Yale University Press, 1939.

Time Capsule/1923, A History of the Year Condensed From the Pages of Time. Time Inc., 1967.

Time Capsule/1929, A History of the Year Condensed From the Pages of Time. Time Inc., 1967.

Time Capsule/1941, A History of the Year Condensed From the Pages of Time. Time Inc., 1967.

Tregaskis, Richard. *Invasion Diary.* Random House, 1944.

Walker, Leo. *Great Dance Bands.* Howell-North, 1964.

Ward, Baldwin. *Nostalgia, Our Heritage in Pictures and Words.* Crusade Bible Publishers.

We Americans. National Geographic Society, 1975, 1980.

Wertheim, Arthur. *Radio Comedy.* Oxford University Press, 1979.

White, W.L. *They Were Expendable.* Harcourt Brace and Company, 1942.

Williams, John. *This Was Your Hit Parade.* Courier-Gazette, Inc., 1973.

Wilson, Edmund. *The Twenties.* Bantam, 1976.

Winslow, Susan. *Brother, Can You Spare a Dime? America From the Wall Street Crash to Pearl Harbor.* Paddington Press, 1976.

Young, Peter. *The World Almanac of World War II.* World Almanac, 1986.

More Great Books for Writers!

The Writer's Guide to Everyday Life in the Middle Ages—This time-travel companion will guide you through the medieval world of Northwestern Europe. Discover the facts on dining habits, clothing, armor, festivals, religious orders and much more—everything you need to paint an authentic picture. *#10423/$17.99/256 pages*

The Writer's Guide to Everyday Life in the 1800's—From clothes to food, social customs to furnishings, you'll find everything you need to write an accurate story about this century. Plus, the entries are dated so you don't invent something before its creation. *#10353/$18.99/320 pages*

Writer's Market—This edition brings you over 4,000 listings of buyers of freelance work—their names, addresses, submission requirements, contact persons and more! Plus, helpful articles and interviews with top professionals make this your most essential writing resource. *#10432/$27.99/1008 pages*

The Writer's Ultimate Research Guide—Save research time and frustration with the help of this guide. 352 information-packed pages will point you straight to the information you need to create better, more accurate fiction and nonfiction. *#10447/$19.99/352 pages*

How to Write Like an Expert About Anything—Find out how to use new technology and traditional research methods to get the information you need, envision new markets and write proposals that sell, find and interview experts on any topic, and much more! *#10449/$17.99/224 pages*

The Writer's Digest Guide to Good Writing—In one book, you'll find the best in writing instruction gleaned from the past 75 years of *Writer's Digest* magazine! Successful authors like Vonnegut, Steinbeck, Oates, Michener and over a dozen others share their secrets on writing technique, idea generation, inspiration and getting published. *#10391/$18.99/352 pages*

Thesaurus of Alternatives to Worn-Out Words and Phrases—Rid your work of trite clichés and hollow phrases for good! Alphabetical entries shed light on the incorrect, the bland and the overused words that plague so many writers. Then you'll learn how to vivify your work with alternative, lively and original words! *#10408/$17.99/304 pages*

Writing for Money—Discover where to look for writing opportunities—and how to make them pay off. You'll learn how to write for magazines, newspapers, radio and TV, newsletters, greeting cards, and a dozen other hungry markets! *#10425/$17.99/256 pages*

The Writer's Digest Character Naming Sourcebook—Forget the guesswork! 20,000 first and last names (and their meanings!) from around the world will help you pick the perfect name to reflect your character's role, place in history and ethnicity. *#10390/$18.99/352 pages*

Write Tight—Discover how to say exactly what you want with grace and power, using the right word and the right number of words. Specific instruction and helpful exercises will help you make your writing compact, concise and precise. *#10360/$16.99/192 pages*

National Writer's Union Guide to Freelance Rates & Standard Practice—A must-have for all freelancers! Tables and charts compiled from surveys of freelance writers, editors and agents give you the going rates for six major freelance markets. Plus, information on rights, the electronic future and more! *#10440/$19.95/200 pages/paperback*

Get That Novel Started! (And Keep It Going 'Til You Finish)—If you're ready for a no excuses approach to starting and completing your novel, then you're ready for this get-it-going game plan. You'll discover wisdom, experience and advice that help you latch on to an idea and see it through, while avoiding common writing pitfalls. *#10332/$17.95/176 pages*